Constitution Making:
Conflict and Consensus
in the Federal Convention of 1787

Calvin C. Jillson

University of Colorado
Boulder

AGATHON PRESS, INC.

New York

© 1988 by Calvin C. Jillson

Published by
Agathon Press, Inc.
111 Eighth Avenue
New York, NY 10011

Library of Congress Cataloging-in-Publication Data

Jillson, Calvin C., 1949–
    Constitution making: conflict and consensus in the Federal
Convention of 1787 / Calvin C. Jillson.
        p.   cm.
    Bibliography: p.
    Includes index.
    ISBN 0-87586-081-8 (cloth)   ISBN 0-87586-082-6 (paper)
    1. United States. Constitutional Convention (1787)   2. United
States—Constitutional history.   I. Title.
KF4520.J55 1987
342.73'0292—dc19
[347.302292]

Printed in the U.S.A.

Contents

	Preface	ix
	Acknowledgments	xiv
1.	Perspectives on the Federal Convention of 1787	1
2.	Debate, Deadlock, and Issue Resolution in the Convention	18
3.	James Madison and the Origins of the Virginia Plan	35
4.	The Nature of Government in the New Republic	49
5.	The Representation Question: Madison and His Opponents	64
6.	The Role of the Executive in Republican Government	101
7.	Localist Periphery and Nationalist Center: On Restraining Government	121
8.	Small State Fears and the States' Rights Caucus	151
9.	The Brearley Committee Report and a New Northern Majority	169
10.	Summary and Conclusion	193
	Notes	208
	Bibliography	209
	Appendix A: The Data	215
	Appendix B: The Virginia Plan	221
	Appendix C: The New Jersey Plan	223
	Appendix D: Committee of Detail Report	226
	Appendix E: The Constitution of the United States	229
	Index	237

List of Tables and Figures

Tables   *found on page*

2.1 Empirical Attempts to Identify Voting Groups in the Convention   25

4.1 Extended Republic versus Small Republic: Power and Principle; Two-Factor
    Solution to Roll-Call Votes 1–36, May 29–June 9, Varimax Rotation (Ortho)   55

5.1 Large States versus Small States: Power and Interest; Two-Factor Solution to
    Roll-Call Votes 37–156, June 11–July 17, Rotation (Ortho)   70

5.2 Twenty-Nine Critical Votes between 1 and 156 as Identified by Factor Scores
    1.25 on Either Factor or 1.0 ɔn Both Factors of the Two-Factor Varimax
    Solution in Table 5.1   71

5.3 Large States versus Small States: Power and Interest; Five-Factor Solution to
    Roll-Call Votes 37–156, June 11–July 17, Varimax Rotation (Ortho)   73

5.4 Two-Factor Solution To 71 Votes Selected by Issue Area Taken May 30–
    July 16, Varimax Rotation (Ortho)   75

6.1 Localist Periphery versus Nationalist Middle States; Two-Factor Solution to
    Roll-Call Votes 157–231, July 17–July 26, Varimax Rotation (Ortho)   103

6.2 Two-Factor Solution to 16 Executive-Issue Votes prior to the Connecticut
    Compromise, Varimax Rotation (Ortho)   108

6.3 Two-Factor Solution to 39 Executive-Issue Votes between 157 and 231,
    July 16–July 26, Varimax Rotation (Ortho)   112

6.4 Nine Critical Votes between 157 and 231 Identified by Factor Scores 1.25 on
    One Factor or 1.0 on Both Factors of the Two-Factor Varimax Solution in
    Table 6.1   113

6.5 Four-Factor Solution to 39 Executive-Issue Votes between 157 and 231,
    July 16 and July 26, Varimax Rotation (Ortho)   114

7.1 Localist Periphery versus Nationalist Center: On Restraining Government;
    Two-Factor Solution to Roll-Call Votes 157–402, July 17–August 29,
    Varimax Rotation (Ortho)   123

7.2 Thirty-One Critical Votes between Roll Calls 232 and 375 as Identified by
    Factor Scores of 1.25 on Either Factor or 1.0 on Both Factors of the
    Two-Factor Varimax Solution in Table 7.1   124

7.3 Localist Periphery versus a Divided Nationalist Center; Three-Factor Solution
    to Roll-Call Votes 157–402, July 17–August 29, Varimax Rotation (Ortho)   127

7.4 Localist Periphery versus Cosmopolitan Center; Two-Factor Solution to
    Roll-Call Votes 232–329, August 6–August 20, Varimax Rotation (Ortho)   131

7.5 Expanded Periphery versus Nationalist Core: On Commerce and Slavery;
    Two-Factor Solution to Votes 330–402, August 21–August 29, Varimax
    Rotation (Ortho)   141

Tables (continued)

found on page

7.6 Localist Periphery versus Divided Nationalist Center: On Commerce and Slavery; Three-Factor Solution to Votes 330–402, August 21–August 29, Varimax Rotation (Ortho)   143

8.1 Three-Factor Solution to Roll-Call Votes 403–441 Taken between August 30 and September 3, Varimax Rotation (Ortho)   154

8.2 Twenty-Four Critical Votes between 352 and 441 as Identified by Factor Scores of 1.25 on Either Factor or 1.0 on Both Factors of the Two-Factor Varimax Solution in Table 8.1   158

9.1 Two-Factor Solution to 58 Executive Votes among Votes 442–569 Taken between September 4 and September 17, Varimax Rotation (Ortho)   172

9.2 Four-Factor Solution to 58 Executive Votes among Votes 442–569 Taken between September 4 and September 17, Varimax Rotation (Ortho)   173

9.3 Two-Factor Solution to Roll-Call Votes 442–569 Taken between September 4 and September 17, Varimax Rotation (Ortho)   175

9.4 Twenty-Nine Critical Votes Taken during the Convention's Closing Days, between Roll-Call Votes 442 and 569, September 4–17, as Identified by Factor Scores of 1.25 on Either Factor or 1.0 on Both Factors of the Two-Factor Solution in Table 9.3   176

Figures

2.1 The decision universe with single cleavage   19

2.2 The decision universe with multiple, cross-cutting cleavages   20

2.3 Coalition realignment in the American Constitutional Convention   29

6.1 Comparison of cleavage structures between representation and executive issues   105

6.2 Two positions on the structure of the executive branch   109

8.1 Comparison of cleavage structures between representation and empowerment issues   156

8.2 Comparison of cleavage structures between representation, empowerment, and the newly dominant states' rights issues   162

10.1 Cleavage lines active during the Convention   200

Preface

This study explores both the empirical and the substantive validity of the traditional historical and philosophical interpretations of the creation of the American Constitution. Advocates of differing interpretations of the Constitution's drafting have taken two distinct views, some arguing that the Convention created the Constitution out of a commitment to ideas and political principles, others arguing that the participants designed the Constitution to aid and protect their social, political, and economic interests. This study looks more closely at the roll-call voting record of the Constitutional Convention than any previous study and concludes that an accurate understanding of the constitution-making process must acknowledge that both philosophical *and* material concerns were at work in the Federal Convention.

I will demonstrate that constitution making is an elaborate and delicate, yet elegantly simple, process in which the participants refer to distinctly different sources of knowledge and information to reach judgments about two fundamental aspects of constitutional design. Thus, I will show that the Founding Fathers acted out of broad, though distinct and competing, philosophical perspectives concerning the working relationships between human nature, particular political institutions, and the resulting social order, when they struggled to design the general institutional structure for the new national government. On these issues of basic governmental organization and design, the nationalist delegates from the Middle Atlantic states, generally supporting Madison's vision of an "extended" republic, opposed the delegates from New England and the lower South, who held tenaciously to Montesquieu's warning that free institutions could survive only in "small" republics.

The delegates, on the other hand, pursued narrow material interests when they voted on specific mechanisms for implementing various aspects of the constitutional design. When debate touched upon the distribution of power and influence within the institutions of the new government, coalitions based upon interest posed the large states against the small, the northern states against the southern, and the states with large claims to the lands in the West against the states that had no such claims to future wealth and power. This movement from the consideration of broad principles to a concern with narrow interests conforms to the general expectation of modern social choice theory, particularly in the work of James Buchanan, Gordon Tullock, and Vincent Ostrom. I will argue, however, that there was more frequent movement back and forth from philosophical principles to material interests than social choice theory would seem to anticipate. Such recurring movement indicates that constitution making is a more delicate and complex process than either the traditional historical analysts or the contemporary social choice theorists have realized. This complexity arises from the broad range of issues raised in constitution making, the lack of a single natural majority coalition across all issues, and the consequent tendency of delegates and state delegations to realign during constitution making as the Convention moved from one set of critical and controversial issues to another set.

Underlying the complexity of the constitution-making process in the Federal Convention of 1787, there nonetheless existed a very simple and widely shared goal. The delegates, though drawn from different cultural and material contexts, sought to create a common constitutional framework through which representative decision-making could resolve their legitimate political differences. They disagreed on the appropriate design of the Constitution, and on the distribution of political power and influence within and across particular institutions, but the general goal of a representative constitution united them and led to a sophisticated and sincere decision process that continues to stand as a model of democratic constitution making.

In elaborating this thesis, I attempt to accomplish three goals. First, I supply an empirical description of the voting coalitions, the stable patterns of cooperation and conflict among the delegates and their state delegations as voting units, that characterized the Convention's work. Particular attention is dedicated to changes in voting coalitions and to the implications of these changes for the substantive issues before the Convention. The goal here is to establish the traditional historical and philosophical discussion of the debates and decisions of the Federal Convention on a firm empirical footing.

Second, I advance an explanation of the underlying rationale (philosophical, sociocultural, economic, or regional) for each division of the states. I will describe the Convention chronologically as a series of confrontations between stable coalitions of states and their delegates over the major issues that confronted the Convention from its opening on May 25 to its final adjournment on September 17, 1787. Questions such as the following will be addressed: What were the major issues that spawned each alignment? What were the theoretical justifications and the practical power implications of each of the principal positions adopted by the delegates? Who finally prevailed and why?

Third, I will demonstrate that the long-standing division in the secondary literature on the Convention between those analysts who stress the impact of philosophical principles and those who stress the influence of political and economic interests is misleading. In fact, a dynamic relationship of mutual interdependence existed—and, in fact, had to exist—between philosophical and material influences in the Convention. I will show that the principled or ideological conflicts that arose in the Convention were generated by the clash of regionally based variations in the republican political culture of the new nation, while the conflicts over power and policy were generated by differences in political and economic interests relating to state size and to region.

The key to my interpretation of the politics of the Federal Convention is the contention that debate moved between two distinct but interrelated levels of constitutional construction and that the relative influence of the delegates' political principles and their material interests on the Convention's debates and decisions was quite different at each level. My thesis is that principles guided action on distinguishable types of questions, while on other sets of questions, personal, state, and regional interests encroached upon, and in some cases overwhelmed and subordinated, the independent impact of ideas. I will argue that questions of each general type dominated the Convention's attention during particular phases of its work, so that at some stages, the dominant voting coalitions were organized around shared principles, while at other times, the dominant coalitions were organized around conflicting material interests.

In developing this revisionist interpretation, I argue that intellectual divisions in the Convention had their basis in regional variations in the republican political culture of the American founding period. This argument is based on the work of Daniel Elazar, Robert Kelley, and many others. Elazar, for instance, has described three related but distinct political subcultures: moralistic in New England, individualistic in the Middle Atlantic states, and traditionalistic in the South. Kelley, while calling his regional subcultures by different names and finding two distinct subcultures active in the Middle Atlantic states, has provided very similar substantive descriptions of the ideas and values at the center of each regional subculture.

Further, I will support this argument by demonstrating—both empirically, through analysis of roll-call voting data, and substantively, through analysis of the Convention's voluminous debates—that when the Convention concentrated on "higher" level questions of constitutional design, voting coalitions among the state delegations formed along lines of intellectual cleavage. During these phases of the Convention's work, the delegates from the more nationally oriented Middle Atlantic states opposed the more locally oriented delegates representing the northern and southern periphery. When the focus shifted to "lower" level choices among specific decision rules, each of which represented an alternative distribution of authority within and over the institutions of government, the states split along lines defined by economic and geographic interest, state size (large versus small), and region (North versus South). But perhaps most importantly, I will show that coalitions, whether based on political principles or on material interests, consistently undercut, disrupted, and weakened one another as debate and decision ranged across the fundamental issues that were the Convention's daily business. What is more, the interplay between coalitions effectively checked and limited the long-term cohesion that any alignment of states could maintain and resulted in the politics of bargaining, compromise, and accommodation for which the Convention is so justly famous.

The ultimate impact of shifting cleavages generating new patterns of allegiance among the participants was that no major group was radically dissatisfied with the product of the Convention's long deliberations. In Charles Warren's words, "One of the most fortunate features of the Constitution was that it was the result of compromises and adjustments and accommodation. . . . It did not represent the complete supremacy of the views of any particular man or set of men, or of any State or group of States. The claims and interests of neither the North nor the South prevailed. . . . Moreover, it represented neither an extreme Nationalist point of view nor an extreme States' Rights doctrine. The adherents of each theory had been obliged to yield" (Warren, 1928, p. 733). Thus, the delegates, almost to a man, departed the Convention convinced that their constitutional glass was at least half full as opposed to half empty.

The impact of factional politics, political compromises, and shifting coalitions has, however, been less happy for scholars seeking to understand and interpret the Convention. Because no consistent set of political principles, no region, no social or economic class interest dominated the Convention's business, and though each of these sources of influence was visibly present and was clearly felt, no simple description of divisions in the Convention or of their sources is available. This has greatly embarrassed most of the sweeping dichotomies—nationalists against federalists, large republic men against small republic men, large states against small states, northern states against southern states, commercial interests against agrarian interests, and many others—that have traditionally been used to explain the work of the Convention. Consequently, we have been inundated by a wealth of contradictory claims concerning divisions within the Convention and their effects, with no firm basis for choice among them. I will attempt throughout this book to explain in some detail, both empirically and substantively, who won (in factional terms), when (at what stage in the Convention's business), and why (in terms of intellectual or practical political advantage) on the major issues faced by the delegates to the Federal Convention of 1787. Ultimately, a conceptually sophisticated and empirically accurate understanding of the politics of constitution making in the Federal Convention will allow us to see the democratic politics of our own age in clearer perspective.

Acknowledgments

In thinking and writing about the American Constitutional Convention for over a decade now, I have incurred many debts and obligations, both personal and intellectual. The deepest debt, and the one of longest standing, is to Professor Thornton Anderson in whose Spring 1975 seminar I was first introduced to the debates of the Federal Convention and to the secondary literature that surrounds them. I am also very grateful to the many friends and colleagues who contributed various forms of support, counsel, and encouragement during this project's long development. Special thanks go to Warren Phillips, Eric Uslaner, Ronald Terchek, and Whitman Ridgway, all of the University of Maryland; to Cecil Eubanks, with whom I have written on the Convention; to Ronald Weber, Wayne Parent, and James Bolner, all of Louisiana State University; and to Lawrence Dodd, David Brady, Rick Wilson, Leroy Rieselbach, Vincent Ostrom, William Riker, Lee Sigelman, Donald Lutz, and Christopher Wolfe.

I would also like to thank the publishers of the following journals for permission to use material originally published in their pages: *Presidential Studies Quarterly*, published by the Center for the Study of the Presidency (Jillson, 1979); *Congressional Studies*, published by The Center for Congressional and Presidential Studies, The American University (Jillson, 1981b); *American Political Science Review*, published by the American Political Science Association (Jillson, 1981a); and *American Journal of Political Science*, published by the University of Texas Press (Jillson and Eubanks, 1984).

And finally, only I can be fully aware of the contribution that my family, my wife Kathy and my children Cal and Susan, made to the completion of this book.

CHAPTER 1

Perspectives on the Federal Convention of 1787

No phase of American political history has absorbed more scholarly attention than the formative period between the Revolution and the rise of the first Washington administration. No event of that founding decade more clearly shaped the course, pattern, and character of the new nation's political development than did the Federal Convention of 1787 and its product: the American Constitution. As a result, a particular strategy is necessary in addressing the events which surrounded the drafting of the American Constitution.

Most topics, particularly those grounded in the past, are clearly limited. Only a few—the Revolution, the Federal Convention, the Civil War, and perhaps the New Deal—have affected everything that came later. In discussing these key events, which have become central to the political mythology and self-understanding of the American nation, one must first control the commentary; one must organize, limit, and define the background noise before one can proceed to a discussion of the event itself. Therefore, we must first ask how scholars have interpreted the work of the Federal Convention and how these interpretations have developed and changed. As we shall see, dramatic changes in the way we have come to understand the founding period have left the literature on the making of the American Constitution in a state of some confusion.

Interpretation of the constitution-making process has seemed to develop inexorably from stark simplicity to great complexity, while the analytic focus has shifted from the role of narrow interests to the role of broadly shared ideological perspectives. George Bancroft, a nineteenth-century eulogist of the Constitution and its authors, claimed that the American people had risen as one against British tyranny and, when free, had adopted an admirably moderate democratic constitution. Later analysts came to view the Constitution as the work of a complicated multiplicity of competing social, regional, and economic interests barely willing to compromise their limited interests to secure the general interest in a more efficient national government. By the late 1950s, interest-based interpretations of the Convention and its work had

1

arrived at such a degree of complexity in describing the disunity engendered by conflicting interests that traditional modes of analysis were virtually overwhelmed. More recently, however, the role of political principles in structuring and guiding the debates of the founding period has been subject to dramatic reevaluation. Scholars have clashed loudly over the relative impact of Lockean liberal and classical republican political principles on the minds of the founding generation. I will first describe the development of these arguments and disputes and then suggest a model that will allow us appropriately to organize, interpret, and understand the issues involved.

The Rise of Interpretations of the Federal Convention Based on Conflict

The "Whig Conception" of history and the men who made it predominated in nineteenth-century studies of the drafting of the Constitution. The decade between the Revolution and the Constitution was consistently described as one in which all right-thinking persons sought the immediate strengthening of the central government so that the nation might more adequately deal with the problems and strains of nationhood on a continental scale. As a result, these patriots were described as defending one of the few remaining strongholds of liberty and democracy in a world in which these values were in perhaps fatal and final decline (Greene, 1967, p. 2; Bailyn, 1967, pp. 63–67; Wood, 1969, pp. 3–45; McDonald, 1985, pp. 9–10).

George Bancroft described the Convention as a critical engagement in the ongoing battle between liberty and tyranny, in which "the statesmen who were to create a new constitution . . . knew themselves to be forerunners of reform for the civilized world" (Bancroft, 1882, pp. 207–208). Opposition to the nationalist or continentalist direction of the Convention was portrayed by Bancroft as the work of narrow, timid, and jealous state and local politicians. He concluded that, in the end, the federalists had been forced to bow before the logic of historical inevitability, working through the persons of Madison, Wilson, Morris, Washington, and the remainder of the nationalist corps.

Americans entered the twentieth century convinced, by Bancroft and a host of others, that British Prime Minister William Gladstone had captured the special character of the American Constitution in describing it as "the most wonderful work ever struck off at a given time by the brain and purpose of man" (P. Smith, 1980, p. 94). Yet, less than a decade into the new century, J. Allen Smith set the tone for a much less flattering interpretation of the Convention's work by arguing that "the American scheme of government was planned and set up to perpetuate the ascendency of the property-holding class" (Smith, 1907, p. 298). Smith and the progressive intellectuals of the early twentieth century articulated a new understanding of the place and importance of the Convention and the Constitution in the founding of the American political system (Smith, 1907; Beard, 1913). Instead of seeing the Constitution as a resounding victory for the general interest of liberty in the world, scholars portrayed interests within the Convention as partial and competitive and as engaged in an essentially zero-sum contest for control of the levers of political and economic power. J. Allen Smith explicitly made this case in arguing that the Constitution "was the outcome of an organized movement on the part of a class to surround themselves with legal and constitutional guarantees which would check the tendency toward democratic legislation" (Smith, 1907, p. 299).

Charles A. Beard, whose name is now synonymous with this "economic interpretation" of the motives of the framers and the outcome of their deliberations, elaborated and extended Smith's argument. Beard concluded that "the members of the Philadelphia Convention which drafted the Constitution were, with a few exceptions, immediately, directly, and personally interested in, and derived economic advantages from, the establishment of the new system" (Beard, 1913, p. 324). Finally, like Smith, Beard thought that there were broad economic and social class interests, as well as direct individual interests, at stake in the Convention. Beard boldly asserted that "the social structure by which one type of legislation is secured and another prevented—that is, the constitution—is a secondary or derivative feature arising from the nature of the economic groups seeking positive action and negative restraint" (ibid., p. 13). In terms of the economic interests involved, Beard was even more specific, interpreting the struggle over the Constitution as a victory for investment capital over capital employed in small-scale agricultural production, calling these two general categories of economic interest "personalty" and "realty" (Lynd, 1967, pp. 10–11).

Although Beard quickly became an imposing presence in the field of constitutional studies, his thesis was attacked from the first (Warren, 1928, pp. 69–72). In fact, since Charles Warren assailed Beard nearly sixty years ago for an "altogether too neat, too simple" picture of the interests that clashed in the Convention, constitutional study had, until recently, employed itself in producing an increasingly complex and sophisticated differentiation of the groups and interests seen as participants in that classic confrontation. If Beard's thesis had been correct, the personalty interests (mobile capital) within each state should have been arrayed against the realty interests (capital invested in land) on opposite sides of the ratification battles that followed the Convention. But the results of several analyses designed to test this interpretation contradicted Beard flatly (Crowl, 1947; Pool, 1950; Thomas, 1953; Brown, 1956). Robert E. Thomas, in his study of the ratification struggle in Virginia, contended that implicit in Beard's personalty-realty dichotomy was "a political contest between the rich and the poor" that relevant data and analysis simply did not support. Thomas concluded that "the data here presented offer substantial proof that the leaders of both the Federalist and Anti-Federalist parties came from the *same* class—slaveowners, large landowners, land speculators, army officers and professional people, in short, the gentry" (Thomas, 1953, pp. 64–65). This and related studies offered solid evidence for the view that there had been virtually no difference in kinds or amounts of property held by supporters and opponents of the proposed Constitution.

Nonetheless, Forrest McDonald attempted to salvage Beard's "economic interpretation" from charges of economic reductionism by redesigning and expanding Beard's analysis to include a broader sense of the kinds of economic interests that might have been active and influential (McDonald, 1958, p. 358). In McDonald's eyes, Beard's greatest shortcoming lay not in his attempt to identify determinant social and economic interests and their adherents in the Convention, but in his unnecessarily simplistic attempt to reduce the complexity of the interests and issues operating in the Convention to "a single set of generalizations that would apply to all the states" (ibid., p. 357). McDonald's analysis reinforced the conclusions arrived at by Warren as early as 1928 and by several of the state ratification studies of the late 1940s and early 1950s. He concluded that "any such attempt [to reduce the Convention's complexity to a single set of generalizations] is necessarily futile, for the various interest groups operated under different conditions in the several states, and their attitudes toward the Constitution varied with the internal conditions of the states" (ibid., p. 357). In fact, after investigating the complicated factional politics of the twelve states that sent delegates to the Convention, McDonald concluded that "Politically, thirty-one of the thirty-four major factions in the twelve states were represented by delegates. . . . Together, then, the delegations constituted an almost complete cross-section of the geographical areas and shades of political opinion existing in the United States in 1787" (ibid., p. 37). Clinton Rossiter has made a very similar point, arguing that "it is possible to identify roughly thirty stable factions in state politics in 1787, of which all but a half-dozen were represented in the Convention" (Rossiter, 1966, p. 140).

These descriptions of the multiplicity of local and regional interests active in the Convention—though only part of the story, as we shall see—are fundamental to understanding the internal dynamics of the Convention as a system and set of processes that produced the American Constitution. Obviously, McDonald did not altogether discard Beard's basic thesis that there were identifiable groups with concrete interests within the American society of 1787. He simply replaced Beard's dichotomous picture with a much more complex and realistic portrayal of the various interests that interacted, each crosscutting and modifying the impact of the others, to produce the complex document that is the American Constitution. McDonald's basic point was that the interplay, the cooperation and opposition, between and among the various interests active in the Convention were complex in the extreme.

John P. Roche applied the modern assumptions concerning interest-group politics, bounded conflict between and among representatives of at least partially incompatible interests, to his analysis of the Convention (Roche, 1961, pp. 799–815). America in 1787 was to be conceived of as a welter of competing interest groups or factions, almost every one of which had representation in the Convention. Not surprisingly, Roche concluded that the Constitution was no more than a particularly impressive "patch-work sewn together under the pressure of both time and events by a group of extremely talented democratic politicians" (ibid., p. 815). This was not to say that there were no serious conflicts or that groups pursuing various and divergent interests did not clash, but that "basic differences of opinion . . . were not ideological; they were *structural*" (ibid., pp. 799–815). On this and similar readings, conflict in the Convention could be interpreted in terms of easy and convenient dichotomies; large states versus small (Bancroft, 1882, p. 228; McLaughlin, 1905, pp. 207–208), northern states versus southern states (Warren, 1928, p. 246; McLaughlin, 1905, pp. 260–261), commercial states versus staple states (Farrand, 1913, pp. 147–148), and the landless or naturally bounded states versus those still claiming extensive tracts of unsettled land, usually in the West (Farrand, 1913, p. 82; Jensen, 1940, pp. 56–57).

Though Roche claimed that he did not intend his reading to "suggest that the Constitution rested on a foundation of impure or base motives," many analysts feared that the cumulative impact of pluralist or interest-based interpretations of the founding had diminished the nation's sense of direction and purpose (Roche, 1961, p. 801; see also Hofstadter, 1954, p. 3). The Constitution as a document of principled purpose providing a clear statement of operative national values had been lost or, at the very least, was in grave danger. Walter Lippmann concluded that, as a direct result of the work of Smith, Beard, Hofstadter, Roche, and many others, American ideals and purposes were in danger: "the public philosophy (that guided the nation's early development) is in large measure intellectually discredited among contemporary men. . . . The signs and seals of legitimacy, of rightness and of truth, have been taken over by men who reject . . . the doctrine of constitutional democracy" (Lippmann, 1955, pp. 136–7; see also Eidelberg, 1968).

The recovery of a sound and effective "public philosophy" did not come quickly. Fully twenty years after Lippmann wrote, Martin Diamond was forced to conclude that "the old root American ideas have been challenged on nearly every front and cast into doubt by the most powerful contemporary intellectual currents" (Diamond, 1976, p. 3). In defense of the Founders and the political system they created, Diamond adopted and promoted a view that clearly, even combatively, emphasized the impact of ideas and political principles over narrow political and economic interests in the Convention. He argued that "the Convention supplies a remarkable example of . . . how theoretical matters govern the disposition of practical matters" (Diamond, 1981, p. 30). In Diamond's view, "the debate over the Constitution was a climactic encounter between two rival political theories of how the ends of democratic consent, liberty, and competent government can best be obtained" (ibid., p. 54). Despite the profound impact of Diamond's work on many students of American political ideas and institutions, others have continued to embrace the economic and pluralist interpretations identified with Smith, Beard, and Roche.

Nonetheless, after decades of concentrating on the essentially static aspects of the American constitution-making process, scholarship has moved steadily toward an interpretation of the Convention that sees a congeries of conflicting, competitive interests, underlain by a basic agreement on the fundamental principles of government (Rossiter, 1966, pp. 58–75; Diamond, 1981, p. 54). These constitutive principles, whatever their exact ideological or intellectual content, provided the parameters within which the competition for advantage, even regional and class advantage secured in a constitutional structure, took place. When joined to McDonald's description of multiple interests in the Convention, and to Roche's recognition of the Founders' willingness to compromise, bargain, and accommodate their varied interests in a search for a workable national government, the growing sense that political principles and ideals played a strong mediating, or perhaps even independent, role in the Convention's work, presents the modern analyst with an incredibly complicated picture.

The Role of Shared Principles
in the Federal Convention

How is one to explain the existence of a Constitution at all if American society in the 1780s was teeming with selfish interest groups bent on directing politics, and particularly the fundamentally constitutive act of constitution making, to the service of their private ends? In recent years, the theme of class conflict and clashing interest groups has been greatly modified by a developing sense of the importance of intellectual, theoretical, and ideological influences on the behavior of Americans in the 1780s (Wood, 1966, p. 3). Lee Benson, as early as 1960, sought to extend Beard's simple economic categories (personalty vs. realty) by outlining two general mind sets, the agrarian and the commercial, visualizing them as opposite ends of a continuum describing the range of American political opinion. His general hypothesis was "that a marked tendency existed for agrarian federalists to oppose, and for commercial nationalists to favor, the Constitution" (Benson, 1960, p. 222). Others, most prominently Louis Hartz, Bernard Bailyn, Gordon Wood, Lance Banning, Joyce Appleby, and John Diggins, have contended that a much more widely shared American mind set, constituting "a general pattern of beliefs about the social process—a set of common assumptions about history, society, and politics," permeated American society in the eighteenth century (Wood, 1969, p. viii). Nonetheless, these authors, and others working along similar lines, have differed profoundly concerning the ideological cast or hue of the American mind during the founding era. That ideas were important they all agree; but about which ideas were important, there is widespread and, by now, long-standing disagreement.

Many descriptions of the role of ideas in American political life have been offered. More than thirty years ago, Louis Hartz provided a powerful and vivid description of the impact of a uniformly Lockean political culture on the origins and future course of American political development. Hartz argued that the nation's early and complete "acceptance of the Lockean creed" was produced by a natural pattern in colonial American life which seemed to confirm Lockean principles at every turn (Hartz, 1955, p. 9). Because Lockean principles seemed to be so commonsensically correct, Americans came rapidly to hold a "fixed, dogmatic liberalism" which was clearly displayed in the "uniform values by which the colonial American was beginning to live" as the Revolution approached (Hartz, 1955, pp. 9, 57). For Hartz, Lockean principles were so pervasive during the founding period that they represented "America's general will" (ibid., p. 59).

The Lockean principles that counted most heavily during the founding period were social, rather than strictly political, though they had clear political implications. For Hartz, the most formidable of the ideas drawn from Locke concerned a radical version of social equality which led directly to a thorough-going individualism. "Here, then, is the master assumption of American political thought, the assumption from which all of the American attitudes . . . flow: the reality of atomistic social freedom. It is instinctive to the American mind" (Hartz, 1955, p. 62). The attachment of America to Lockean principles, as Hartz understands that attachment, is an attachment to competitive individualism, social equality, and unlimited economic opportunity (Devine, 1972, pp. 43–48).

More recently, historians of the revolutionary period have attempted to describe a republican political culture which, while more diffuse than the Lockean consensus described by Hartz, came powerfully together during the decade surrounding 1776 to constitute a volatile revolutionary ideology (Bailyn, 1973, pp. 7–9). In this reading, the roots of the American political culture are not simple and Lockean, as once believed, but are "complex and atavistic, growing out of the rich English intellectual traditions of the Dissenters, radical Whigs, Classical Republicans, Commonwealthmen, Country party, or, more simply, the Opposition" (Appleby, 1978, p. 935). Just as Hartz saw Lockean principles as pervasive in colonial America, so Bailyn saw republican principles as equally pervasive. Bailyn argued that:

> Everywhere in America the tradition that had originated in seventeenth-century radicalism and that had been passed on, with elaborations and applications, by early eighteenth-century publicists brought forth congenial responses and provided grounds for opposition politics. . . . It was in terms of this pattern of ideas and attitudes . . . that the colonists responded to the new regulations imposed by England on her American colonies after 1763. (Bailyn, 1967, pp. 53–54)

The key to the tradition of civic humanism described by Bailyn, Wood, Pocock, and many others is its social or communitarian character. Citizens are not isolated atoms of self-interest; rather, they are participants in a larger social whole. In this republican reading of the American founding, "Public virtue, as the essential prerequisite for good government, was all important . . . Since furthering the public good—the exclusive purpose of republican government—required the constant sacrifice of individual interests to the greater needs of the whole, the people, conceived of as a homogeneous body (especially when set against their rulers), became the great determinant of whether a republic lived or died" (Shalhope, 1982, p. 335).

The Clash of Political Cultures in the American Founding

For a time, it seemed that Bernard Bailyn's (1967) republican interpretation of the revolutionary and early founding periods had replaced Louis Hartz's (1955) Lockean interpretation. More recently, however, scholars such as Joyce Appleby (1978), Isaac Kramnick (1982), E. James Ferguson (1983), Ralph Ketcham (1984), and John Diggins (1984) have reasserted the importance of Lockean liberalism and economic individualism to the political culture of the founding period. Unfortunately, most of this literature has been based on the premise that Locke—rather than the republicans, or to the exclusion of the republicans—holds the key to understanding the early American political culture. I believe that Gordon Wood was fundamentally correct in 1969 to reassert Lee Benson's (1960) suggestion that "what is needed is . . . a broad social interpretation in which the struggle over the Constitution is viewed as the consequence of opposing ideologies rooted in differing social circumstances" (Wood, 1969, pp. 626–627; see also Diggins, 1984, p. 31; McDonald, 1985, pp. viii, 259). A return to Lockean individualism, at the expense of the civic humanism of the republican tradition, is not likely to lead to work that is sensitive to "differing social circumstances."

While Hartz, Bailyn, and many others sought to describe a general American political culture, a second analytic tradition has attempted to distinguish the patterns of "cultural, sectional, and social differences" in postcolonial America in terms of their distinctively regional hues (Wood, 1969, pp. 626–627; see also Lipset, 1963, pp. 2–8; McDonald, 1985, pp. viii, 70). Within political science, much of this work has been inspired by Daniel J. Elazar, while Robert Kelley is the leading historian working along these lines. In moving the analytic focus from the study of the general American character to that of its regional variations, Elazar and Kelley have drawn attention to the interaction of classical republican ideals with the principles of Lockean liberalism (see also McDonald, 1985, pp. 60–80). Elazar has argued that

> The United States as a whole shares a general political culture that is rooted in two contrasting conceptions of the American political order, both of which can be traced back to the earliest settlement of the country. In the first (liberalism), the political order is conceived as a marketplace in which the primary public relationships are products of bargaining among individuals and groups acting out of self-interest. In the second (republicanism), the political order is conceived to be a commonwealth—a state in which the whole people have an undivided interest—in which the citizens cooperate in an effort to create and maintain the best government in order to implement certain shared moral principles. (Elazar, 1972, p. 90–91; see also Huntington,

1982, p. 8; Ketcham, 1984, pp. 184–185; Appleby, 1984, p. 22; McDonald, 1985, pp. 291–292)

However, Elazar has gone beyond Hartz and Bailyn to contend that regional political "subcultures represent the interaction of nuances of differences within larger cultures, separable to a degree but always within the framework of the overall culture" (Elazar and Zikmund, 1975, p. 5). Each regional subculture represents a characteristic synthesis of selected and distinctively weighted values drawn from the general matrix of liberal and republican principles:

> These subcultures may be regarded as . . . manifestations of the ethnic, socioreligious, and socioeconomic differences which existed among residents of the three main sections of the original thirteen colonies. The moralistic political culture is rooted in New England where the Puritans . . . sought to create covenanted communities . . . for the ultimate purpose of saving a degenerate world. The individualistic political culture is rooted in the Middle States where most settlers sought . . . individual opportunities for material wealth and personal freedom. . . . The traditionalistic political culture is rooted in the South where individual opportunity . . . took the form of a plantation economy . . . which . . . created a well-nigh feudal aristocracy. (Kincaid, 1982, p. 9; see also Elazar, 1972, pp. 93–102; Bellah et al., 1985, pp. 27–28)

I will demonstrate the importance to our understanding of the intellectual and political dynamics of the founding period of descriptions of an American political culture composed of several regionally based subcultures, each drawing heavily though distinctively on both liberal and republican political traditions and principles. I will demonstrate that on some issues, specifically those dealing with the general nature and role of government, the factional divisions that consistently appeared in the work of the Federal Convention clearly were grounded in the regional distribution of political subcultures within the new nation. I will argue that both the intellectual composition and the regional distribution of the ideas, values, and attitudes which formed the American political culture during the founding period provide the basis for an understanding of important aspects of the Federal Convention's work.

The substantive descriptions that Elazar and others have offered of the political subcultures dominating the several regions of the new American nation rest directly upon widely accepted bodies of historical interpretation (Rossiter, 1966, p. 23). Elazar's description of New England, for instance, draws heavily on the work of Perry Miller, Edmund Morgan, Alan Simpson, and others in contending that "the Puritans came to these shores intending to establish the best possible earthly version of the holy commonwealth. . . . From the first, they established a moralistic political culture" (Elazar, 1972, p. 108). In this holy commonwealth, "the values, ideas, and attitudes of the Puritan Ethic . . . clustered around the familiar idea of 'calling.' God, the Puritans believed, called every man to serve Him by serving society and himself in some useful, productive occupation" (Morgan, 1967, p. 4). John Kincaid has elaborated the political dimension of the Puritan perspective in explaining that "politics tends to be viewed as a communalistic search for the 'good society' . . . government is regarded as a positive instrument for promoting the public's social and economic welfare. . . . Political activity is treated as a matter of civic duty, and public service is viewed as a responsibility to be carried out honestly, conscientiously, and even selflessly for the sake of public rather than private interests" (Kincaid, 1982, pp. 9–10; see also Hall, 1978, p. 3).

Robert Kelley agrees that "the Congregational New Englanders were sharply distinctive in their *moralistic* republicanism. . . . The Yankee model for America was an idealized version of New England's orderly peasant democracy: communal, pious, hard working, austere, and soberly deferential" (Kelley, 1979, p. 83). Further, the "New England Mind" or the "Puritan Ethic" produced a distinctive form of social life which Timothy Breen has described as "persistent localism" (Breen, 1975, p. 1). Nationalism did not come easily or naturally to New England, where church and government were, and always had been, a local concern. Town meetings and congregationalism encouraged no breadth of vision. Nonetheless, the insular village culture of New England was undergoing disconcerting change in the decades preceding the Revolution (Appleby, 1976, p. 7). Kelley argues that "a crucial transformation from *Puritan* to *Yankee* was in fact underway. . . . By the mid-1700's . . . a growing passion for liberty, a mounting readiness to demand that rulers serve their subjects well or be replaced, and a far more unrestrained search for wealth and individual advancement were shifting the balance in New England's social order. . . . The result was that public life became turbulent, partisan, and uncomfortable for those in authority" (Kelley, 1979, p. 52; Szatmary, 1980, pp. 1–18). Shay's Rebellion and the related disturbances that took place throughout New England during the winter of 1786–1787 are the clearest examples of this new turbulence in the hitherto orderly politics of New England. As the Convention approached, New England's political elite was concerned to enhance stability without appearing directly to deny the region's commitment to local governance based on broad popular participation.

While the political, social, and economic life of the South was not quite so uniform as that of New England, the slave culture of Virginia and the political dominance of her planter elite did set the pattern and tone for the states to her south. If moralistic republicanism was at one pole of America's republican political culture, "at the opposite pole was Southern *libertarian* republicanism. Its representatives . . . were secular men, prickly about personal freedom and hostile to meddling clerics. Most were of the aristocracy" (Kelley, 1979, p. 84; see also Cash, 1941, pp. 31–33; Shalhope, 1982, pp. 45–46; Diggins, 1984, p. 36). Further, Elazar argued that, unlike New England, where the role of government was to serve a generalized version of the public good, the political culture within which Southern politics functioned (which Elazar calls traditionalistic) "tries to limit that role to securing the continued maintenance of the existing social order" (Elazar, 1972, p. 99). Charles Sydnor, Rhys Isaac, and others have also made this point; arguing, in Sydnor's words, that, in the Southern colonies, "the gentry of the county, operating through the county court, the vestry, and the militia, managed the business of the county. . . . In local affairs, the members of the gentry were the government" (Sydnor, 1952, p. 85; see also Isaac, 1982, pp. 88–114). The controversy that centered on the illegal loans and grants made out of the public treasury by Speaker Robinson of Virginia's House of Burgesses to literally scores of the leading figures of the Virginia gentry during the hard economic times of the 1760s is a nearly paradigmatic case in point (Greene, 1978, pp. 86–102).

Once the social order had been secured, the aristocratic libertarians of the South looked for little else from government. Kelley and Cash both make this point very strongly, Kelley arguing that "in its heart . . . Southern republicanism was rural and localist. . . . They believed that government should be small and inactive, limiting itself to the simplest social functions" (Kelley, 1979, p. 84). W. J. Cash is even more forceful, arguing that the political culture of the South stood "powerfully against the development of law and government . . . also, and as its ruling element, an intense distrust of, and, indeed, downright aversion to, any actual exercise of authority beyond the barest minimum essential to the existence of the social organism" (Cash, 1941, p. 33). Of particular concern to southerners was the distinct possibility that a distant national government, controlled by nonsoutherners in all probability, might attempt to alter southern economic and social structures.

In the historical literature dealing with the American founding, something close to consensus exists concerning the distinctive forms of life in New England and the South. Literature concerning the Middle Atlantic states has been less settled. Initially, the complex social, economic, and political design of the Middle Atlantic states led analysts to conclude that this region had no distinctive character of its own.

Frederick Tolles, surveying the literature on the Middle Atlantic states as it stood in the mid-1960s, concluded that "a question might even arise in some minds whether there was a Middle Atlantic region in any other sense than that it was what was left over between New England and the South" (Tolles, 1966, p. 65).

More recently, however, historians and political scientists have begun to conclude that while the Middle Atlantic states had no uniform social or economic character, they had, as a direct result of their diversity, a distinctive political style which anticipated the future course of American development. Patricia Bonomi helped to initiate this line of argument by contending that "the principal contribution of the middle colonies was not—as with the South and New England—to our cultural heritage, but to the formation of our political habits" (Bonomi, 1973, p. 65). Milton Klein has also noted that "this middle region exhibited the traits which were to become characteristic of the nation as a whole: It was national in outlook, easy and tolerant in its social attitudes, composite in its demographic makeup, individualistic and competitive in its manners" (Klein, 1978, p. 181; see also Greenberg, 1979, p. 400). Daniel Elazar agrees that the political culture of the Middle Atlantic states, which he calls individualistic, "established the basic patterns of American pluralism" (Elazar, 1972, p. 109).

In elaborating the explicitly political components of Elazar's individualistic political subculture, John Kincaid has argued that "in this subculture, the political arena tends to be viewed as a 'marketplace' of competing interests acting out of primarily private, often utilitarian motives . . . politics is often treated as a kind of business. . . . Those who make a 'career' in politics are expected and often permitted to profit personally while providing the public . . . with a 'product'—material and symbolic" (Kincaid, 1982, pp. 10–11). Robert Kelley, taking a somewhat different, though not incompatible, view, attributes part of the complexity and distinctive character of politics in the Middle Atlantic states to the fact that "the Middle States . . . [supported] two different [and conflicting] modes of republicanism. One was strongly *egalitarian*. Its leaders were hostile to Philadelphia and New York business interests, localistic, and predominantly Scotch-Irish. The other mode of republicanism was *nationalist* and elitist. . . . Nationalist republicans were impatient with localists, for the American nation could realize its great future only if it developed a strong central government" (Kelley, 1979, pp. 84–85). In the Convention, as we shall see, the nationalist republicans thoroughly dominated most of the Middle Atlantic states' delegations.

In sum, the social, economic, and ideological diversity of the Middle Atlantic region encouraged a different kind of political behavior than did the more narrowly ideological cast of the political cultures of New England and the South) The political culture of New England said that politics was about service to society; the political culture of the South said that politics was about securing the stability and continuity of the existing aristocratic social order; and the political culture of the Middle Atlantic states said that politics was about power and influence, about how to get them and how to wield them in pursuit both of public benefit and of private advancement. In the end, this distinction is fundamental indeed; the moralistic and traditionalistic political subcultures point out what to pursue (the public good or stability) and for whose benefit (society's or the established elite's), while the individualistic political subculture acknowledges and even encourages the pursuit of public office as an avenue to private opportunity and advantage (Kincaid, 1982, pp. 8–12; see also Adams, 1889, pp. 77–94).

The regional subcultures thesis offers a distinctive hypothesis concerning the general nature of the divisions between the states that should have characterized the business of the Convention when it dealt with issues in which intellectual or ideological differences were critical. In this instance, we wish to know whether the factional patterns displayed in the Convention comport with the regionalism thesis, show some other pattern, or show no pattern at all. Substantively, this study will demonstrate that some of the most important political disputes to arise in the Convention were molded and shaped by the interplay of distinct regional political subcultures, both among themselves and with the events and pressures of the American founding.

Principles and Interests: Levels of Constitutional Choice

As I have suggested at several points in this discussion, I am convinced that different kinds of issues and choices were before the Convention and that the delegates reacted to them on different levels and on the basis of different influences and motives (Jillson and Eubanks, 1984). Therefore, I will seek to demonstrate that debate moved between two levels of constitutional construction and that these levels represented significant shifts in the relative importance of broad political principles and narrower political and economic interests in the Convention. Though this insight has been suggested before, it has never been developed at any length. For example, Robert Dahl observed that:

> Indeed, as one reads Madison's reports of the debates at the Convention, one senses two rather different levels of debate. At one level there were practical problems of designing a system of government that would . . . work well enough to endure: Should there be one executive or three? How many

representatives should there be in the legislative body? What specific powers should be given to Congress.

But underlying and greatly influencing the debates on these practical matters, there were differences in political objectives that seemed to reflect differences in political ideas and ideology, for the Founders were simply not of one mind in their beliefs as to what kind of political system was desirable, possible, or likely to endure in America. (Dahl, 1967, p. 33)

This general reading of the Convention's work, that in some important sense it took place at two distinguishable though related levels of debate and decision, has been given impressive theoretical support by two important analytical distinctions concerning the logical structure of constitutional choice made some twenty years ago by James Buchanan and Gordon Tullock and elaborated more recently by Vincent Ostrom. Buchanan and Tullock began their attempt to develop a "positive" or "economic theory of constitutions" by distinguishing between the "operational" level of practical politics and the "ultimate constitutional level of decision-making" (Buchanan and Tullock, 1962, p. 6). Ostrom has elaborated on this distinction by explaining that choice at "the *constitutional* level focuses upon alternative sets of rules or institutional arrangements . . . that apply to the taking of future operational decisions" (Ostrom, 1979, p. 2). At the *operational level,* on the other hand, "one is concerned with who gets what, when, and how," and at this level, "the primary preoccupation of inquiry is with the play of the political game within a given set of rules" (ibid., p. 1).

Where concern focuses exclusively upon choice and decision at the constitutional level, Buchanan and Tullock suggest that the constitution maker must address two related but analytically distinct sets of issues or questions: "Individuals choose, first of all, the fundamental organization of activity. Secondly, they choose the decision-making rules" (Buchanan and Tullock, 1962, p. 210). This distinction highlights the fact that the first order of business during constitutional construction is to address what will here be called "higher" level questions of regime type and of the basic options for institutional design. Only when these decisions have been made does choice pass to what will be referred to as a "lower" level of constitutional design, where the decision rules that will regulate and order behavior within the regime's primary institutions are selected. These "lower" level choices specify the ways in which later operational decisions will be made, by whom, and over what range of issues. Nonetheless, as we shall see below, the two levels of debate, one dealing with principles and the other with their practical implementation, were not as closely related in the Convention as Dahl suggests. Rather, the two levels seemed regularly to diverge, almost as if the debates were on separate tracks altogether. Why should this be so?

At the "higher" level of constitutional choice, the constitution makers wrestled with general questions concerning the scope, scale, and form appropriate to government and to its several institutions (McDonald, 1965, pp. 166, 184). It was in dealing with issues at the "higher" level of constitutional choice that the differences in assumptions and perspectives at the core of the several regional subcultures discussed above became most evident. In the instance of the Federal Convention, the Founders had to decide whether the new government that they were creating would be strictly popular, with the attendant risks of volatility and instability, or whether it would lean toward aristocracy in order to insure order and stability. Should the regime be an aristocratic, democratic, or mixed republic? Should the executive be one man or several; serving for a fixed term or for life; empowered to declare war and make treaties independently or not? Should the Congress be unicameral or bicameral? Should judges be removable by Congress or appointed for life? These questions were less likely to be decided with reference to the economic status, the social role, or the personal characteristics of the constitution makers than with reference to their general assumptions concerning the interplay among human nature, political institutions, and the good society. This was not because the constitution makers disregarded their personal interests in favor of broader social interests while considering questions at the "higher" level of constitutional choice, but because they were unlikely to see clearly what difference choices concerning such broad structural questions would make to them as individuals, or to their states and regions. Therefore, the constitution makers had no alternative but to base their decisions on impressions regarding the more diffuse and general interests of the community.

As the general institutional design of the regime and the relationships that would pertain among its component parts became clear, the individual constitution makers moved closer to the realm of practical politics. The questions that dominated this "lower" level of constitutional design concerned the regulation of political behavior and the distribution of political power through rules governing such specific matters as citizenship, suffrage and voting, eligibility to office, and representation. For instance, on the critical issue of the allocation among the states of seats in the national Congress: Should the states be represented equally there? If not equally, should the allocation be based on population? If so, should slaves be counted? At what proportion to whites should the blacks be calculated: one to one, one to two, three to five? Should wealth be given a role? How should the value of urban versus rural property, of improved versus unimproved land, be measured? The choices made concerning these matters would determine the power relationships that would pertain in day-to-day politics at the operational or practical level. Therefore, questions at this level were much more likely to be decided with direct reference to the political, economic, and social characteristics of the choosers, their states, or their regions than with reference to their philosophical principles.

My intention is to suggest that the division of scholarly opinion into principle versus interest interpretations of the Convention's work derives from a tendency of scholars to focus on one level of constitutional choice or the other. Those who posit the dominance of ideas in the Convention have concentrated their attention almost exclusively on the "higher" level of constitutional choice, where the delegates were choosing among regime types (as in aristocratic versus democratic republics). Those analysts who posit the dominance of interests in the Convention have focused on questions at the "lower" level of constitutional choice, where debate over specific decision rules (as in proportional versus equal representation in the legislature) tended to bear much more the interest-laced character of practical politics.

I will show that when the Convention concentrated on "higher" level questions of constitutional design, coalitions formed along lines of intellectual cleavage. During these phases of the Convention's work, the delegates from the more nationally oriented Middle Atlantic states opposed the more locally oriented delegates representing the northern and southern periphery (McDonald, 1965, pp. 1–6). When the focus shifted to "lower" level choices among specific decision rules, each of which represented an alternative distribution of authority within and over the institutions of government, the states split along lines defined by economic and geographic interest, state size and region (large versus small or North versus South).

CHAPTER 2

Debate, Deadlock, and Issue Resolution in the Convention

Chapter 1 delineated a clear pattern in the development of constitutional studies over the past two centuries as that body of literature has considered the origins of the Constitution and the process of its drafting. Recently, scholars have moved toward a view of the Convention as a congeries of conflicting, competitive interests, underlain by a very general, though at times quite tenuous, agreement on the fundamental principles of republican government. These republican principles provided the restraining parameters within which the competition for control over and advantage in a strengthened national government occurred. Yet, when one looks more closely, below the very general agreement on broad republican ideals, the delegates to the Federal Convention of 1787 clearly were divided by their adherence to regionally distinct visions of the republican government that they all professed to desire.

A Model of Factional Politics

We can explore the implications for the Convention of this complex interaction among independent agents by attempting to develop further E. E. Schattschneider's explanatory framework for the characteristic processes of conflict in democratic decision-making (Schattschneider, 1960, pp. 62–77). This dynamic model, applied to the roll-call voting record of the Convention and interpreted in light of the intricate debates recorded by James Madison and others, will contribute to the development of a more sophisticated understanding of the accomplishments of that historic conclave (Jillson, 1981a).

Schattschneider argued that a decision taken in any voting system composed of independent actors requires the participants to join forces to create the requisite majority. In the act of joining forces, the participants necessarily form a cooperation-opposition pattern on at least this individual event or decision. If the same cooperation-opposition patterns are evident across a series of decisions on the same, or

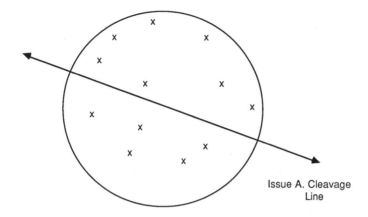

Figure 2.1. The decision universe with single cleavage. *Source:* Prepared by the author. Drawn from Schattschneider (1960), pp. 62–77.

perhaps even on different, issues, one can begin to speak of coherent decision groups or voting coalitions (Pomper, 1970, pp. 209–213).

Schattschneider uses an illustration such as Figure 2.1 to demonstrate the argument that active decision systems are characterized by both cooperation and unity on the one hand, and by conflict and cleavage on the other (Schattschneider, 1960, pp. 62–68). When a question representing an issue of importance to the members of the decision system is presented for discussion, debate, and final resolution, two related aspects of a dynamic process are set in motion. First, a division of the participants takes place between those who favor and those who oppose Issue A, those above the cleavage line versus those below it. Obviously, this indicates some measure of conflict in the system—the two groups disagree. But simultaneously, within each group, some measure of cooperation or agreement on Issue A is being displayed. The more cohesive groups become internally, the more effectively and confidently they can act in the between-group conflict that is the continuous battle over political issues in an open and ongoing decision system. Finally, the circle itself represents the boundedness of conflict and disagreement in ongoing decision systems. Systems would breakdown and decisions would be impossible if the participants were separated by cleavages so deep that consensus even on general principles and processes were not securely in place.

One such decision system is that discussed by V. O. Key, Walter Dean Burnham, James Sundquist, Gerald Pomper, and others: the national electoral system in which the presidential or congressional election is the common unit of analysis (Key, 1959, pp. 198–210; Burnham, 1970, pp.

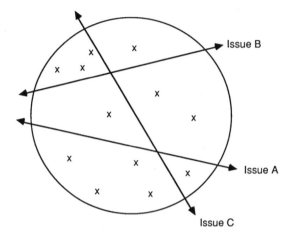

Figure 2.2. The decision universe with multiple, cross-cutting cleavages.
Source: Prepared by the author. Drawn from
Schattschneider (1960), pp. 62–77.

1–10; Pomper, 1967, pp. 535–566; Sundquist, 1973, pp. 1–10). Extensive research has already been brought to bear in analyzing the characteristic functions and processes of electoral decision-making as these are reflected in aggregate voting statistics at the national, state, and local levels (Key, 1959, pp. 198–200; Burnham, 1970, pp. 1–10). Clearly, critical realignment in the American party system can profitably be viewed as a particular case of Schattschneider's more general argument that competing issues may divide a body of voters along a number of different lines. The voting body in question may be the American mass electorate as it participates in a presidential election or the average of thirty-five delegates from eleven states that gathered daily during the American Constitutional Convention. In each case, the single decision event, the election or the roll-call vote, provides the unit of analysis, and the serial consideration of these units provides a picture of the dynamic development of the decision system over time. Therefore, in the analysis of an ongoing decision process, the interesting case concerns a system in which a number of salient issues are simultaneously present (see Figure 2.2).

Since each major issue taps a more or less different set of questions or problems, the participants may find it convenient to join with different allies as the business moves forward. When this occurs, the power of effective decision is redistributed within the system, creating new cooperation-opposition patterns, new allies and enemies, and most importantly, new winners and losers on the substantive issues. As

Schattschneider argues, when the issue changes, so does the line of cleavage that divides the participant members within the decision universe:

> The political universe remains the same in spite of the shift, but what people can do and what they cannot do depends on how they are divided. Every shift of the line of cleavage affects the nature of the conflict, produces a new set of winners and losers and a new kind of result. Thus a change in the direction and location of the line of cleavage will determine the place of each individual in the political system, what side he is on, who else is on his side, who is opposed to him, how large the opposing sides are, what the conflict is about and who wins. Since this is the process by which majorities and minorities are made, it may be said that every change in the direction and location of the line of cleavage produces a new majority and a new allocation of power. (Schattschneider, 1960, p. 63; see also, Sundquist, 1973, p. 5)

The fact that the Constitution has traditionally been characterized as a "bundle of compromises" strongly suggests that the Convention fulfilled the minimal requirements of Schattschneider's model of an ongoing decision system facing multiple issues. Gerald Pomper even finds that behavior in the Convention meets the more rigorous demands of coalition theory to the extent that "we are justified at least in an initial assumption that its behavior is of a coalitional quality" (Pomper, 1970, p. 210).

The prevalence of compromise in the Convention is of particular interest because the very need for a compromise decision indicates that voting groups have formed on opposite sides of an issue; that conflicts over a period of time in the normal decision process have sharpened the differentiation between groups and the unity within groups; but that neither side has been able to win cleanly. On the other hand, the ability to compromise at all was dependent upon the presence and strength of certain broadly shared ideas and interests (Diamond, 1981, p. 35). The decision to accept a compromise solution very rapidly dissipates the energy behind the conflict and allows a new issue to rise to preeminence, perhaps activating a new cleavage line, and dividing the participants differently. As Diamond notes, and as I will demonstrate throughout this book, "complex political struggles often come down to some single issue in which all the passions, all the forces find their focus. When that single issue is settled it is as if all the passions and forces are spent. Both sides seem somehow obliged fully to accept the outcome and matters move quickly thereafter" (Diamond, 1981, p. 31).

The delegates themselves understood quite clearly that the Convention would be characterized by conflict bounded by a broad, though perhaps quite thin and vulnerable, consensus. George Mason wrote to his son just a week before the Convention convened, saying, "upon the great principles of it, I have reason to hope there will be greater unanimity and less opposition, except from the little States, than was at first apprehended. The most prevalent idea in the principal States seems to be a total alteration of the present federal system. . . . It is easy to foresee that there will be much difficulty in organizing a government upon this great scale. . . . yet with a proper degree of coolness, liberality and candor (very rare commodities by the bye), I doubt not but it may be effected" (Farrand, ed., 1911, *Records of the Federal Convention of 1787*, vol. 3, p. 23; hereafter cited as *Records*). And on the very day that the Convention took its first roll-call vote, James Madison, in a letter to Edward Pendleton, expressed the impression that, "in general the members seem . . . averse to the temporising expedients. I wish they may as readily agree when particulars are brought forward" (ibid., p. 27).

Nonetheless, Madison and his colleagues knew that, even though the broad principles of republican government were widely accepted within the Convention, they faced many dangerous battles and confrontations over these potentially divisive "particulars." Republicanism, as a form of the mixed state, never visualized a single, determinate, governmental structure. All that republicanism necessarily demanded was that the government be somehow, directly or indirectly, derived from and responsible to the people. The Founding Fathers saw a continuum along which many variations on the republican theme might be plotted.

Obviously, the McDonald-Roche-Diamond view of the Convention as a field of conflict bounded by tenuous agreement on the broad principles of republican government is consonant with the firsthand observations of both Mason and Madison, particularly in stressing that many of the differences in the Convention over the details of constitutional construction would very likely be of a practical interest-balancing and interest-accommodating nature. Yet, at the ideological level, clear regional differences existed among the delegates concerning the kind of republican government that they wanted to create. Robert Shalhope made precisely this point when he observed that "republicanism represented a general consensus solely because it rested on such vague premises. Only one thing was certain: Americans believed that republicanism meant an absence of an aristocracy and a monarch. Beyond this, agreement vanished. . . . Different groups or factions in various sections of the nation defined 'republicanism' as they perceived it and could only view their opponents as dangerously antirepublican" (Shalhope, 1972, p. 72; see also Bailyn, 1973, p. 19; Greene, 1982, p. 15; Ketcham, 1984, pp. 200–201).

Therefore, my task requires an analytic approach that takes cognizance of a reading of the Convention's basic structure that is both confirmed by so prescient a pair as Madison and Mason and consonant with the dominant trends of recent scholarship. That structure was determined by the Convention's need to reach agreement, always within the general parameters provided by a government in the republican form, on a broad range of constitutional detail. Each point, though necessarily interrelated with the other points by the need to form a consistent whole in the final document, was a matter of some discretion during debate. This discretion, this room for debate, argument, and potential advantage, provided in each case the opportunity, not to say the promise, for conflict and disagreement. I will show that resolution of major issues triggered coalition realignments as the delegates and their states organized to confront new issues, with new implications, requiring new patterns of cooperation and opposition among the participants (Farrand, 1904, pp. 481–482).

The Convention and the Model

The circular models outlined in Figures 2.1 and 2.2 clearly display the logic inherent in the McDonald-Roche-Diamond description of a highly fractious convention sustained by an underlying ideological compatibility. The circle itself represents bounded disagreement (Rossiter, 1966, p. 51). In the Convention, this meant that fundamental agreement on two major points served to limit the divisive impact of disagreement on all other points. First, there was broad agreement on the desirability— indeed, the political necessity, given the existing distribution of political opinion in the new American society—of offering a government in the republican form (Smith, 1965, p. 56; Banning, 1974, p. 170; *Records*, vol. 3, p. 23; and Madison's *Federalist*, No. 9). This consensus on fundamental principles allowed the dialogue to begin, but widespread agreement on a second set of facts greatly facilitated successful completion of the Convention's business. The dominant interpretation of the existing political situation was summarized in James Madison's impression that "in general the members seem to accord in viewing our situation as peculiarly critical" (*Records*, vol. 3, p. 27).

George Washington, writing to Thomas Jefferson in France, echoed Madison's assessment, saying, "The business of this convention is as yet too much in embryo to form any opinion of the conclusion. . . . That something is necessary, none will deny; for the situation of the general government, if it can be called a government, is shaken to its foundation, and liable to be overturned by any blast. In a word, it is at an end; and, unless a remedy is soon applied, anarchy and confusion will inevitably ensue" (*Records*, vol. 3, p. 31). This view of the immediacy of the danger and of the consequent necessity for the Convention to present the nation with an acceptable alternative to the near-defunct Articles of Confederation held the Convention together and positively pulled it through its most dangerous periods.

Largely due to this widely shared belief that the nation's health, perhaps even its very survival, depended upon producing a broadly acceptable Constitution, one conflict scenario became very familiar. Conflict or disagreement within the Convention began with the rise of a critical and divisive issue or set of related issues. As initial debate clarified the available options, opposing coalitions quickly formed and engaged in extended debate, often characterized by impassioned pleas, demands, and threats of withdrawal until deadlock and stalemate threatened the Convention with dissolution. Whenever they were faced with a conflict that seemed to be insoluble under normal decision procedures, the delegates would deliberately select a compromise committee composed of moderates on the issue. After a relatively brief deliberation, this committee would return to the floor with a proposal acceptable to neither extreme but supported by a majority. Such a compromise solution, when accepted by the Convention, rapidly deflated the salience, centrality, and potential for further divisiveness on the issue. Further, the compromise created an emotional and substantive vacuum in the Convention's business that was rapidly filled by a new cluster of critical issues with new and different coalitions to contest them. On several occasions, as the Convention seemed to approach too violent an altercation, cooler heads drew it back from the abyss. The issue was compromised, the circle of shared consensus remained unbroken, and the Convention proceeded to new issues, new conflicts, new decisions (Diamond, 1981, p. 31).

Nonetheless, previous research gives us surprisingly little insight into the coalition patterns, the actual power relationships, that pertained in the Convention, particularly following the Connecticut Compromise. Virtually every author in the historical tradition of constitutional studies—including Bancroft (1882, p. 228), Fiske (1888, p. 289), McLaughlin (1905, p. 207), Farrand (1913, p. 82), Warren (1928, p. 293), Jensen (1964, p. 54), McDonald (1958, p. 102), Pomper (1970, pp. 209–213), and Wolfe (1977, pp. 112–117), to mention only a few of the most prominent—has identified the same opposing coalitions contesting the representation issue. Yet, this same literature tells us very little about voting groups that operated later in the Convention. In other words, during the various stages of the Convention's work, who had the clout, the votes, the actual ability to get their preferences adopted? When the

TABLE 2.1.   **Empirical Attempts to Identify Voting Groups in the Convention**

Ulmer's Alignment[a]			
1	2	3	4
North Carolina	New York	New Hampshire	Virginia
South Carolina	New Jersey	Massachusetts	Pennsylvania
Georgia	Delaware		
	Maryland		
	Connecticut		

McDonald's Alignments[b]		
1	2	3
New Hampshire	Delaware	Pennsylvania
Massachusetts	New Jersey	Virginia
North Carolina		
South Carolina	New York	
Georgia		

("Maryland and Connecticut acted as two lone wolves")

[a]Derived from "Sub-Group Formation in the Constitutional Convention," p. 296.
[b]Derived from McDonald, *We The People*, pp. 95–97.

rhetoric died away, and the votes were actually cast, who won, and how consistently did they win? When it became clear that no one could win unless the choices were redefined, how did this happen, when, and to whose ultimate benefit? This gap in our understanding is surprising because readily available and widely accepted statistical and mathematical techniques for identifying and delineating coalition structure and activity have been very successfully applied in such related areas of study as state legislatures, the United Nations, the U. S. Congress, judicial behavior, and party development (Harris, 1948; Schubert, 1962; Grumm, 1963; Alker, 1964; Alker and Russett, 1965; and Russett, 1966).

The most prominent attempts to employ the aids of quantitative analysis to confront the data (the roll-call votes) left by the Constitutional Convention are those of S. Sidney Ulmer and Forrest McDonald (see Table 2.1). Though methodologically sound, these studies suffer from important conceptual shortcomings (McDonald, 1958; Ulmer, 1968; Stoudinger, 1968). While Ulmer is surely correct to argue that one "need not suggest in advance the lines along which the states should divide in voting on Convention issues," both he and Forrest McDonald structure the outcome of their analyses by confining the search for alignments among the states to those that existed throughout the Convention (Ulmer, 1968, p. 293). Implicit in any analysis of all 569 roll-call votes as one undifferentiated group is the very strong assumption that the voting blocs so identified operated throughout the Convention with equal authority, or that temporary variations in the alignments did not prove crucial and that the disturbed coalitions somehow returned to their characteristic form.[1]

On the other hand, if the voting alignments changed during the course of the Convention as our model would lead us to expect, then the attempt to define one general coalition structure would not result in a definitive pattern, but in the homogenization of a number of coalition structures that might have been valid on particular issues, but not universally so. Such an analysis might also identify a number of small voting blocs that would have had to vary their associations and constantly recombine to form, dissolve, and reform working majorities as issues changed. If this latter possibility pertains, and as we shall see it does, the analytic task becomes one of describing when, how, and why these coalition realignments took place (see roll-call vote data in Appendix A).

The Model and the Methodology

The widespread use of factor analysis to confront problems of dimensionality in the social sciences is well known. To define empirically both the consensus and the conflict that characterized the Convention, and that has been described by earlier studies, I have attempted to build several concerns into the adaptation of factor analysis employed in this study (Rummel, 1967, 1970; Harman, 1976; Anderson et al., 1966). First, there must be an explicit time dimension so that the methodology can identify coalition realignments across time in the Convention. Second, the methodology must allow us to distinguish between levels of commitment and to observe changes in the levels of commitment demonstrated by particular states to general coalitions. Third, if it is true, as I have argued, that issues engender alignments and that the substitution of one critical issue for another may engender a realignment, then it is of considerable importance to determine with confidence what the central issues under discussion at each stage in the Convention's business were, when they changed, and whether a coalition realignment ensued.

Factor analysis will allow us to address each of these concerns very directly.[2] A two-factor solution to the patterned variation that underlies and organizes the surface complexity in the roll-call voting record of a particular phase of the Convention's business will display the general voting coalitions that confronted one another over the issues contested during that period.[3] The factor loading for each state on each factor will display the level of intensity or degree of commitment of each state to its coalition.[4] Factor scores, on the other hand, indicate the extent to which the general coalition alignments pertained to or were reflected in each particular roll-call vote. High factor scores identify those questions confronting the delegates that most directly touched upon the dominant issues of the period, allowing us to address the following question: which individual roll-call votes, dealing with which substantive issues, contributed most to creating the coalition patterns that dominated a given period of the Convention's work? In other words, what were the critical issues around which the coalitions formed and over which they did battle?

Obviously, since the questions we are attempting to answer vary, so must our use of factor analysis as an analytic tool.[5] First, in the sense that it must temporally precede other facets of this study, factor analysis will be employed to establish an initial definition of the nature, number, and timing of the coalition realignments that occurred during the Convention. Once this has been accomplished, factor analysis will be used to specify dominant coalitions during the periods of relative stability between the major realignments. I will also look within the stable periods for coalition changes that might not be uncovered by the broader analysis. In this way, I should be able to avoid the criticism that I have leveled at others of seeking to identify a single coalition structure for the entire Convention. Rather, I seek to describe a number of coalition structures, but only during those periods when they actually held sway over the business of the Convention.

Once these broad gauge questions have been answered, a number of more specific questions will arise concerning each of the major coalition patterns. For instance, what was the extent of each state's commitment to its coalition? Were the two major coalitions made up of smaller, more cohesive voting groups (protocoalitions)? Do the Convention's debates suggest that the subgroups had at least partially conflicting aims that may have led to stress within the coalition? And finally, what actions or events, what bargains or compromises, eventually led to the degeneration and final dissolution of the coalitions that dominated each phase of the Convention's business?

Coalition Formation and Realignment in the Convention

An initial step in this attempt to be explicit about the operation of voting coalitions in the Constitutional Convention involves specifying those periods during the course of the debates at which coalition realignments occurred. To do this, a temporal dimension must be added to the clustering capabilities of factor analysis (Rummel, 1970, pp. 192–202). To allow the factor methodology to identity stable realignments in the voting coalitions as issues and interests changed over time in the Convention, one need only limit the number of votes considered on each run. Rather than using a single run covering all 569 roll-call votes, this study has acknowledged the data's temporal dimension by performing twenty-five separate factor analysis runs of 100 votes each (see similar method used on vastly different data by Burnham, 1970, pp. 13–14).

Run number 1 covers votes 1 through 100. On the second run, the first 20 votes, 1 through 20, are dropped and the next twenty, 101 through 120, are added. Thus, the second run covers the 100 votes between 21 and 120. The process proceeds by 20-vote increments until all 569 roll-call votes have been included in the analysis. It is important to note that by run number 6, no vote that was included in run number 1 is still in the 100-vote bloc under consideration. Since two completely different sets of votes are being subjected to analysis in runs 1 and 6, if the coalitions that opposed one another over the first 100 votes were not the same as those that controlled the second 100, that fact should be detected. This logic should hold up for any coalition change from the Convention's opening to its adjournment. The decision to base the analysis on 100-vote blocs, rather than on some smaller number, was designed to allow a measure of stability in the coalitions, while the addition and subtraction of 20-vote increments was designed to allow realignments to emerge, rather than to appear abruptly as they would have done if larger increments had been employed.

Figure 2.3, entitled "Coalition realignment in the American Constitutional Convention," displays the initial results of this dynamic approach. Three distinct coalition realignments are identified as having occurred during the course of the Convention's proceedings, suggesting that there were—before, between, and after these realignments—at least four periods of relative stability during which various coalition alignments dominated the Convention's affairs. In addition, I will demonstrate through other means that a fourth coalition realignment occurred, this one very early in the Convention, that is not captured by the technique employed to create Figure 2.3.

Figure 2.3. Coalition realignment in the American Constitutional Convention.
Facing Page.

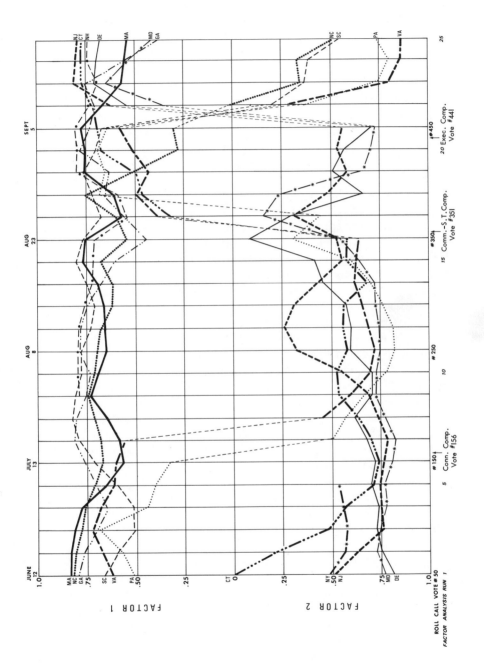

As is always the case when a great deal of information is consolidated for graphic presentation, much of that information may be lost if the design of the graph and the nature of its contents are not carefully explained. The most important facets of Figure 2.3 are the following. Each vertical line represents an individual two-factor solution to 100 sequential roll-call votes. Notice that at the bottom lefthand corner of the graph are two labels, "Roll-Call Vote" and "Factor Analysis Run," the first two labels being numbers 50 and 1. From left to right along the bottom of the graph, votes are explicitly labeled at intervals of 100 (50, 150, 250, 350, 450), but each vertical line represents an interval of 20; for instance, the lines between 50 and 150 represent 100-vote sets, with 70, 90, 110, and 130 as their middle or pivot votes. The factor analysis runs are labeled in increments of 5 (1, 5, 10, 15, 20, 25). At the top of the graph are specific dates on which the corresponding votes at the bottom of the graph were taken in the Convention. This arrangement should aid readers in placing themselves in relation to the Convention's ongoing activities.

A hypothetical case will help to explain why the middle vote in each set of 100 is highlighted. If the coalitions in the Convention changed significantly at vote number 100, the first run, on votes 1 through 100, would define an unambiguous coalition pattern. Of the 100 votes considered on the second run, votes 21 through 120, 80 would still be characterized by the original coalition alignment, while the 20 new votes, 101 through 120, would be characterized by the new and different pattern. Nonetheless, one would expect the factor solution for the second run to describe the original pattern, since the 80 votes would outweigh the 20 new votes. On run number 3, the same thing would happen, as the 60 votes would overbalance the 40, though one would expect the old coalitions to blur as the new pattern made itself felt. However, on the fourth run, a dramatic coalition shift would be registered. For the first time, the number of votes characterized by the new pattern would be greater than the number reflecting the original pattern. This is why the middle vote in each set is explicitly labeled. The pivot or middle vote in a 100-vote set marks the approximate point at which a coalition shift is registered by this methodology.

Figure 2.3 presents both a fluid picture of coalition realignment in the Convention and an initial definition of the structure of the principal opposition patterns that operated at any time during the course of the Convention's work. Each run displays the dominant coalition pattern during the period in which the 100 votes under consideration were debated and recorded. The sensitivity of this dynamic factor analysis approach is obvious. The first coalition realignment to be registered in Figure 2.3 began with run number 6, of which the middle or pivot vote is 150. The Connecticut Compromise was approved in the Convention at vote number 156. The second realignment displayed here began with run number 16, of which the middle vote is 350. The Commerce and Slave Trade Compromise was passed in part by vote number 352. The final realignment began with run number 21, of which the middle vote is 450. The Executive Branch Compromise was passed with vote number 441. In no case is there a discrepancy of more than 9 roll-call votes between one of these three major realigning compromises and its reflection by this adaptation of the factor methodology.

The horizontal lines on the graph are of equal importance, as they indicate the extent to which individual states participated in the opposing coalitions defined by each two-factor solution. The middle horizontal line is labeled 0 and the loadings of each state on each two-factor solution are laid out above and below the 0 point. Factor 1 and the states that coalesced on it are found above the 0 point, and Factor 2 and those that grouped together on it in opposition to the Factor 1 states are found below. The loadings on both factors are labeled at intervals of .25 (0, .25, .50, .75, 1.0). The stronger the state's factor loading (the nearer to 1.0), the greater its commitment to its coalition. The abbreviation for each state identifies a distinctive line symbol which can be traced across the entire graph from the Convention's opening to its final adjournment.

A brief example may help clarify the range of information contained in the graph. The two-factor solution to factor analysis run number 1 indicates that within the six-member factor 1 coalition, three states load very strongly, between .75 and .85, while three others load less strongly, between .50 and .75. The opposition, found on factor 2, is made up of four states, two of which load strongly, and two moderately, with a fifth state, Connecticut, initially uncommitted but soon unambiguously to fill the factor 2 ranks. Each of the twenty-five separate factor analysis runs displays both the broad coalitions that opposed one another over the issues facing the Convention in the 100 roll-call votes in question and the intensity of each state's commitment to its coalition.

Obviously, the most striking aspect of Figure 2.3 is the identification of several very clear periods of coalition realignment. But of equal importance are the long and well-defined periods of stability in the voting coalitions between realignments. These promise to enhance our ability to understand and interpret the realignments themselves. During the periods of relative stability, it is possible to define the major issues under debate and each state's position on each issue. Further, we can follow debate on the issue or issues that ultimately deadlocked the Convention and created the necessity for compromise and reevaluation. The result, at least in the cases highlighted in Figure 2.3, was a decision by some to realign and cooperate with states which before the compromise, were vehemently opposed on other issues.

On the basis of Figure 2.3, we can confidently state the following initial conclusions. First, voting patterns or coalitions did change during the course of the Convention, with states leaving one coalition to join another. Second, the cause of each realignment can very directly be tied to three of the major compromises taken at the Convention, two of which, the Connecticut Compromise and the Commerce and Slave Trade Compromise, are well known, while the third and final, the Executive Branch Compromise, has been much underestimated in its impact on the final document.

Those who are familiar with the history of the American Constitutional Convention will not be surprised to find these three compromises enumerated as crucial or of special interest (Farrand, 1904, pp. 488–489). But their familiarity is deceptive, because there were other well-known compromises made in the Convention—only a few of which involved the judiciary, the western lands, ratification procedures, and the militia—that did not instigate wholesale realignments of the voting coalitions. Only a few of the hundreds, even thousands, of decisions taken by the delegates had that degree of impact on the business of the Convention.

The first coalition realignment to occur in the Convention is not captured in Figure 2.3. Chapter 4 demonstrates quite clearly that the Convention's opening days, from May 25 to June 9, saw a critical clash between those delegates who wished to move immediately to the construction of a powerful and independent national government and those delegates who wished merely to modify the existing Articles of Confederation. During this initial phase of the Convention's work, the nationalists of the Middle Atlantic region battled with the more tentative and parochial delegates from New England and the lower South. Though these regime questions at the "higher" level of constitutional choice held the Convention's attention through the first ten days of substantive debate, only thirty-five roll-call votes were taken during that time. By June 9, the supporters of a powerful national government had established their point, and debate shifted to the question of who would control this new government, particularly its powerful legislative branch. When the Convention's focus shifted to these "lower" level decisions concerning the distribution of power and control within the legislature, the large states faced off against the small. Though the coalitions that confronted one another during the Convention's opening days are not clearly displayed in Figure 2.3 (because in run number 1 the thirty-five votes taken before June 9 are overbalanced by the sixty-five votes taken after June 9), they are separately analyzed and fully discussed in Chapter 4.

The first realignment to be displayed in Figure 2.3 was generated by a compromise solution to the critical representation question that dominated the Convention's business from June 9 to July 17. Figure 2.3 shows that the realignment began on or about July 13, with Pennsylvania leaving the nationalist coalition on factor 1 to join the opposition on factor 2. Virginia followed a few days later. The specification of which states moved (and which chose not to move) between coalitions and when they moved raises many interesting questions that have gone unanswered in previous studies of the Convention and its work. For instance, why did Pennsylvania leave when it did, before the compromise had actually decided the question, and before Virginia did so? What interests did Virginia serve by remaining with her colleagues on factor 1 for those few extra days in mid-July? And why did Massachusetts, a large northern state, after wavering in the early weeks of July, choose to stick with the states of the deep South even after the critical issues facing the Convention had changed from representation to slavery, commerce, and the structure of the executive branch? Our considerably more detailed understanding of exactly how this realignment occurred—Pennsylvania leaving, followed later by Virginia, with everyone else standing firm—make these questions much easier to address. Chapter 5 treats in great detail the rise, operation, and ultimate decline of the coalitions that dominated the Convention's treatment of the representation issue.

The second major coalition alignment highlighted in Figure 2.3, discussed in Chapters 6 and 7, once again, as during the Convention's opening days, pitted the wings of the new nation, the Northeast and the deep South, against the nation's solid middle in a periphery-versus-center coalition pattern. This opposition pattern dominated the Convention's business from July 17 until it was dramatically altered as a direct result of the resolution of issues achieved in mid-August in the Commerce and Slave Trade Compromise. This coalition realignment finds Virginia, Pennsylvania, and Connecticut abandoning the Middle Atlantic state group on factor 2 to rejoin Massachusetts and the deep South on factor 1. Chapter 8 analyzes the results of these movements as they occasioned a short lived, but powerful, coalition of large and medium size states that were vehemently opposed by three smaller states' rights oriented delegations.

The third and final realignment shown in Figure 2.3 was the most dramatic and has been the least understood of the major compromises of the Convention. Run number 21, covering votes 401–500, marks the beginning of this final phase of realignment. New Jersey, Delaware, and Maryland, the small states of the Middle Atlantic region, which had always been very sensitive to the potential danger of being overwhelmed by the larger states, became the core of a dominant group of small northern states, while Virginia and Pennsylvania again fell into opposition along with North and South Carolina. Fully chronicled in Chapter 9, this new alignment, which was maintained until the end of the Convention, was the result of a set of compromise propositions reported on September 4. These propositions dealt with the selection process for the Chief Executive, as well as, and perhaps even more importantly, with the balance of power between the Chief Executive, the Senate, and the states that sought to control these institutions. Finally, Chapter 10 summarizes the findings and reanalyzes the phenomenon of coalition realignment in the Federal Convention in light of this study.

Considerable progress has been made toward answering some of the questions outlined above and toward laying the groundwork for answering the others. Nonetheless, much remains to be done. Satisfactory organization of the data really only opens the door to our primary task. But only when the first task of data organization has been completed can personal interpretations, conclusions, and observations about the data, and about the dynamic processes that structure and give meaning to them, be undertaken with any degree of confidence and specificity. A convincing structure of argument must be erected on the firm foundation which has been created. Now that we know what happened, who voted with whom, and when, we can assess in some detail the impact of voting coalitions and changes in these voting coalitions over time on the final resolution of those questions that imparted to the American Constitution its distinctive character.

CHAPTER 3

James Madison and the Origins of the Virginia Plan

Chapter 2 highlighted three periods during the Convention's work when significant changes occurred in the voting alignments that clashed over the critical issues under review. In later chapters, our task will be to explain this process of coalition formation, operation, degeneration, and subsequent realignment in terms of the different intellectual, political, social, and economic issues that were before the Convention during each period. But how do we explain the early appearance of the large-state–small-state opposition alignment?

I will argue that James Madison's preconvention strategy, shared in letters to several of his Virginia colleagues, anticipated the fundamental importance of the representation question. The most detailed letters, identifying both the key problem with current American governmental forms and the solution that he thought most eligible, were to Edmund Randolph, dated April 6, and to George Washington, dated April 16. Madison began with what he and many others took to be the root of the problem: "Conceiving that an individual independence of the States is utterly irreconcileable with their aggregate sovereignty . . . I would propose as the ground-work that a change be made in the principle of representation." Madison then went on to indicate that he was "ready to believe that such a change would not be attended with much difficulty" (Meyers, 1973, p. 95). In addition, Madison correctly predicted that the coalitions likely to form around this issue would find a coalition of the large and southern states in a slim but solid majority.

Madison believed that "a majority of the States, and those of greatest influence, will regard it as favorable to them. To the Northern States it will be recommended by their present populousness; to the Southern by their expected advantage in this respect. The lesser States must in every event yield to the predominant will" (Hunt, 1901, vol. 2, p. 345). Once the small states had yielded to the reality of the larger states' greater weight, Madison told Washington, this would "obviate the principal objections of the larger States to the necessary concessions of power" (ibid.). Yet, as the Convention drew near, Madison, listening closely to his Virginia colleagues and to others gathering for the Convention, came increasingly to fear the potential impact of this disruptive, perhaps even destructive, issue and eventually sought to delay direct consideration of it during the Convention's opening days. In the end, Madison's proposal for proportional representation in both houses of the Congress did not prevail. More importantly, the coalition that Madison called forth in support of proportional representation and that dominated the Convention's business into mid-July failed to regain control of the Convention when the representation issue faded and new issues became paramount.

Madison's Developing Constitutional Thought

James Madison was the principal author and tactician of the Virginia Plan (see the Virginia Plan in Appendix B). Madison's foremost concern throughout the 1780s, and even more single-mindedly after he left the Congress in 1783, was with the theoretical and practical shortcomings of the Confederation government and of the several state governments. As early as March 16, 1784, Madison wrote to Thomas Jefferson, then in Paris, to "particularize" Jefferson's mandate to buy for him "rare and valuable books. . . . to whatever may throw light on the general constitution & droit public of the several confederacies that have existed. . . . The operations of our own must render all such lights of consequence" (ibid., p. 43). A year later, on April 27, 1785, Madison expanded his request of Jefferson to include, "treatises on the ancient or modern federal republics—on the law of Nations—and the history natural & political of the New World" (ibid., p. 134).

Madison's scholarly interest in these questions was reinforced by a constant and increasingly urgent concern for practical application. These endeavors contributed mightily to making Madison the most thoroughly prepared and knowledgeable member of the Federal Convention. William Pierce of Georgia provided a "character sketch" of each delegate in attendance. His sketch of Madison seems to capture a general consensus that "he blends together the profound politician, with the Scholar. . . . From a spirit of industry and application which he possesses in a most eminent degree, he always comes forward the best informed Man of any point in debate. The affairs of the United States, he perhaps, has the most correct knowledge of, of any man in the Union" (*Records*, vol. 3, p. 94).

Both Madison the "scholar" and Madison the "profound politician" had been bringing that "spirit of industry and application" to bear on matters of constitutional theory and design since his student days at

Princeton. His interest and expertise in these matters were so widely known in Virginia and beyond that George Muter and Caleb Wallace of Kentucky, in anticipation of that state's separation from Virginia, approached him in August of 1785 with a series of specific questions concerning constitutional design. Three later examples of Madison's developing thought are found in letters to Jefferson, Randolph, and Washington in March and April of 1787. These letters to his fellow Virginians on the eve of the Convention outline Madison's understanding of the problems facing the architects of a national government in the republican form and his strategy for pushing large-scale changes designed significantly to strengthen the national government through a convention in which they were certain to encounter formidable opposition. In addition, Madison formalized and elaborated his critique of existing political institutions, particularly those at the state level, in his famous "Vices of the Political System of the United States," which also appeared in April of 1787. From these diverse sources the origins, growth, and intent of the Virginia Plan can be reconstructed.

A Constitution for Kentucky: State-Level Solutions

In the instance of the Kentucky Constitution, Madison was only concerned to suggest adjustments to the basic institutional structure of the state governments. Following the Revolution, state constitutions were written which removed power from the aristocratic and monarchical branches of government and added them to the more popular branch. State executives came commonly to be appointed by state legislatures, often for short terms and with no reeligibility. Frequently, their powers of appointment and veto were removed or dramatically restricted. State senates were made elective, with eligibility and powers similar to those of the lower house. Everywhere, the lower houses were powerful, if not predominant and unchecked (Main, 1973, pp. 186–221). Although Madison also saw serious problems plaguing relations between the states, and between the states and the Confederation government, these would have to wait for treatment in another place. Like most of his countrymen, Madison was convinced that the structure of the legislative branch held the key to the chronic injustice and instability that had historically afflicted republican governments. Therefore, in order to confront this characteristic instability directly, his first point of advice was that "the legislative Department ought by all means. . . . to include a Senate constituted on such principles as will give wisdom and steadiness to legislation. The want of these qualities is the grievance complained of in all our republics." Maryland's strong upper house was held up as a favorable example, while Virginia's weaker Senate was derided. Nonetheless, even the Virginia Senate was said to act on occasion as "a useful bit in the mouth of the house of Delegates."

The central thrust of Madison's concern with the legislative branch, strengthening the senate, was made clear by his offhand disposal of the more popular house. He simply observed in passing that "for the other branch models enough may be found" (Hunt, 1901, vol. 2, p. 167). Madison and many others were convinced that the key problem confronting American constitutional development involved constructing an effective counterweight to the aggressive and volatile lower houses. To add further stability to the legislative process, Madison noted that "as a security against fluctuating & indigested laws the Constitution of New York has provided a Council of Revision. I approve much of such an institution" (ibid., p. 168). A similar council was to loom both large and impossibly controversial in Madison's later plans for an adequate national government.

Turning to the executive branch, Madison confronted a problem that he was never to solve to his own satisfaction and that was to confound the Federal Convention through most of its debates, that is, the selection, tenure, reeligibility, and powers of the Chief Magistrate. The memory of George III and his royal governors was still too fresh in the American mind to allow enhancing the office without generating substantial apprehension. A statement very similar to the following appears in this and each of his subsequent plans: "I have made up no final opinion whether the first Magistrate should be chosen by the Legislature or the people at large or whether the power should be vested in one man assisted by a council or in a council of which the President shall be only primus inter pares. There are examples of each in the U. States and probably advantages and disadvantages attending each" (ibid., p. 169).

Despite the safe operation of strong executives in New York and South Carolina throughout the 1780s, most Americans still found it very difficult to conceive of a strong executive who would not eventually pervert legitimate discretion into arbitrary and aggressive power (Jillson, 1979). Worse yet, the popular view held that even those executive institutions wielding power short of a kingly prerogative, but with authority sufficient to restrain the legislative branch, would be very difficult to effectively bind within their constitutional parameters. The great fear was that an executive strong enough to be efficient and useful might be too strong to be guided and limited by an interest broader than its own position and power (Thach, 1923).

Madison shared these concerns with the great majority of his countrymen in 1785. His conclusion was that little more could be achieved at the state level than a redistribution of authority away from the popular House and toward a more stable (aristocratic) Senate. These views changed very little prior to the Federal Convention. Nonetheless, critical elements were added to them in order to justify an overarching national government to which the several state governments clearly would be subordinate.

Principles Justifying a Strong National Government

To supplement these structural considerations, which applied to both the state and the national governments, Madison outlined his sense of the theoretical principles that might justify the allocation of authority sufficient to establish a supreme national government in a March 18, 1787, letter to Jefferson. Madison's first point was that ratification of a national constitution should be by the people at large, rather than by the state legislatures or any intermediate body. Only such a national referendum would establish a firm basis in popular sovereignty for the supremacy of the national Constitution and the government that it defined. Second, in addition to control over "matters in which uniformity is proper" (such as commerce and coinage), Madison contended that "the federal head" must be armed "with a negative *in all cases whatsoever* on the local Legislatures." Third, he argued that the principle of representation at the federal level should be changed from equality among the states to a measure that would recognize "the inequality of importance and influence in the States." And finally, so that dominance by the popular assemblies might be avoided at the national level, care should be taken to "organize the federal powers in such a manner as not to blend together those which ought to be exercised by separate departments" (Hunt, 1901, vol. 2, pp. 324–327).

Madison hoped to base the proposed national government on these far-reaching and fundamental principles. However, precisely because they constituted far-reaching and fundamental adjustments in the existing system, Madison's ideas were quite beyond the expectations of some powerful members of his own Virginia delegation. Edmund Randolph, recently elected governor of Virginia and therefore titular head of that state's very distinguished delegation to the Convention, suggested in a March 27 letter to Madison the incremental approach that he hoped to see the Convention take: "At present, I conceive— 1. that the alterations should be grafted on the Old Confederation. 2. That what is best in itself, not merely what can be obtained from the Assemblies be adopted. 3. That the points of power to be granted be so detached from each other, as to permit a State to reject some part, without mutilating the whole. 4. With these objects, ought not some general proposition be prepared for feeling the pulse of the Convention on the subject at large?" (Hunt, 1901, vol. 2, pp. 336–340).

Madison disagreed fundamentally with Randolph because he thought the governor's second point was completely at variance with his first and third points. In addition, Madison had already developed "some general propositions" that were dramatically at variance with Randolph's preferred approach to the business. In view of Governor Randolph's preference for an incremental approach to the Convention's business, Madison was undoubtedly very much heartened upon his receipt of George Washington's letter of April 1, which outlined Washington's very different sense of the Convention's task. Washington was adamant in his view "that a thorough reform of the present system is indispensable." But like most Americans, and even most delegates to the rapidly approaching Convention, Washington had not progressed far enough in his thinking to set down the structure and principles upon which a viable alternative might be based. He said only that he doubted "whether any system, without the means of coercion in the sovereign, will enforce due obedience to the ordinances of a general government. . . . But the kind of coercion you may ask. This indeed will require thought" (Ford, 1891, vol. 11, pp. 132–134). Madison knew that Washington's "wish . . . that the Convention may adopt no temporizing expedient, but probe the defects of the Constitution to the bottom, and provide radical cures," would constitute more than a counterweight to Randolph's timidity in the scales of the other men's judgment. Therefore, Madison set rapidly about marrying his thoughts concerning the institutional structures required to address the chronic instability that had plagued ancient and modern confederacies to his thoughts on the principles that would justify the strong national government that both he and Washington desired.

Vices of the Political System of the United States

Madison's detailed analysis of the deficiencies in the American political experience under the Articles of Confederation resulted in a short essay entitled, "Vices of the Political System of the United States," dated April 1787 (Meyers, 1973, pp. 83–92). "Vices" consisted of eleven numbered paragraphs that constituted both an indictment of the existing system and a short list of the most pressing problems that would have to be overcome in any new system. Madison's fundamental concern was that thoughtless and frequently misdirected state governments were abusing their own citizens, each other, and the weak Confederation government. The eleven counts of Madison's indictment were as follows (from Meyers, pp. 83–88):

1. Failure of the States to comply with the constitutional requisitions.
2. Encroachments by the States on the federal authority.
3. Violations of the law of nations and of treaties.
4. Trespasses of the States on the rights of each other.
5. Want of concert in matters where common interest requires it.
6. Want of guaranty to the States of their constitutions & laws against internal violence.
7. Want of sanction to the laws, and of coercion in the government of the confederacy.
8. Want of ratification by the people of the articles of confederation.
9. Multiplicity of laws in the several States.
10. Mutability of the laws of the States.
11. Injustice of the laws of the States.

Although each of these shortcomings contributed to the impotence of the Confederation, the eleventh point, the "injustice of the laws," was the focal point of Madison's critique of the popular assembly dominated state governments: "If the multiplicity and mutability of laws prove a want of wisdom, their injustice betrays a defect still more alarming," because it brings into doubt the most "fundamental principle of republican Government, that the majority who rule in such governments are the safest Guardians both of the public Good and private rights" (Meyers, 1973, p. 88).

Madison deployed arguments that would later form the core of *Federalist* no. 10 in identifying two primary causes of the evils that seemed to befall republics with such regularity. The first derived from the self-interested behavior of the people's elected representatives; but since basic human nature is largely fixed, a cure would have to be sought elsewhere. Happily, the principles of separation of powers and checks and balances, widely known if not yet completely understood by Madison and his soon to be colleagues at the Convention, were available to pose interest against interest within the institutional structure of a national government. The second, and historically less tractable, cause of social and political instability originated in divisions among the people themselves. Madison argued that

all civilized societies are divided into different interests and factions, as they happen to be creditors or debtors—rich or poor—husbandmen, merchants or manufacturers—members of different religious sects—followers of different political leaders—inhabitants of different districts—owners of different kinds of property & &. In republican Government the majority however composed, ultimately give the law. Whenever therefore an apparent interest or common passion unites a majority what is to restrain them from unjust violations of the rights and interests of the minority, or of individuals? (Meyers, 1973, p. 89).

This brief statement summarized the problem that Madison saw confronting the delegates soon to arrive in Philadelphia.

As the Convention approached, Madison stood ready with the radical cure that both he and Washington thought necessary. Nothing less than a continental republic with a national government strong enough to control the volatile local authorities and sufficiently well constructed to control itself would provide the requisite stability. Madison believed that a potential solution to the factionalism that seemed so endemic to republican governments lay in the fact that "an enlargement of the sphere is found to lessen insecurity . . . because a common interest or passion is less apt to be felt and the requisite combinations less easy to be formed by a great than by a small number. The Society becomes broken into a great variety of interests, of pursuits of passion, which check each other, whilst those who feel a common sentiment have less opportunity of communication and concert" (Meyers, 1973, p. 91). With an enlargement of the geographical sphere as a partial defense against majority tyranny, the next great consideration involved insuring against the rise of tyranny from within the national government itself (Carey, 1978). Madison called the basic problem confronting the constitution makers at Philadelphia "the great desideratum in Government;" that is, "such a modification of the sovereignty as will render it sufficiently neutral between the different interests and factions, to controul one part of the society from invading the rights of another, and at the same time sufficiently controuled itself, from setting up an interest adverse to that of the whole Society" (Meyers, 1973, p. 91).

The firm ground from which Madison moved off in search of a solution to this "great desideratum of Government" was his conviction, noted earlier, "that an individual independence of the States is utterly irreconcilable with the idea of an aggregate sovereignty." The critical question facing the Convention was "whether any middle ground can be taken which will at once support a due supremacy of the national authority, and leave in force the local authorities so far as they can be subordinately useful" (Hunt, 1901, vol. 2, p. 46).

Madison's 'Grand Plan' for the Federal Convention

Madison sought to describe his initial conception of the contours of this stable middle ground between tyranny and license to Randolph and to Washington in the form of a nine-point plan for establishing a new national government. Many aspects of this plan had been articulated earlier in his proposals for a Kentucky constitution and in his letter to Jefferson on federal principles (Hunt, 1901, vol. 2, pp. 336–340). These letters to Randolph and Washington constitute both an early draft of the Virginia Plan and a statement of Madison's strategy for the upcoming Convention. Nonetheless, Madison was somewhat circumspect with Randolph, while he spoke more freely and bluntly with Washington.

First, we have noted that Madison thought that it was critical to the tactical element of his plan for addressing the Convention that "the first step [would] be a change in the principle of representation." The equality of voting rights that pertained among the states under the Articles of Confederation had to be changed to some principle that would, as he had suggested to Jefferson some three weeks earlier, reflect "the inequality of importance and influence in the States."

Second, a viable national government would require "a positive and complete authority in all cases where uniform measures are necessary, as in trade &c." Third, in addition to the positive powers required by the national government, "let it have a negative, in all cases whatsoever, on the Legislative acts of the States, as the King of Great Britain hitherto had." Although the proposal for a negative, "in all cases whatsoever," appears in the letters to both Randolph and Washington, it is much expanded and emphasized in the letter to the more sympathetic Washington. The negative appeared to Madison "to be absolutely necessary, and to be the least possible encroachment on the authority of the States." Madison thought that such a negative was necessary because "without this defensive power. . . . The States will continue to invade the National jurisdiction, to violate treaties and the law of nations & to harass each other with rival and spiteful measures dictated by mistaken views of interest." But even more significantly, Madison thought that the negative contained the answer to that "great desideratum of Government," that stable middle ground, that he had been seeking in the books that Jefferson had sent him and in his thoughts on the vices of the current system. He promised Washington that "another happy effect of this prerogative (the negative) would be its control on the internal vicissitudes of State policy, and the aggressions of interested majorities on the rights of minorities and of individuals."

Clearly, the potential that the "negative" carried for limiting legislative injustice at the state level was the critical point for Madison because this behavior had brought the very wisdom and safety of republican government into direct question. Failure to achieve the "negative," even in an otherwise broadly strengthened federal structure, might leave these "vices" dangerously alive. Carefully feeling his way in the presence of

Washington, Madison tentatively argued that "the great desideratum that has not yet been found for Republican Governments seems to be some disinterested & dispassionate umpire in disputes between different passions & interests in the State. The majority who alone have the right of decision, have frequently an interest, real or supposed in abusing it. . . . Might not the national prerogative (the negative) here suggested be found sufficiently disinterested for the decisions of local questions of policy, whilst it would itself be sufficiently restrained from the pursuit of interests adverse to those of the whole Society?"

I will demonstrate that the change in the principle of representation, along with a "complete negative" for the national government on state legislation, were the linchpins of Madison's plan and were clearly the provisions with which his Convention strategy was most directly concerned. This letter to Washington makes it clear that Madison envisioned a national government not appreciably less powerful than the British king had been prior to the Revolution. The problem as he saw it was not to limit this authority but to distribute it through the primary institutions of the government in such a way as to make it efficient without being dangerous, effective without being threatening.

Fourth, Madison thought it critical that the judges of the national courts be tied to the national government, rather than the states, by both their oaths and their pocketbooks, lest the states apply pressure in important cases. Not surprisingly, Madison did not want disputes between the national and state governments over authority and prerogative to be settled in the state courts by state appointed judges. Madison simply proposed that "this national supremacy be extended also to the Judiciary department."

Points five through nine provide no surprises. Fifth was the proposal that "the Legislative department may be divided into two branches. One of them to be chosen every____years by the Legislatures or the people at large; the other to consist of a more select number, holding their appointments for a longer term, and going out in rotation." Sixth was Madison's suggestion that "a Council of Revision may be superadded, including the great ministerial officers." Seventh, that "a national Executive will also be necessary." But, in words very similar to those he had used two years earlier when advising his friends in Kentucky, Madison again confessed that he had "scarcely ventured to form my own opinion yet, either of the manner in which it ought to be constituted, or of the authorities in which it ought to be clothed." Eighth, was Madison's suggestion than "an article ought to be inserted expressly guaranteeing the tranquility of the States against internal as well as external dangers."

And finally, ninth was his conviction that "to give the new system its proper energy, it will be desirable to have it ratified by the authority of the people, and not merely by that of the Legislatures" (Hunt, 1901, vol. 2, pp. 336–340). This would unequivocally establish its superiority to the state constitutions.

Madison's plan envisioned proportional representation in both houses of a bicameral legislature, with one branch elected by the people and the other selected by the first branch out of a list of candidates submitted by the state legislatures. Acting together, the two branches of the legislature would have wide powers to intervene wherever the states were incompetent or the national harmony was threatened. State incompetence and threats to the national harmony were to be judged by the national legislature, which could enforce its judgment through the exercise of a negative over any and all state laws. A national executive and judiciary were also proposed, but the locus of power would lie in the legislative branch, and so, as all well knew, the crucial battles in the Convention would be fought over this ground.

How did Madison expect to secure approval for this radical centralization of authority when the whole history of the previous decade had been one of the states consistently refusing to sanction even quite moderate and incremental additions of power to the central government (Jensen, 1950; Wood, 1969; Henderson, 1974; Davis, 1977)? Madison had both an analysis of the probable balance of forces confronting his plan and an explicit strategy for accomplishing the several elements of it. Madison's forecast was that "the change in the principle of representation will be relished by a majority of the States, and those too of most influence. The northern States will be reconciled to it by the *actual* superiority of their populousness; the Southern by their *expected* superiority on this point. This principle established, the repugnance of the large States to part with power will in a large degree subside, and the smaller States will ultimately yield to the predominate will" (Hunt, 1901, vol. 2, p. 340).

This, then, was Madison's Grand Plan, developed over the decade of the 1780s and outlined to Washington and Randolph five and six weeks prior to the Convention's opening. The first order of business would be to change the existing equality of voting rights to one proportioned to some measure of weight and power, population and wealth being the obvious possibilities. This change would be "relished" by those states currently most populous (Massachusetts, Pennsylvania and Virginia) and those states of the deep South (North Carolina, South Carolina and Georgia) in whose favor the population trends seemed to be moving.

These six states formed a majority of the eleven states likely to appear for the Convention's opening; therefore, the proposal should carry even though the small states might vehemently oppose. Such a redistribution of authority in the central government, while just in itself, would also serve to correct the fundamental weakness of the Confederation. Once their importance was formally recognized, the larger states would be much less reticent to part with the power needed to give a requisite energy to that "aggregate sovereignty" that Madison, Washington, and their nationalist colleagues had sought since the Revolution.

With this plan in hand, Madison arrived in Philadelphia for the Convention on May 3, fully eleven days before it was to begin and over three weeks before it would actually achieve a quorum. Several of the Pennsylvania delegates resident in Philadelphia were available for immediate consultation concerning the upcoming business. Other Virginia delegates also arrived early, including Washington on May 13, providing plenty of time for consultation with and the lobbying of members not earlier privy to Madison's plan. On May 14, when the Convention was scheduled to convene, only eight or ten delegates were present, and only Pennsylvania and Virginia had legal quorums. Although a quorum in the required seven delegations was not attained until May 25, Madison and his Virginia colleagues did not allow the time to go to waste. As George Mason recorded in a letter of May 20 to his son; "The Virginia deputies (who are all here) meet and confer together two or three hours every day, in order to form a proper correspondence of sentiments" (*Records*, vol. 3, p. 23).

Mason's description of this "correspondence of sentiments" within the Virginia delegation shows Madison's clear influence (Collier and Collier, 1986, p. 55). Mason indicated that: "The most prevalent idea in the principal States seems to be a total alteration of the present federal system, and substituting a great national council or parliament, consisting of two branches of the legislature, founded upon the principles of equal proportionate representation, with full legislative powers upon all the subjects of the Union; and an Executive: and to make the several State legislatures subordinate to the national, by giving the latter the power of a negative upon all such laws as they shall judge contrary to the interest of the federal Union" (*Records*, vol. 3, p. 23).

Nonetheless, Madison's plan did not pass directly from his hand to the Convention floor. The daily meetings of the Virginia delegation made significant additions by way of fleshing out his basic outline. For instance, where Madison called for proportional representation to replace equality, the Virginia caucus specified that representation "be

Proportioned to the Quotas of contribution, or to the number of free inhabitants." In another very visible instance, that of the process for selection of the Chief Executive, upon which Madison had never formed a solid opinion, the caucus specified an Executive "to be chosen by the National Legislature for a term of____years. . . to be ineligible a second time."

Though the Virginia caucus made many other additions to and specifications of Madison's basic structural design, it is perhaps more important to note that the strategic element of the plan was reversed. In preparing for the Convention, Madison had come to believe that two critical questions had to be decided by the Convention and that the order in which they were addressed was fundamentally important. One was the question of the relative weight of the states in the new government, and the other was the question of the powers that the new government would wield. Madison's great fear was that if the Convention went directly to the question of expanded powers, the pattern of the previous decade would take hold and the nationalist cause would be nibbled to death by both timidity and uncertainty. But if the representation question could be quickly settled in favor of proportional representation, the largest and most influential states would feel quite secure in allocating to the new government the broad powers it would need to play the stabilizing role that Madison and the nationalists envisioned for it in American politics. As the Convention approached, Madison declared to Randolph and Washington that he "was ready to believe that such a change would not be attended with much difficulty" (Hunt, 1901, vol. 2, p. 345).

Despite Madison's early optimism, his convention strategy did not survive the Virginia delegation's caucuses over his plan. Randolph's timidity, since, as governor, he would be called upon to present his state's plan, was probably decisive. Once the Convention did open on May 25 and the credentials of the delegates were read, the fate of Madison's strategy was sealed. Madison recorded that "on reading the Credentials of the deputies it was noticed that those from Delaware were prohibited from changing the Article in the Confederation establishing an equality of votes among the States" (*Records*, vol. 1, p. 4). The delegates from Delaware indicated to their colleagues that they might be forced to withdraw from the Convention if a proposal denying equal votes to the several states were passed.

In view of the timidity within his own delegation and the apparent inability of the Delaware men to adopt what Madison had earlier called the "ground-work" of his new system, Madison sought to adapt to the new reality. In an explanatory footnote attached to the debates of May 28, a day dedicated to discussion and adoption of the rules to be followed by the Convention, Madison explained that:

> Previous to the arrival of a majority of the States, the rule by which they ought to vote in the Convention had been made a subject of conversation among the members present. It was pressed by Gouverneur Morris and favored by Robert Morris and others from Pennsylvania, that the large States should unite in firmly refusing to the small States an equal vote, as unreasonable, and as enabling the small States to negative every good system of Government, which must in the nature of things, be founded on a violation of that equality. The members from Virginia, conceiving that such an attempt might beget fatal altercations between the large & small States, and that it would be easier to prevail on the latter, in the course of the deliberations, to give up their equality for the sake of an effective Government, than on taking the field of discussion, to disarm themselves of the right & thereby throw themselves on the mercy of the large States, discountenanced & stifled the project. (*Records*, vol.1, p. 10–11)

Initially, Madison would certainly have agreed with the Morrises and others of the Pennsylvania delegates that the move to proportional representation should come early and be strongly pursued. When the Virginia caucus "discountenanced & stifled the Project," Madison's strategy, as well as the impetuousity of the Pennsylvanians, was brought into question.

CHAPTER 4

The Nature of Government
in the New Republic

The Convention's first two weeks of substantive debate, May 29 to
June 9, saw a fundamentally important clash of ideas at the "higher"
level of constitutional choice (Jensen, 1964, p. 43; Smith, 1965, pp.
36–41). Questions of broad regime type or general institutional outline
came first before the Convention, while issues of detail that might
engender premature and uncontrollable conflicts were actively avoided.
James Madison, among others, had become quite strongly committed to
the idea that general principles favoring broad scale change needed to
be firmly established before the more divisive details of power distribution could be broached safely. In fact, at several points early in the
Convention, questions posing dangerous issues of detail, particularly
those touching upon proportional representation in the legislature, were
pushed to the background and postponed.

Martin Diamond, Douglass Adair, and others have argued that the
American Constitution was born in a clash between a new science of
republican politics, spawned by the Scottish Enlightenment, and more
traditional versions of republicanism (McDonald, 1985). In addition,
Adair contended that "the most creative and philosophical disciple of
the Scottish school of science and politics in the Philadelphia Convention
was James Madison," and "his most amazing political prophecy . . . was
that the size of the United States and its variety of interests could be
made a guarantee of stability and justice under the new constitution"
(Adair, 1957, p. 346). Madison's theory of the "extended republic"
sought to offer a positive new approach to providing "a republican
remedy for the diseases most incident to republican government" (Earle,
1937, p. 62).

Nonetheless, Madison's "new science" met substantial opposition from
delegates who clung to the traditional versions of republicanism that had
informed the Revolution, the early state constitutions, and the Articles
of Confederation. As Martin Diamond correctly noted, "the main thrust
of the opposition resulted from the more general argument that only the

state governments (small republics), not some huge central government, could be made effectively free and republican" (Diamond, 1972, p. 635).

These alternative visions of the appropriate scope and scale for republican government did not stand on equal terms as the Convention opened. After a decade of upheaval and turbulence at the state level and impotence at the level of the Confederation, traditional republican solutions had come to be questioned by nearly everyone and rejected by many. Whereas Madison arrived in Philadelphia with a new understanding of the governing potential inherent in the republican form, the traditional republicans arrived clinging to old nostrums whose credibility seemed clearly to be on the wane. Cecilia Kenyon has captured the predicament of the dispirited republicans by describing them as "men of little faith" (Kenyon, 1955, p. 3). Perhaps more to the point, they were "men of shaken faith," men whose political principles many now thought more appropriate to spawning a revolution than to providing the proper basis for just and stable republican government (Wood, 1969, pp. 396–413; Diggins, 1984, pp. 32, 63). Nonetheless, these traditional republicans, hailing principally from New England and the lower South, supplied formidable opposition to the idea of a powerful national government that Madison and the Middle Atlantic state nationalists had in view. They were firmly convinced, as they had been since before the Revolution, that concentrated power, particularly when exercised at too great a distance from local concerns, represented a dire threat to liberty.

The Initial Conflict: A New Fabric or Mere Amendment

The initial structure of debate and conflict in the Convention was, in large measure, determined by Alexander Hamilton's very effective move to control the early definition of the general alternatives before the Convention. Madison's notes indicate that on the morning of May 29, "Mr. Randolph (then) opened the main business" with a long speech analyzing the defects of the existing Confederation and the curative measures that might be beneficial. Randolph closed his remarks by bringing forward fifteen resolutions "which he proposed to the convention for their adoption, and as leading principles whereon to form a new government." The resolutions presented by Randolph and generally known as the Virginia Plan, together with a similar set of resolutions authored by Charles Pinckney of South Carolina, were bound over to the following day, when the Convention was to "resolve itself into a Committee of the whole House to consider of the State of the American Union" (*Records*, vol. 1, pp. 18–23). The Pinckney Plan quickly disappeared, but the Virginia Plan, widely understood to be the nationalist program for a greatly strengthened central authority, served as the Convention's agenda during its first nine weeks. Each resolution was considered, many of them several times, until every point had been either accepted, compromised, or rejected.

Madison's notes contain no reference to opposition to treating the resolutions presented by Randolph on May 29 as the basis for the Convention's initial discussions. Yates, however, does record a very important reservation voiced by Alexander Hamilton. Yates records that "it was observed by Mr. Hamilton before adjourning that it struck him as a necessary and preliminary inquiry to the propositions from Virginia whether the united States were susceptible of one government, or required a separate existence connected only by leagues offensive and defensive and treaties of commerce" (*Records,* vol. 1, p. 27). Hamilton wanted first to deal with the very basic question of a national versus a federal government. His position was that if the goal was to be to create a truly national government, mere amendment to the existing Articles would likely be insufficient to achieve the goal. When the Convention reconvened on the morning of May 30, Hamilton's ideas were carried forward by other nationalists, chiefly by Gouverneur Morris of Pennsylvania.

The adoption, on May 29, of Madison's Virginia Plan, soon to be enhanced and strengthened by Hamilton and others, gave the "extended republic" men an initial edge because their general principles obviously underlay its specific provisions. On May 30, they sought, as Hamilton had proposed, to solidify this potential advantage by putting the Convention on record in favor of radical change. Hamilton, Morris, and those members of the Convention who sought to enhance dramatically the authority and independence of the national government moved decisively and successfully to capture the Convention's agenda and therewith to set the tone of its early deliberations. The nationalists' opening gambit saw Randolph, at the urging of Gouverneur Morris, move to consider, in place of the Virginia Plan's first resolution, three more strongly phrased alternatives. The skeletal record provided by Madison's notes show precisely how this result was achieved. Madison recorded that on the morning of May 30:

> The propositions of Mr. Randolph which had been referred to the Committee being taken up. He moved on the suggestion of Mr G. Morris that the first of his propositions to wit ('Resolved that the articles of Confederation ought to be so corrected & enlarged, as to accomplish the objects proposed by their institution; namely, common defence, security of liberty & general welfare.') . . . should be postponed in order to consider the 3 following.
> 1. that a Union of the States merely federal (will not accomplish the

objects proposed by the articles of Confederation, namely common defence, security of liberty, & genl. welfare.)

2. that no treaty or treaties among the whole or part of the States, as individual sovereignties, would be sufficient.

3. that a *national* Government (ought to be established) consisting of a *supreme* Legislative, Executive & Judiciary. (*Records*, vol. 1, p. 33)

The new resolutions, designed to place the initial question confronting the Convention in starkest terms, made no mention of marginally improving the old structure of the Articles. Instead, they explicitly proposed a government "national" and "supreme." Clearly, these resolutions constitute the nationalist delegates' specific answers to the questions posed by Hamilton late on the twenty-ninth.

Predictably, use of the words "national" and "supreme" in the new resolutions evoked fear within the still inchoate federalist opposition. For the nationalists, the substitute resolution served to gauge the temper of the house toward radical change rather than minor alteration and amendment. Only Connecticut opposed the resolution; New York divided between Hamilton and Yates; and the six remaining delegations cast their votes in favor. With this affirmative vote behind them, the nationalists went directly to the matter of representation. Madison's notes clearly display an attempt to secure general approval of measures embodying broad change while avoiding the explicit details that might bog the discussion down in interstate rivalries and jealousies. Madison recorded that immediately following acceptance of the substitute first resolution:

> The following Resolution being the 2d. of those proposed by Mr. Randolph was taken up. viz—'that the rights of suffrage in the National Legislature ought to be proportioned to the quotas of contribution or to the number of free inhabitants. . . . '
>
> Mr. M(adison) observing that the words ('or to the number of) free inhabitants.' might occasion debates which would divert the Committee from the *general question* whether the principle of representation should be changed, moved that they might be struck out. (*Records*, vol. 1, pp. 35–36)

Madison's immediate reaction was that this was getting into too much detail too early. He clearly wanted to forestall the obvious—and at some point, unavoidable—clash between large and small states and slave and free states over the distribution of legislative representation among themselves. Madison understood that the southern states would not accept a version of proportional representation that did not count their slaves in some degree. He wished to avoid this messy scrap while insuring that the general principle of proportional as opposed to equal representation of the states in the proposed national legislature was firmly established. Therefore, Randolph and Madison offered a more generally phrased amendment to the second resolution which proposed "'that the rights of suffrage in the national Legislature ought to be proportioned,'" to which it was moved to add, "'and not according to the present system.'"[1] The motion passed by the unanimous vote of 7-0, with Delaware refusing to vote because its instructions forbade it to relinquish equality (*Records*, vol. 1, p. 36). Read of Delaware, citing the restrictions imposed on him by the instructions of his state legislature (he did not mention that this restriction had been imposed at his request for use in precisely this situation), then quickly secured an adjournment before a final vote on the resolution as amended could be taken. Nonetheless, the nationalists considered the sense of the house to have been taken on the central issue. Madison confidently jotted in his notes: "no objection or difficulty being started from any other quarter (than from Delaware)" (ibid., vol. 1, p. 38).

Clearly, Madison, Hamilton, Morris, and their colleagues, though moving carefully in order to avoid engendering undue opposition, thought that their plan was on track against minimal opposition. But when one begins to look beyond Madison's notes, to accounts of these same debates recorded by other delegates, the impression grows that Madison's confidence led him to underestimate the initial signs of an ominously developing opposition. This small state opposition coalesced around a contrasting view of the approach that the Convention should take to its business. By adjournment on May 30, the first full day of substantive debate, the delegates clearly had two, rather than just one, general approaches to the business before them. McHenry recorded that Rufus King concluded the day's debates with the summary observation that "In order to carry into execution (the design of the States in this meeting)," two approaches had surfaced: "the object of the motion from Virginia, an establishment of a government that is to act upon the whole people of the U.S. The object of the motion from Delaware seems to have application merely to the strengthening of the confederation by some additional powers" (*Records*, vol. 1, pp. 43–44).

Many delegates sympathized with the root and branch approach being pursued by Madison, Hamilton, and Morris, but others were wary, preferring the incremental approach to the Convention's business enunciated by John Dickinson of Delaware. Dickinson, a thorough nationalist by temperament, simply began from the idea that wholesale change was unnecessary and that a more conservative and careful approach, which would not endanger the equality of the small states, was readily available. Notes taken by Maryland's James McHenry make this countercurrent particularly clear. McHenry recorded that as soon as the strong nationalist alternative for the first resolution of the Virginia Plan and the favorable reaction to proportional representation in the second resolution were adopted, Dickinson rose to suggest that the entire approach embodied in the plan, particularly as it had been amended by Hamilton and Morris, was misguided. Dickinson argued that rather than the broad questions then under consideration (obviously offered in anticipation and justification of wholesale change to come):

> We may resolve . . . in order to let us into the business. That the confederation is defective; and then proceed to the definition of such powers as may be thought adequate to the objects for which it was instituted. . . . This inquiry should be—
>   1. What are the legislative powers which we should vest in Congress.
>   2. What judiciary powers.
>   3. What executive powers. (*Records*, vol. 1, p. 42)

This is the cautious approach that one might have expected on the opening day of substantive debate as the delegates sought to take some measure of each other's concerns prior to constructing an agenda. It is almost certainly the approach anticipated by the Congress that had approved the Convention, the state legislatures that had appointed the delegates, the population from whom the delegates had been drawn, and most of the delegates themselves even as they made their way to Philadelphia. On the other hand, Madison and his nationalist colleagues undoubtedly had come to realize that to bog down in a detailed discussion of additional increments of power to be granted to the old Confederation would put an end to their hopes for a radical and thorough reform. To assuage the doubts and anxieties of those to whom Dickinson's incremental approach seemed persuasive, Madison argued that the strongly nationalist substitute motion was designed only "to bring out the sense of the house" and even "if agreed to it will decide nothing" (*Records*, vol. 1, p. 44). With these assurances and explanations, the Convention had, by adjournment on May 30, voted 6-1-1 in favor of a government national and supreme and 7-0 in favor of proportional representation.

Table 4.1 highlights the dramatic division within the Convention over how to proceed and over the purposes and intentions that underlay the alternative approaches. The nationalists, favoring Madison's extended republic (factor 1), sought to undertake immediately the radical changes necessary to institute a truly national government, while the localists, adhering to the small republic vision associated with Montesquieu (factor 2), favored incremental changes in the existing Confederation. The fact that nearly two-thirds (64.3%) of the variance in the roll-call

TABLE 4.1.   Extended Republic versus Small Republic: Power and
Principle; Two-Factor Solution to Roll-Call Votes 1–36, May 29–June 9,
Varimax Rotation (Ortho)

	1 Extended Republic	2 Small Republic	h^2
New Hampshire	absent	absent	absent
Massachusetts	(.60)	(.67)	.81
Connecticut	−.21	(.63)	.44
New York	(.76)	.29	.66
New Jersey	absent	absent	absent
Pennsylvania	(.82)	−.10	.68
Delaware	(.70)	.08	.49
Maryland	(.77)	−.12	.60
Virginia	(.66)	.32	.54
North Carolina	(.51)	(.68)	.73
South Carolina	−.04	(.86)	.74
Georgia	.27	(.81)	.73
Sum of squares	3.50	2.93	6.43
% Var. explained	35.00	29.30	64.30

voting over the Convention's first two weeks is captured by this two-factor solution indicates that this cleavage was both deep and stable.

The extended republic men from the Middle Atlantic region, led by New York's Alexander Hamilton, Virginia's James Madison, and Pennsylvania's James Wilson and Gouverneur Morris, obviously held the early initiative. This largely reflected the fact that the small republic men had yet to formulate an acceptable balance between national and state authority that could be offered as a coherent alternative to Madison's Virginia Plan. As a consequence, their opposition lacked the conviction and cohesion that characterized the support for Madison's extended republic (McDonald, 1985, p. 201). This uncertainty was evident in the fact that two of the small republic delegations, Massachusetts and North Carolina, gave substantial support to the extended republic cause. These two states split their support almost evenly between the two factors, while no state on the first factor provided even modest support for the incremental approach favored by the locally oriented delegates still cleaving to the small republic imagery.

The First Confrontation: Madison
versus Dickinson on the Scope of Government

The first order of business on May 31, whether the people or the state legislatures should select the members of what would come to be called the House of Representatives, further demonstrates the difference in approach and perspective being taken by the nationalists from the Middle Atlantic states and the localists or federalists from New England and the South. Under discussion was the fourth resolution of the Virginia Plan, which read, "that the (members of the first branch of the National Legislature) ought to be elected by the people of (the several) States" (*Records*, vol. 1, p. 48).

Connecticut's Roger Sherman immediately objected to "election by the people, insisting that it ought to be by the (State) Legislatures." He contended that "The people . . . (immediately) should have as little to do as may be about the Government. They want information and are constantly liable to be misled" (ibid.). Elbridge Gerry, from neighboring Massachusetts, with Shay's Rebellion still clearly in mind, supported Sherman, noting that "In Massts. it has been fully confirmed by experience that they (the people) are daily misled into the most baneful measures" (ibid.). Pierce Butler of South Carolina, the only southern delegate to speak on this question, simply noted that he "thought an election by the people an impracticable mode" (*Records*, vol. 1, p. 50). These delegates and their colleagues from New England and the lower South would consistently support selection by the state legislatures as opposed to the people.

The delegates from the Middle Atlantic states, represented on this issue by Wilson and Madison, argued passionately for popular selection: "Mr. Wilson contended strenuously for drawing the most numerous branch of the Legislature immediately from the people. He was for raising the federal pyramid to a considerable altitude, and for that reason wished to give it as broad a basis as possible" (*Records*, vol. 1, p. 49). Madison reinforced Wilson, arguing that he "considered popular election of one branch of the national Legislature as essential to every plan of free Government. . . . He thought too that the great fabric to be raised would be more stable and durable if it should rest on the solid foundation of the people themselves, than if it should stand merely on the pillars of the Legislatures" (ibid., p. 49–50). Following the debate the measure was passed, six states voting yes, two voting no, and two dividing evenly. Madison then recorded that "the (remaining) Clauses (of Resolution 4th.) relating to the qualifications of members of the

National Legislature (being) postpd. nem. con. as *entering too much into detail* for general propositions" (ibid., p. 50–51; see also p. 60).

The Convention then moved immediately to the fifth resolution, which dealt with selection of members of the Senate. The fifth resolution read: "'that the second, (or senatorial) branch of the National Legislature (ought to) be chosen by the first branch out of persons nominated by the State Legislatures'" (*Records*, vol. 1, p. 51). Arguments very similar to those made concerning selection of members to what would become the House of Representatives were again made concerning selection to the Senate. Spaight of North Carolina and Sherman of Connecticut argued in favor of the appointment of Senators by the state legislatures, while Wilson again argued for popular election. While the delegates did not like the complicated process outlined in the Virginia Plan, neither did they immediately approve any of the alternatives "so the clause was disagreed to & a chasm left in this part of the plan" (ibid., p. 52).

The Convention then began to move quickly—given the content of the issues under review—through the clauses of the sixth resolution of the Virginia Plan. The sixth resolution read:

> Resolved that each branch ought to possess the right of originating Acts; that the National Legislature ought to be impowered to enjoy the Legislative Rights vested in the Congress by the Confederation & moreover to legislate in all cases to which the separate States are incompetent, or in which the harmony of the United States may be interrupted by the exercise of individual Legislation; to negative all laws passed by the several States, contravening in the opinion of the National Legislature the articles of Union; and to call forth the force of the Union agst. any members of the Union failing to fulfill its duty under the articles thereof. (*Records*, vol. 1, p. 21)

They first approved, unanimously and without discussion, the right of both houses to originate legislation, and of the new Congress to enjoy the legislative rights and powers of the Confederation Congress. The next clause, empowering the Congress "to legislate in all cases to which the separate States are incompetent," led to a brief but interesting and portentous discussion. The southern delegates were particularly nervous: "Mr. Pinkney, & Mr. Rutledge objected to the vagueness of the term *incompetent*, and said they could not well decide how to vote until they should see an exact enumeration of the powers comprehended by this definition" (*Records*, vol. 1, p. 53). Butler, also of South Carolina, was also wary, repeating "his fears that we were running into an extreme in taking away powers from the States, and called on Mr. Randolp(h) for the extent of his meaning" (ibid., p. 53). When pressed similarly on another issue earlier in the day, Randolph had responded that "he had at the time of offering his propositions stated his ideas as far as the nature of general propositions required; that details made no part of the plan, and could not perhaps with propriety have been introduced" (ibid., p. 51). On this occasion, Randolph simply "disclaimed any intention to give indefinite powers to the national Legislature, declaring that he was entirely opposed to such an inroad on the State jurisdictions," but he offered no clarification of the phrase's meaning or enumeration of the powers to be granted (ibid., p. 53). Madison also sought to soothe the South Carolinians. He assured them that he, like they, had entered the Convention with "a strong bias in favor of an enumeration and definition of the powers necessary to be exercised by the national Legislature; but had also brought doubts concerning its practicability." Nonetheless, Madison declared that "he should shrink from nothing which should be found essential to such a form of Govt. as would provide for the safety, liberty and happiness of the Community" (ibid.). Madison clearly believed that national control over state legislatures was "essential" to the "safety, liberty and happiness of the Community."

These statements and declarations from Randolph and Madison did virtually nothing directly to satisfy the South Carolinians' request for more specificity. Nonetheless, the nationalist bandwagon was rolling almost unopposed at this point, and the clause was approved 9-0-1, all of the states voting in favor of this sweepingly nationalizing clause—except Connecticut, whose vote was divided, with Sherman voting no and Ellsworth voting yes. Following this overwhelmingly favorable vote, the remainder of the clause, including the power "to negative all State laws contravening in the opinion of the National Legislature the articles of Union," was, at the suggestion of Benjamin Franklin, approved without discussion and debate.

It took some time before the initiative and momentum captured by the nationalists early in the Convention could be slowed and then turned back; and when it occurred, it would not be solely the work of the small state men worried about the loss of political power that the states they represented would suffer if proportional representation were to be put into effect. In the end, the small state men would be decisively reinforced by a few small republic men worried about the threat that the national negative on state laws would pose to the power and position of the states, large and small, in the new system. All of the delegates had experienced the insufficiencies of the Confederation government and favored some degree of consolidation. But unlike the nationalists, the federalist opposition had yet to answer a number of crucial questions: How much consolidation was required? How far must they go in granting additional authority to the nation? How far must they reduce the states? Since the issue of national supremacy was phrased abstractly in these first few votes, it received nearly unanimous support. But as the abstractions became real choices in the allocation of power between the nation and the states, the focus of debate moved from principle to interest, and the opposition steadily grew.

Madison's vision of a great commercial republic, ruled by a powerful national government that would regulate with competence and justice the activities of the several states, was directly challenged by John Dickinson on June 2. In Dickinson's view, the critical problems confronting government in a free society were the twin dangers that authority, on the one hand, might be debilitatingly weak and vacillating, and on the other, might concentrate and become tyrannical (Bailyn, 1967, pp. 55–93; Wood, 1969, pp. 410–414). To minimize these constant dangers, Dickinson argued, the national government should be built on the foundation of the states, while structurally "the Legislative, Executive, & Judiciary departments ought to be made as independt. [separate] as possible" (*Records*, vol. 1, p. 86).[2]

June 2 was the second full day of debate on the selection, organization, and powers of the executive. These topics will be discussed fully in Chapter 6, but for now, we can glean from Dickinson's comments on impeachment the nature of the alternative that he offered to Madison's extended commercial republic. Debate on June 1 and 2 concerned the appointment of the Chief Executive, the length of his term, and whether he would be eligible to serve consecutive terms. On the matter of impeachment, Dickinson moved "'that the Executive be made removeable by the National Legislature on the request of a majority of the Legislatures of the individual States'" (*Records*, vol. 1, p. 85). Dickinson, beginning from traditional republican assumptions, argued that power in government should rest principally in the hands of the people's representatives in the legislature, not with the powerful executive that Wilson and others seemed to envision. He also believed that the role of the states, small republics already in existence, should be acknowledged wherever possible.

Dickinson warned his colleagues that "he had no idea of abolishing the State Governments as some gentlemen seemed inclined to do. The happiness of this Country in his opinion required considerable powers to be left in the hands of the States" (*Records*, vol. 1, p. 86). Madison and Wilson then argued against the Dickinson proposal on the grounds that "they both thought it bad policy (to introduce such a mixture) of the State authorities" into the impeachment process (ibid.). Dickinson clearly recognized that Madison and Wilson opposed a significant role for the states, not just here, but generally and as a fundamental principle of their alternative vision. Therefore, Dickinson took this occasion to state at some length his ideas concerning both the appropriate structure of the national government and the relationship between the national government and the states.

First, Dickinson argued in favor of a strict separation of powers, even though this seemed to require an executive strictly subservient to the legislature. He argued "that the Legislative, Executive, & Judiciary departments ought to be made as independt. as possible; but that such an Executive as some seem to have in contemplation was not consistent with a republic; that a firm Executive could only exist in a limited monarchy" (*Records*, vol. 1, p. 86). Second, Dickinson more clearly outlined his view of the critical role to be played by the states in the new system. He agreed with most of the delegates that instability and injustice at the state level had necessitated the meeting of the Convention. Nonetheless, he thought that important stabilizing forces were readily at hand. In fact, he contended that a moderately empowered national legislature would operate to turn the states from agents of instability into key sources of stability in the new nation. "One source of stability," he noted "is the double branch of the Legislature. The division of the Country into distinct States formed the other principal source of stability. This division ought therefore to be maintained, and considerable powers to be left with the States. This was the ground of his consolation for the future fate of his Country" (ibid.).

On June 4, Madison set about dismantling Dickinson's argument that the defense of republican liberty required a strict separation of responsibilities between the departments of a modestly empowered national government resting directly upon the individual states. In this important speech, Madison carefully presented and explained the theoretical underpinnings of his "extended republic." William Pierce of Georgia recorded that "Mr. Madison in a very able and ingenious Speech . . . proved that the only way to make a (national) Government answer all the end of its institution was to collect the wisdom of its several parts in aid of each other [by blurring a pure separation of powers] whenever it was necessary" (*Records*, vol. 1, p. 110). By stressing the principle of "Checks and Balances" as a supplement and buttress to a strict "Separation of Powers," the extended republic men sought to create a governmental structure in which each department was fully capable of and motivated to self-defense. If the integrity of the structure and its ability to forestall tyranny by maintaining separate centers of power could be depended upon, then great power could be given to the national government in the knowledge that one branch would check potential abuses of the other.

As the full implications of Madison's program became clearer to the small republic men, they struggled with increasing determination against the idea that substantial authority at the national level could be either necessary or safe. George Mason, perhaps the most consistent spokesman in the Convention for traditional republicanism, spoke movingly and at length in its defense and in opposition to the strong executive envisioned by Hamilton, Wilson, and others who found Madison's extended republic argument convincing. Mason noted that "the chief advantages which have been urged in favor of unity in the Executive, are the secresy, the dispatch, the vigor and energy which the government will derive from it, especially in time of war," yet he urged his colleagues to question "whether there is not some pervading principle in republican government which sets at naught and tramples upon this boasted superiority" (*Records*, vol. 1, p. 112). Not surprisingly, Mason was convinced that there was such a fundamental principle and that it most clearly was not the energy and dispatch that Hamilton and Wilson expected from a powerful executive; rather, "this invincible principle is to be found in the love, the affection, the attachment of the citizens to their laws, to their freedom, and to their country" (ibid.). Most delegates, including Hamilton and Wilson, joined Mason, Dickinson, and Sherman in assuming that the emotional attachments of citizens would be much stronger toward their state and local governments than toward some new and distant national government. Traditional republicans wanted to foster and to build upon these natural local attachments, while the nationalists wished to sever the national government from the constraints that the states might attempt to impose upon it.

On June 6, Roger Sherman, supplementing Dickinson's faith in the states as "small republics" on which the future happiness of the new nation hinged, contended that great power at the national level could not be well used because "the objects of the Union . . . were few" (*Records*, vol. 1, p. 133). Moreover, great power should not be housed at the national level because most "matters civil & criminal would be much better in the hands of the States" (ibid.). Therefore, Sherman concluded, "the Genl. Government (should) be a sort of collateral Government which shall secure the States in particular difficulties . . . I am agst. a Genl. Govt. and in favor of the independence and confederation of the States" (*Records*, vol. 1, pp. 142–43).

Madison met Sherman's opposition to a "Genl. Government" by challenging his assumption that the responsibilities of the national government would be few. In addition to those objects noted by Sherman (defense, commerce, and disputes between the states), Madison "combined with them the necessity, of providing more effectually for the security of private rights, and the steady dispensation of Justice"

(*Records*, vol. 1, p. 134). Most of the delegates agreed when Madison argued that interested local majorities had been "the source of these unjust laws complained of among ourselves" (ibid., p. 135). Madison proposed a solution to the problem of majority tyranny that few others understood and that many saw as dangerously speculative: "The only remedy is to enlarge the sphere . . . as far as the nature of Govt. would admit. This was the only defence agst the inconveniences of democracy consistent with the democratic form of Govt" (ibid., pp. 134, 136).

Madison's opponents knew that additional powers would have to be granted to a central government, but the idea of a truly national government clashed directly with the philosophical assumptions with which they (and most Americans with them) had been operating since before the revolution. Yet, bereft of viable alternatives, these "men of shaken faith" could oppose only half-heartedly when Madison contended that "it was incumbent on (them) to try this (extended republic) remedy, and . . . to frame a republican system on such a scale & in such a form as will controul all the evils wch. have been experienced" (*Records*, vol. 1, p. 136). While the conflict remained at this "higher" level of constitutional choice, the small republic men cast about for alternatives to Madison's frighteningly radical approach. None came readily to hand (Diamond, 1981, p. 27).

The Second Confrontation: Madison versus Paterson on the Place of the States

On June 7 the tenor of the questions before the Convention began to drift from the high plane of theory to the rough and tumble of practical, interest-driven power politics. Dickinson opened the discussion on June 7 by restating the modest commitment of the small republic men to "the preservation of the States in a certain degree of agency" (*Records*, vol. 1, pp. 152–153). James Wilson, on behalf of the supporters of the Virginia Plan, observed that the "doubts and difficulties" surrounding the place of the state governments in the proposed system derived from the threat that they seemed to pose to the independence and effectiveness of the national government; "he wished to keep them from devouring the national Govt." (ibid., p. 153).

Those delegates who followed the logic of Madison's extended republic expected any initiative left with the state governments to be misused. Their theoretical principles told them that small republics had always been violent and short-lived because interested local majorities, possessed of the means, invariably acted unjustly. Therefore, Charles Pinckney proposed "'that the National Legislature shd. have authority to negative all (State) Laws which they shd. judge to be improper'" (*Records*, vol. 1, p. 164). Madison seconded the Pinckney motion, saying that he "could not but regard an indefinite power [Pinckney had called it a "universality of power"] to negative legislative acts of the States as absolutely necessary to a perfect system" (ibid.). Further, by June 8, Madison's extended republic arguments had begun to tell on Dickinson. Dickinson grudgingly accepted the argument that the "objects" of the national government would be many, and that to accomplish these objects, the national government would have to exercise substantial powers over the governments of the states. Nonetheless, as we shall see, Dickinson's conversion to the national negative on state laws sparked an even more violent form of opposition to Madison's general program. Following arguments by Madison, Wilson, and others in favor of the negative, Dickinson informed his colleagues that he

> deemed it impossible to draw a line between the cases proper & improper for the exercise of the negative. We must take our choice of two things. We must either subject the States to the danger of being injured by the power of the Natl. Govt. or the latter to the danger of being injured by that of the States. He thought the danger greater from the States. (*Records*, vol. 1, p. 167)

Elbridge Gerry, Gunning Bedford, and William Paterson sprang to the defense of the states. Gerry scornfully rejected the idea of "an indefinite power to negative legislative acts of the States" as the work of "speculative projector(s)" whose theory had overwhelmed their experience and their judgment (*Records*, vol. 1, pp. 164–65). Bedford reminded his small state colleagues of the dangers inherent in such a plan. Paterson reinforced Bedford's remarks by holding up "Virga., Massts., & Pa. as the three large States, and the other ten as small ones" (ibid., p. 178). He concluded that "the small States will have every thing to fear . . . N. Jersey will never confederate on the plan before the Committee. She would be swallowed up" (*Records*, vol. 1, pp. 178–179). James Wilson responded in kind for the large states. He said that "if the small States (would) not confederate on this plan, Pena. & he presumed some other States, would not confederate on any other" (ibid., p. 180). This exchange indicates how quickly and decisively the Convention's focus shifted from general theories about the nature of republican government to the impact of various modes of representation on particular states and regions. It also highlights the interest-laced character (who gets what, when, and how) of discussion at the "lower" level of constitutional choice.

CHAPTER 5

The Representation Question: Madison and his Opponents

During the Convention's first two weeks, the states of the deep South (the Carolinas and Georgia) and of New England (Massachusetts and Connecticut) had been wary of Madison's plan to place great power at the national level. Nonetheless, the extended republic men had successfully overcome the objections of the delegates from the Northeast and the deep South to establish firmly the principle of a strong national government. Now the questions were, Who would wield this power, and What role would remain for the states in the new system? Table 5.1 (see below) shows how dramatically the voting alignments changed when the Convention's attention shifted from "higher" to "lower" level questions of constitutional choice. Under these new circumstances, the rapidly growing states of the deep South and Massachusetts joined Pennsylvania and Virginia to pursue proportional representation in both houses of the national legislature. The large states were opposed by five smaller states from the Middle Atlantic region, demanding equal representation in at least one branch of the proposed legislature (Farrand, 1913, p. 82; Warren, 1928, p. 246; McDonald, 1958, p. 102; Jensen, 1964, p. 54; Wolfe, 1977, pp. 112–117).

Empirical evidence will be presented to support the argument that the confrontation over representation occurred in three phases. First came a contest over the role of the states in the new system. Initially, the delegates supporting Madison's extended republic wanted a limited role for the states, but as the debates progressed, several delegates from the large states of the lower South, particularly those from South Carolina, and the delegates from Massachusetts became uneasy over the broad powers given to the national government to control the states. Their increasingly frequent defections to the federalist coalition on votes to secure a prominent role for the states in the new system weakened the dominant nationalist coalition. Then, almost simultaneously and largely as a result of the first battle, came a second battle: the classic confrontation between the large states and the small that culminated in the achievement of a compromise committee report that included equal representation in the Senate. This partial solution to the representation issue only served to focus attention more closely on a third aspect of the question: the distribution of suffrage in the House of Representatives, where the states and regions would be distinctly, and perhaps dangerously, unequal. This third battle was primarily contested between the large populous states of the North and South, with the smaller states of each region cleaving to their larger brothers out of regional interest. Thus, three related but variously motivated battles were fought: two closely related battles were fought from the second week of June to early July to secure a prominent role for the states and equal voting rights for the small states in the Senate, while a third confrontation occurred from early to mid-July to decide the distribution of suffrage in the House of Representatives.

The Politics of Power: Large States versus Small

Although the proponents of the Virginia Plan won consistently during the Convention's first two weeks, the issues confronting the delegates were carefully cast in general terms. By June 5, all fifteen propositions of the Virginia Plan had been before the Convention. Already, the outlines of a powerful national government exercising a negative over the state governments were in place. These early developments served to mobilize those delegates wishing to defend the position of the states in the new system. In addition, while nationalists such as Madison, Hamilton, Morris, and Wilson had rushed to Philadelphia (if it was not their home), often arriving several days before the Convention was scheduled to begin, many other delegates, particularly those with reservations about the motives of the nationalists, were slower in arriving. On May 21, as the delegates awaited the presence of a quorum, George Read wrote to Dickinson, warning him that "the gentlemen who came here early, particularly Virginia, that had a quorum on the first day, express much uneasiness at the backwardness of individuals in giving attendance." Read concluded with the observation that he expected "it to be of importance to the small States that their deputies should keep a strict watch upon the movements and propositions from the larger States, who will probably combine to swallow up the smaller ones. . . . If you have any wish to assist in guarding against such attempts, you will be speedy in your attendance" (*Records*, vol. 3, pp. 25–26).

Two issues, both coming under discussion late on June 5, indicate a growing sense of concern among delegates committed to a federalist system built on strong state governments. First, resolution fifteen, the last of the Virginia Plan resolutions to be treated, proposed "conventions

under appointment (of the people) to ratify the new Constitution"
(*Records*, vol. 1, p. 122). The delegates from New England, with Sherman
leading the way, moved to oppose popular ratification, preferring
ratification by the state legislatures. Gerry, however, went to the core of
New England's reticence to depend on popular action by observing that
"the people in that quarter (New England) have (at this time) the wildest
ideas of Government in the world. They were for abolishing the Senate
in Massts. and giving all the other powers of Govt. to the other branch
of the Legislature" (ibid., p. 123). Not surprisingly, Madison and Wilson
spoke in favor of popular ratification. The Convention then voted
without objection to postpone the fifteenth resolution. With this vote,
each resolution had been before the Convention at least once.

With New England's reservations about a popular basis for government before the Convention, the southerners, or more specifically the
South Carolinians, also sought to weigh in for a dependence of the
national government on the state governments as opposed to the people.
Pinckney and Rutledge moved that tomorrow be assigned for a reconsideration of the fourth resolution, dealing with elections to the first
branch. On June 6, Pinckney moved "'that the first branch of the
national Legislature be elected by the State Legislatures, and not by the
people'" (*Records*, vol. 1, p. 132). Pinckney supported his proposal with
the argument that "the people were less fit Judges (in such a case)" than
were the members of the state legislatures. Gerry and Sherman spoke in
support of Pinckney's resolution, Sherman reasoning that

> if it were in view to abolish the State Govts. the elections ought to be by the
> people. If the State Govts. are to be continued, it is necessary in order to
> preserve harmony between the national & State Govts. that the elections to the
> former shd. be made by the latter. The right of participating in the National
> Govt. would be sufficiently secured to the people by their election of the State
> Legislatures. (ibid., p. 133)

General Pinckney agreed with Sherman and with his South Carolina
colleagues. Pinckney "wished to have a good national Govt. & at the
same time to leave a considerable share of power in the States. . . . He
differed from gentlemen who thought that a choice by the people wd. be
a better guard agst. bad measures, than by the Legislatures." The
people, he argued, were "notoriously" undependable, while legislators
"had some sense of character and were restrained by that consideration"
(ibid., p. 137). When the vote was taken, only Connecticut, New Jersey,
and South Carolina voted in favor of appointment of House members by
the state legislatures, while eight states voted against it.

This discussion highlights the critical problem that faced Madison and

Wilson and those who wished to base a powerful national government directly on the people. Significant elements within the large state coalition, which was the only vehicle available to Madison and Wilson, though they wanted proportional representation, did not want to see the states dismantled or even dramatically reduced in influence. In the end, their desire for both proportional representation (p.r.) and for protection of the states led them to compromise along lines already being suggested by the delegates from Connecticut; p.r. in one house and equality in the other.

Though defeated on state legislative selection of members of the national House, the advocates of the states worked assiduously from June 6 to June 27 to enhance the role of the states in the new system. June 7 opened with a reconsideration of means of selecting members of the Senate. Dickinson moved "'that the members (of the 2d. branch ought to be chosen) by the individual Legislatures'" (*Records*, vol. 1, p. 150). Dickinson offered two arguments in support of his motion. Both were widely shared among delegates who wanted to maintain a significant role for the states. Dickinson proposed selection by the state legislatures "1. because the sense of the States would be better collected through their Governments; than immediately from the people at large. 2. because he wished the Senate to consist of the most distinguished characters . . . and he thought such characters more likely to be selected by the State Legislatures" (ibid.). Though Madison, Read, and Wilson spoke against this mode, only Pennsylvania voted to postpone Dickinson's motion in favor of one by Wilson calling for popular election. Ten states, Pennsylvania included, then voted in favor of selection of national senators by the state legislatures. The states would have a role.

Gerry immediately followed this favorable vote on the selection of senators with "notice that he wd. tomorrow move for a reconsideration of the mode of appointing the Natl. Executive in order to substitute an appointm. by the State Executives" (*Records*, vol. 1, p. 156). Gerry did so move on the morning of June 8 and reconsideration was granted for June 9. The remainder of June 8 was taken up by a vituperative debate over an attempt to broaden the national negative on state laws. When Dickinson, to this point a champion of the federalist desire to limit the inroads of national power on state prerogatives, agreed with Madison and Wilson that a broad national power over state legislatures was necessary, the Convention was abruptly drawn into a bitter confrontation between the large states and the small over power and control in the proposed national government. These two battles would run parallel to each other throughout the month of June. In the end, decisions to strengthen the role of the states would eventually make it easier, in early July, to decide to allow each state an equal vote in the Senate.

Madison initially faced an easy, because only half-hearted, opponent in John Dickinson. Dickinson was a longtime nationalist. Madison can even be seen as winning the intellectual battle with Dickinson and Sherman over the "objects" of the national government, whether they would be few or many (Diamond, 1981, pp. 26–27). Over the two days following June 6, the debate revolved around the "partial agency" that the national government would leave to the states. On June 8, however, the vote for an enhanced national negative on all state legislation, which Dickinson was convinced to support, ignited an increasingly vehement opposition from the small state men and from some large state federalists who valued the state governments as "small republics." Madison's key problem from this point forward was to hold together a slim 6-5 majority in favor of proportional representation in both the House and the Senate against slippage among New England (Massachusetts) and deep South delegates, who were afraid of an overly powerful and intrusive national government.

Dickinson, who to this point had been leading the moderate opposition to Madison's plan, moved over to support an expanded negative: "Mr. Dickinson deemed it impossible to draw a line between the cases proper & improper for the exercise of the negative. We must take our choice of two things. We must either subject the States to the danger of being injured by the power of the Natl. Govt. or the latter to the danger of being injured by that of the States. He thought the danger greater from the States" (*Records*, vol. 1, p. 167). Gunning Bedford, Dickinson's young colleague in the Delaware delegation, answered him immediately and vehemently—and in doing so, he swept the opposition to Madison's program onto a much different and, for the Convention, more dangerous path. With Bedford and New Jersey's Paterson now in the lead, the opposition to Madison's program became much less amenable to theoretical argument and to being won over by explanations based in principle. Bedford argued, "in answer to his colleagues question, where wd. be the danger to the States from this power, would refer him to the smallness of his own State which may be injured at pleasure without redress. It was meant he found to strip the small States of their equal right of suffrage. . . . Will not these large States crush the small ones whenever they stand in the way of their ambition or interested views" (ibid.).

June 9 was an important day in the Convention's development because it represented a radicalization of the opposition to the nationalism of the first week. Paterson jumped in to take over from Bedford in leading the opposition to Madison. Paterson, the voice of antifederalism in the Convention, wrenched the Convention into a large-state–small-state stance with a very long and powerful speech. Paterson moved "that the Committee resume the clause relating to the rule of suffrage in the Natl. Legislature" (*Records*, vol. 1, p. 176). Both Paterson and Brearley proposed an equality of suffrage or an abolition of the current state boundaries to be followed by an equalization. The discussion was very intense and was directed at the issue of the power to be given to the three largest states and the danger that this might pose to the smaller states. Paterson threatened that New Jersey would never agree to a plan based on proportional representation, and Wilson countered that Pennsylvania would accept no other basis. With tempers flaring, adjournment was secured before a vote could be taken.

Nonetheless, over the early days of June, the balance of forces among the states and between the regions in the rapidly building confrontation over the distribution of seats in the new government's legislature became ever more balanced as delegates continued to arrive from the smaller states. Max Farrand described the development of the opposition to proportional representation in this way: "With the arrival of additional delegates from day to day the opponents of the Virginia Plan were increased. Lansing of New York sided with Yates against Hamilton and cast the vote of that state accordingly. New Jersey and Maryland being represented were entitled to vote and were found in the opposition. Delaware also went over to the other side, which was partially accounted for by the fact that the combination had become strong enough to make opposition worth while" (Farrand, 1913, p. 73; see also Jensen, 1964, p. 48). Thus, as early as June 9, the battle lines that would be staunchly defended into July were clearly drawn. In Table 5.1 is shown a two-factor solution to the votes taken in the Convention between June 11 and July 17 that display these divisions with particular effectiveness.

The table shows the precise alignments that Madison foresaw in his letters to Randolph and Washington more than a month before the Convention met. The first factor (large states) demonstrates that the three largest states, Massachusetts, Pennsylvania, and Virginia, joined with the three states of the deep South in generally favoring proportional representation. They were opposed by the five smaller states of the Middle Atlantic region (small states), which stood in favor of equal representation for the states in the new national government. This two-factor description of opposing voting coalitions accounts for over one-half (50.7%) of the variance in the voting of all of the states represented in the Convention between June 11 and July 17.

The extent to which representation was the critical issue confronting

TABLE 5.1.   Large States versus Small States: Power and Interest;
Two-Factor Solution to Roll-Call Votes 37–156,
June 11–July 17, Rotation (Ortho)

	1 Large States	2 Small States	h^2
New Hampshire	absent	absent	absent
Massachusetts	(.80)	.13	.66
Connecticut	.13	(.59)	.37
New York	−.02	(.52)	.27
New Jersey	−.13	(.75)	.58
Pennsylvania	(.65)	.09	.43
Delaware	−.08	(.74)	.56
Maryland	.25	(.78)	.68
Virginia	(.73)	.08	.54
North Carolina	(.79)	.12	.64
South Carolina	(.55)	−.23	.36
Georgia	(.69)	−.10	.49
Sum of squares	3.13	2.45	5.58
% of variance explained	28.45	22.25	50.70

the Convention during the five weeks under discussion here has been widely recognized (Birkby, 1966, pp. 127–128; Pomper, 1970, p. 213; Jensen, 1964, p. 52). Nonetheless, the true pervasiveness of the representation question can be fully appreciated only when it is formally demonstrated that fully twenty-four of the twenty-nine roll-call votes identified by high factor scores as defining the critical issues around which the coalitions of Table 5.1 were organized dealt explicitly with the issue of representation (see Table 5.2). Equally striking is the fact that all the remaining five roll calls highlight the nationalist attempt to institutionalize the supremacy of the nation to the separate states by, for example, demanding that state officials be bound by oath to support the national Constitution.

Though the two-factor solution identifies the principal division between the states, neither Madison, nor his colleagues, expected the coalitions to function as monolithic wholes. The three most populous states, Massachusetts, Pennsylvania, and Virginia, could pursue proportional representation without constraint, since they would control a new government so constituted. Demographic trends indicated that the three states of the deep South would soon benefit from proportional repre-

TABLE 5.2.   Twenty-Nine Critical Votes between 1 and 156 as Identified
by Factor Scores[a] 1.25 on Either Factor or 1.0 on Both Factors of the
Two-Factor Varimax Solution in Table 5.1

Vote No.	Factor Score	Factor No.	Voting Split	Issue Content	Date of Vote	*Records,* v.1, p.
7	1.25	2	3-7	2nd branch to be elected by the 1st branch.	May 31	47
37	−1.31	1	7-3-1	Suffrage in House to be according to some equitable rule.	June 11	195
40	1.77 −1.40	1, 2	5-6	Equal vote in Senate.	11	195
41	−1.29 1.67	1, 2	6-5	Suffrage in Senate to be same as in House.	11	195
42	−1.30 1.20	1, 2	7-4	To add the words 'voluntary junction of partition' to the resolution concerning division of states.	11	195
43	−1.30 1.25	1, 2	7-4	Add the words "National Government."	11	195
44	1.77	1	4-7	State officers to be bound by oath to support constitution.	11	195
45	−1.29 1.67	1, 2	6-5	State officers to be bound by oath to support Constitution.	11	195
65	1.78 −1.13	1, 2	4-6-1	Adopt Dickinson motion as substitute for Paterson's New Jersey Plan.	19	313
67	−1.13	1	7-3-1	Reject New Jersey Plan, report Virginia Plan.	19	313
68	1.78 −1.31	1, 2	4-6-1	Postpone 2nd resolution to take up Lansing's.	20	335
69	1.77	1	4-7	To adjourn.	20	335
70	−1.31	1	7-3-1	Legislature to consist of two houses.	21	354
71	1.35	1	4-6-1	1st branch to be elected as state legislatures direct.	21	354

TABLE 5.2. *(Continued)*

Vote No.	Factor Score	Factor No.	Voting Split	Issue Content	Date of Vote	*Records,* v.1, p.
82	1.37	1	2-8-1	Legislators to be ineligible for offices they create.	23	385
85	1.31	2	4-7	Postpone resolution on 2nd branch.	25	397
103	1.33	2	3-8	Legislators to be ineligible for state offices while holding national office.	26	420
105	1.78	1	4-6-1	Equal vote in the Senate.	29	461
106	−1.31 1.30	1, 2	6-4-1	Equal vote in the Senate.	29	461
110	1.48 −1.32	1, 2	5-5-1	Equal vote in the Senate.	July 2	511
115	−1.31	1	7-3-1	Refer distribution of suffrage in the House to a new compromise committee.	6	539
120	−1.36	2	6-3-2	Equal vote in the Senate.	7	549
125	1.78	2	3-8	Raise N.C. from 5 to 6.	10	565
127	1.75	2	4-7	Raise Ga. from 3 to 4.	10	565
139	1.48	2	5-5	Census "at least" every 15 years.	11	577
143	1.29	1	5-4-1	Replace 2 with 6 years before first census.	12	591
148	1.77	1	4-6	Postpone motion to tie tax to census.	13	600
149	1.45	2	5-5	Tax by number of representatives until first census.	13	600
150	1.45	2	5-4-1	Vote No. 149 moved again.	13	600

[a]Rummel, *Applied Factor Analysis*, pp. 172–173, 433–436. Rummel outlines the close relationship between factor loadings and factor scores as follows: "The identification of the loadings showing which factors [coalitions] are related to what variables [states] may be the goal of the factor analysis. For this the factor loading matrix is sufficient. It should be clear, however, that when . . . the relationship between variables and factors are considered, it is the vectors of factor scores [on each roll-call vote] . . . that are involved. The factor loadings measure only the dependence of variables [states] on factor scores [roll-call votes]."

**TABLE 5.3.   Large States versus Small States: Power and Interest;
Five-Factor Solution to Roll-Call Votes 37–156, June 11–July 17,
Varimax Rotation (Ortho)**

	1 Large States	2 Deep South	3 Lower Middle	4 Upper Middle	5 Conn. Compromise	h^2
New Hampshire	absent	absent	absent	absent	absent	
Massachusetts	(.71)	.34	.04	−.05	.33	.74
Connecticut	.01	.03	.23	.13	(.89)	.87
New York	−.21	.31	.29	(.75)	−.10	.79
New Jersey	.05	−.23	.20	(.83)	.26	.86
Pennsylvania	(.91)	−.06	.01	.02	−.11	.83
Delaware	.01	−.21	(.80)	.21	.08	.73
Maryland	.21	.05	(.78)	.21	.27	.77
Virginia	(.70)	.30	.34	−.15	−.19	.75
North Carolina	.47	(.59)	.18	−.15	.32	.73
South Carolina	.02	(.87)	−.11	−.04	.02	.77
Georgia	.43	(.66)	−.20	.30	−.12	.77
Sum of squares	2.30	1.95	1.62	1.48	1.21	8.61
% Total	20.90	17.73	14.73	13.45	11.00	78.20

sentation, but they felt constrained to demand at least temporary protection of their dominant interests because they would initially be a minority, and therefore vulnerable. So from the beginning, the delegations pursuing proportional representation were a coalition made up of smaller, more naturally cohesive voting blocs, with at least partially competing and divergent interests. The same can obviously be said of the small states, as their number cut across regional boundaries and the slave-free dichotomy. But, unlike the delegates from the larger states, there was one issue on which the small state delegates believed that their authority in the new system absolutely hinged. They could not afford to split on equality of suffrage in at least one house of the proposed Congress.

A five-factor solution to the votes recorded between June 11 and July 17 (see Table 5.3) allows one to identify the smaller voting groups that combined to form the more general voting coalitions identified in Table 5.1. Of particular interest in the remainder of this analysis are the reactions of Pennsylvania, South Carolina, and Connecticut to the differentiation of the broader coalitions. These three states go from having very modest loadings in the two-factor solution to having the highest loadings of any of the states on any of the factors in the five-factor solution.

Clearly, factor 1 of Table 5.1 is shown to be a large state coalition of two smaller, more intuitively plausible, voting blocs. One of the smaller blocs was made up of the three largest states, with Pennsylvania leading the way, and the other was composed of the three states of the deep South, with South Carolina most committed to that position. Not surprisingly, the tables indicate that those most committed to the smaller groups were least committed to the coalition.

A similar situation characterized the small state group on factor 2 of Table 5.1. The five-factor solution differentiates the five smaller states across three factors, seemingly on the basis of geographic or regional affinity. Delaware and Maryland, whose populations contained a significant number of slaves (15% and 32% respectively), share factor 3 and are separated from New York and New Jersey on factor 4, both of which had minimal (6%) slave populations. Factor 5 displays the independent behavior of Connecticut (Wolfe, 1977, pp. 108–112).

Votes coded 2, 2a, and 2b serve to show where the large state wall was first decisively breached. Code 2 encompasses the seventy-one votes (nearly half the whole number taken before the Connecticut Compromise) dealing with the legislative branch. The fifty-three votes coded 2a are those taken before July 11 (the point at which the southern states seized the initiative from the large northern states on the proportional representation issue). The code 2a votes highlight the regional conflict among the larger states on Factor 1 over the counting of slaves for the purposes of representation and taxation. These votes show the early dominance of the northern view that representation should be based on population and wealth (in all its forms: slaves, commerce, and industry). The votes taken after July 11 (code 2b) demonstrate the southern attempt to define population alone as the sole criterion by which representation should be apportioned, if three-fifths of all slaves, the principal form of southern wealth, could be included in the count.

The regional strains within the large state coalition can be understood best by analyzing the votes of the Pennsylvania and South Carolina delegations as displayed in Table 5.4. These two states were the most vehemently committed to the partially conflicting northern and southern positions on the representation issue, as demonstrated by their separation into factors 1 and 2 of Table 5.3. While the northern orientation dominated the large-state coalition, South Carolina refused to participate (2a votes), loading at only .28 on factor 1 (a figure matched by such staunch opponents of the states loading on factor 1 as Connect-

Table 5.4. Two-Factor Solution To 71 Votes Selected by Issue Area Taken May 30–July 16, Varimax Rotation (Ortho)[a]

	Code 2 (N = 71) 1st Branch	Code 2a (N = 53) Pre–July 11	Code 2b (N = 18) Post–July 11
Massachusetts	(.81)	(.81)	(.90)
Connecticut	.14	.28	−.18
New York	.12	.15	Absent
New Jersey	−.09	.08	−.35
Pennsylvania	(.68)	(.76)	(.50)
Delaware	.01	.01	.24
Maryland	.21	.29	.20
Virginia	(.73)	(.74)	(.73)
North Carolina	(.78)	(.75)	(.83)
South Carolina	.41	.28	(.76)
Georgia	(.75)	(.74)	(.76)
Sum of squares	3.07	3.17	3.69
% Total variance	27.91	28.82	36.90
Massachusetts	.17	.17	.08
Connecticut	(.53)	.38	(.71)
New York	(.58)	(.56)	Absent
New Jersey	(.69)	(.61)	(.81)
Pennsylvania	.33	.26	(.55)
Delaware	(.71)	(.74)	(.65)
Maryland	(.79)	(.79)	(.73)
Virginia	.32	.30	.19
North Carolina	.10	.05	.07
South Carolina	−.33	−.47	−.02
Georgia	−.21	−.23	−.32
Sum of squares	2.62	2.45	2.56
% Total variance	23.82	22.27	25.60

[a]This table is made up of three separate two-factor analyses. In each case, Factor 1 is displayed above Factor 2 of the same run. The table is constructed this way so the reader can follow the movement of individual states on these issues by reading left to right. Code 2 votes: 5, 6, 26, 29, 37–39, 47–55, 71–84, 105–106, 113–118, 122–130.

icut and Maryland). But South Carolina was far from joining the small state opposition, as that state actually loaded at −.47 on factor 2. South Carolina's seeming isolation stemmed from its uncompromising demand for full representation for blacks at 1 for 1, rather than the old federal ratio of 3 for 5.

After July 11 (the 2b votes), when the initiative within the large state coalition shifted to the southern states, led by South Carolina, the perspective from which the proposals for proportional representation were made also changed. Pennsylvania, concerned that the South was demanding institutional structures that it would surely dominate in a few years, began to shift away from its allies of the last four weeks and towards cooperation with a geographically contiguous group of Middle Atlantic states. Pennsylvania's movement is made particularly striking by the stability of the rest of the large state coalition. Four of its six members change their loading across the 2, 2a, and 2b votes by less than .1. These delegations were committed to proportional representation in either its northern or its southern guise. Thus, the clash between Pennsylvania and South Carolina over the question of counting slaves for representation provides a clear demonstration of Pennsylvania's fear that demographic trends were sweeping power to the South.

The behavior of Pennsylvania and South Carolina on the code 2, 2a, and 2b votes demonstrates that the basic weakness within this coalition was one of northern versus southern parochial interest. This stress finally separated the large state coalition on factor 1 of Table 5.1 so that the steady opposition of the small states on factor 2, supplemented by the occasional, though often timely, defections of Massachusetts, the Carolinas, and Georgia, resulted in equal voting rights in the Senate and cleared the way for a subsequent regional battle over the power relationships to pertain in the first House of Representatives.

Confrontation and Stalemate on the Convention Floor

The confrontation between the delegates from the large states and those from the small states on the representation issue intensified on June 11, when Roger Sherman of Connecticut suggested that the House of Representatives be apportioned according to the number of a state's free inhabitants, while each state would have one vote in the Senate. The large state forces still demanded proportional representation in both houses. Madison recorded that "Mr. King and Mr. Wilson (in order to bring the question to a point) moved 'that the right of suffrage (in the first branch of) the national Legislature ought not to be according to the rule established in the articles of Confederation (equality), but according to some equitable ratio of representation,'" which after some discussion passed in the affirmative, 7-3-1 (*Records*, vol. 1, p. 196). The large state coalition unanimously voted yes and was joined by Connecticut in pursuit of Sherman's suggested compromise. New York, New Jersey, and Delaware opposed, while the Maryland delegates were divided on the issue.

Wilson then sought to solidify the allegiance of the southern states to the large state coalition by assuring them of the traditional three-fifths representation for their slaves. The Convention accepted this by a vote of 9-2. New Jersey and Delaware opposed (*Records*, vol. 1, p. 201). Even though the South had been strengthened by the counting of three-fifths of their slaves, Sherman still called for the second half of his proposed compromise, equal voting rights in the Senate. The small states were denied by a vote of 6-5, with the six factor 1 states unanimously opposing the five factor 2 states of Table 5.1. Pressing the large state advantage, Wilson and Hamilton moved that "the right of suffrage in the 2nd branch ought to be according to the same rule as in the 1st branch" (ibid., p. 202). They were successful by the same 6-5 alignment. Thus proportional representation in both houses, for a time, had been achieved by a head-on clash between the large states and the small.

June 12 was spent in debating details concerning the length of the terms, reeligibility to office, and assorted limitations on members of both houses of the national Congress. On the term for the House, New England wanted to follow its tradition of yearly elections, while the South favored a longer, three-year term. For the Senate, New England called for a five-year term, while the South favored a longer, seven-year term. In both instances, the longer term was adopted. These debates show that though both New England and the lower South wished to focus the new government on the states, New England wanted to maintain its tradition of frequent elections, while the South wanted elite control with broad discretion. The remainder of June 12 and most of June 13 were given over to consideration of details in the Virginia Plan that earlier had been passed over or left unresolved. At the end of business on the thirteenth, Gorham, chairing the Committee of the Whole, "reported from the Committee that the Committee having considered and gone through the propositions offered to the House by the honorable Mr Randolph, and to them referred, were prepared to report thereon—and had directed him to submit the report to the consideration of the House" (*Records*, vol. 1, p. 223). Discussion of the report, once it was read, was postponed to the next day.

The Virginia Plan, as amended through the first two and one-half weeks of debate, envisioned a very powerful national government. This was to be a government "consisting of a Supreme Legislative, Judiciary, and Executive." The legislature clearly was envisioned to be the dominant branch. It would consist of two houses, the first elected by the people, the second by the state legislatures. The numbers in each branch were to be proportional to the populations of the various states, including three-fifths of all slaves, and each branch was to have equal rights to initiate legislative action. The powers to be exercised by this national legislature were awesome, particularly when viewed against the pale backdrop of the Confederation Congress. The proposed Congress would have authority to legislate in all areas where *it* might judge the individual states to be "incompetent" or in which *it* conceived that their individual legislation might disrupt the "harmony" of the new nation. In addition, the Congress would have the power "to negative all laws passed by the several States contravening, in the opinion of the national legislature, the articles of union; or any treaty subsisting under the authority of the Union." Both the executive and the judiciary would derive their appointments from the legislature. The executive would be a single person "with power to carry into execution the national laws." He would be chosen by the national legislature, for a term of seven years, and would be ineligible a second time. A national judiciary, to consist of one supreme tribunal, would be appointed by the Senate, with inferior tribunals to be empowered and appointed by the national legislature. Finally, the amendments composing the new Constitution were to be ratified by popularly elected state conventions while "the Legislative, Executive, and judiciary powers within the several States ought to be bound by oath to support the articles of union" (*Records*, vol. 1, pp. 225–228).

Clearly, the political interests of the states generally, and of the smaller states in particular, had been systematically dismantled in the initial pass through the Virginia Plan. The equality of suffrage that had pertained in the Continental and Confederation Congresses since before the Revolution was now completely removed. Further, the states as political entities, irrespective of their size, had been reduced in stature far below their previous role as the sovereign units upon which the utterly dependent Confederation government had been based. Both Madison and his opponents must have known—and if not, they would soon discover—that a coalition of small states demanding equality in at least one branch of the legislature and of delegates from the larger states (Gerry and Strong from Massachusetts and the delegates from South Carolina are the best examples) who wished to see the dominance of the national government over the state legislatures somewhat reduced posed a major threat to the slim majority (6-5) held by the states supporting Madison's plan for a strong national government dominated by a powerful legislature in which the large states would exercise decisive influence.

Luther Martin of Maryland reported in his "Genuine Information"

(*Records*, vol. 3, pp. 172–232) that opponents had been biding their time and consulting on alternative courses of action while Madison's Virginia Plan was receiving its early favorable treatment in the committee of the whole. Martin reported that while the Virginia Plan was before the committee "a number of members, who disapproved them, were preparing *another system*, such as *they thought more conducive to the happiness and welfare of the States*" (ibid., p. 174). Therefore, when the Virginia Plan was reported from the Committee back to the full Convention on the morning of June 14, "Mr. Patterson, observed to the Convention that it was the wish of several deputations, particularly that of N. Jersey, that further time might be allowed them to contemplate the plan reported from the Committee of the Whole, and to digest one purely federal, and contradistinguished from the reported plan. He said they hoped to have such an one ready by tomorrow to be laid before the Convention: and the Convention adjourned that leisure might be given for that purpose" (*Records*, vol. 1, p. 240).

The nine propositions comprising the New Jersey Plan were presented by Patterson to the Convention on June 15 (see the New Jersey Plan in Appendix C). "Mr. Lansing & some other gentlemen" then secured an adjournment until the next day, "by which delay the friends of the plan proposed by Mr. Patterson wd. be better prepared to explain & support it, and all would have an opportunity of taking copies" (*Records*, vol. 1, p. 242). Madison, always the legislative tactician, appended a footnote to these debates explaining the nature and motives of the support for the New Jersey Plan:

> this plan had been concerted among the deputations or members thereof, from Cont. N. Y. N. J. Del. and perhaps Mr Martin from Maryd. who made with them a common cause on different principles. Cont. and N. Y. were agst. a departure from the principle of the Confederation, wishing rather to add a few new powers to Congs. than to substitute, a National Govt. The States of N. J. and Del. were opposed to a National Govt. because its patrons considered a proportional representation of the States as the basis of it. The eagourness displayed by the Members opposed to a Natl. Govt. from these different (motives) began now to produce serious anxiety for the result of the Convention.—Mr. Dickenson said to Mr. Madison you see the consequence of pushing things too far. Some of the members from the small States wish for two branches in the General Legislature, and are friends to a good National Government; but we would sooner submit to a foreign power, than submit to be deprived of an equality of suffrage, in both branches of the legislature, and thereby be thrown under the domination of the large States. (ibid.)

The New Jersey Plan was undoubtedly much more what the delegates arriving in Philadelphia thought they would be discussing than was the

Virginia Plan. The New Jersey Plan, based securely on the existing states, sought, through amendment to the Articles of Confederation, to allocate those new powers to Congress that had long been under discussion. The first resolution was a slight modification of the first resolution of the Virginia Plan as initially read by Randolph: "Resd. that the articles of Confederation ought to be so revised, corrected & enlarged, as to render the federal Constitution adequate to the exigencies of Government, & the preservation of the Union" (ibid.). Resolutions two and three outlined what new powers the proponents of the New Jersey Plan thought were necessary. First, the Congress would "be authorized to pass acts for raising a revenue" through duties on imports, stamps on paper, and postage on letters and packages "passing through the general post-Office." In addition, Congress would have the power "to pass Acts for the regulation of trade & commerce as well with foreign nations as with each other" (*Records*, vol. 1, p. 243). The absence of these powers and resources, an independent revenue and commercial regulation, were widely seen as the key deficiencies in the Confederation government. The New Jersey Plan would grant these, but even here, it would hedge them in with state power and discretion.

It was clear to everyone that the federal revenue sources granted in the New Jersey Plan would not be sufficient. The deficiency would be filled through the traditional means of requisitions on the states. Requisitions on the states had been the bane of the Confederation Congress, being only rarely complied with, they left the Congress always dependent and most often penniless. Similarly, the commercial power of the Congress was hedged in by state authority. The New Jersey Plan gave Congress the power to regulate foreign and interstate commerce, but "all punishments, fines, forfeitures & penalties to be incurred for contravening such acts rules and regulations shall be adjudged by the Common law Judiciarys of the State in which any offence . . . shall have been committed" (*Records*, vol. 1, p. 243). Though appeals could be had to federal courts, initial judgments concerning violations of national commercial regulations would be rendered in state courts.

The federal judiciary, to be appointed by the Executive, was "to consist of a supreme Tribunal of Judges," having original jurisdiction only in cases involving impeachment of federal officers; cases dealing with the rights of ambassadors, captures, and piracies and felonies on the high seas; or cases involving foreigners or the interpretation of treaties. In addition, the federal high court would have appellate jurisdiction in cases involving violations of the Congress' revenue and commercial policies (*Records*, vol. 1, p. 244). Clearly, virtually all original jurisdiction over American citizens was to be exercised by the state courts.

The sixth resolution did, however, seem to grant the national government broad coercive powers to defend its authority against recalcitrant states. The sixth resolution declared that all legitimate acts and treaties of the national government "shall be the supreme law of the respective States" and that "the Judiciary of the several States shall be bound thereby in their decisions." Further, the sixth resolution declared that the "federal Executive shall be authorized to call forth ye power of the Confederated States . . . to enforce and compel an obedience to such Acts, or an Observance of such Treaties" (*Records*, vol. 1, p. 245). While the powers of the national government would be severely limited and would be checked by state power at every turn, where power was granted it was to be supreme and was to be enforceable against the states through the direct application of military power.

When debate opened in the Committee of the Whole on June 16, both plans were before the Committee, and the day was dedicated to their close comparison. The debate was opened by New York's John Lansing: "Mr. Lansing called for a reading of the lst. resolution of each plan, which he considered as involving principles directly in contrast; that of Mr. Patterson says he sustains the sovereignty of the respective States, that of Mr. Randolph distroys it: the latter requires a negative on all the laws of the particular States; the former, only certain general powers for the general good" (*Records*, vol. 1, p. 249). James Wilson, while speaking in opposition to the New Jersey Plan, agreed that the key difference was as Lansing had described it, noting that "representation of the people at large is the basis of the one; the State Legislatures the pillars of the other" (ibid., p. 252). Randolph also agreed on the basic point in dispute between the two plans, arguing that "the true question is whether we shall adhere to the federal plan, or introduce the national plan" (ibid., p. 255). Randolph and Wilson, together with Madison and several of the delegates from the larger states, clearly wished to move to the "national" plan. Yates recorded Paterson, however, as speaking cogently and at length in favor of the "federal" alternative:

> The doctrine advanced by a learned gentlemen from Pennsylvania (Wilson), that all power is derived from the people, and that in proportion to their numbers they ought to participate equally in the benefits and rights of government, is right in principle, but unfortunately for him, wrong in the application to the question now in debate.
>
> When independent societies confederate for mutual defence, they do so in their collective capacity; and then each state for those purposes must be

considered as *one* of the contracting parties. Destroy this balance of equality, and you endanger the rights of the *lesser* societies by the danger of usurpation in the greater." (*Records*, vol. 1, p. 259)

Alexander Hamilton, largely silent since the Convention's opening days, took almost all of June 18 to respond in depth to Paterson's arguments in favor of the New Jersey Plan. Hamilton declared himself to be "unfriendly to both plans. He was particularly opposed to that from N. Jersey, being fully convinced, that no amendment of the confederation, leaving the States in possession of their sovereignty could possibly answer the purpose" (*Records*, vol. 1, p. 283).

Nonetheless, Hamilton was much more clear on what he opposed and on his doubts than on what he could support with confidence or with even the remote hope of political success. Hamilton's key concern derived from his doubts concerning Madison's "extended republic" solution to the instability attendant on popular government. Clearly, if Hamilton was unconvinced by Madison's "extended republic" arguments, we cannot expect that Sherman, Bedford, or Paterson could have been profoundly swayed. Hamilton's personal notes concerning Madison's speech are terse but clear:

Maddisons Theory—
    Two principles upon which republics ought to be constructed—
    I. that they have such extent as to render combinations on the ground of interest difficult—
    II. By a process of election calculated to refine the representation of the People—
    Answer—There is truth in both these principles but they do not conclude so strongly as he supposes." (*Records*, vol. 1, p. 146)

After declaring himself opposed to both the Virginia and New Jersey Plans, Hamilton pointed to the source of his distress: "he confessed he was much discouraged by the amazing extent of Country in expecting the desired blessings from any general sovereignty that could be substituted" (*Records*, vol. 1, p. 283). Hamilton recurred twice more during this speech to his doubts concerning the governability on republican principles of a nation of continental scope.

After reviewing the deficiencies of the two plans before the Convention, Hamilton asked, "What then is to be done? Here he was embarrassed. The extent of the Country to be governed discouraged him" (ibid., p. 287). Hamilton then went on to declare that "in his private opinion he had no scruple in declaring . . . that the British Govt. was the best in the world: and that he doubted much whether any thing short of it would do in America" (ibid., p. 288). Therefore, Hamilton concluded his speech with the observation "that we ought to go as far in order to attain stability and permanency, as republican principles will admit. Let one branch of the Legislature hold their places for life or at least during good behaviour. Let the Executive also be for life" (ibid., p. 289).

Hamilton, frustrated by the fact that Yates and Lansing had carried New York's vote against him on most matters of consequence, was speaking his mind even though "he was aware that it [his plan] went beyond the ideas of most members" (ibid., p. 291). Though his calls for life terms for the executive and for senators fell on deaf ears, others of his comments struck the federalists as more worrisome. For instance, Yates recorded Hamilton as concluding that "all federal governments are weak and distracted," and as proposing that "to avoid the evils deducible from these observations, we must establish a general and national government, completely sovereign, and annihilate the state distinctions and state operations; and unless we do this, no good purpose can be answered" (ibid., p. 297). Finally, Hamilton's own notes express eloquently the source of his distress with both the Virginia and the New Jersey Plans: "a democratic assembly is to be checked by a democratic senate, and both these by a democratic chief magistrate. The end will not be answered—the means will not be equal to the object. It will, therefore, be feeble and inefficient" (ibid., p. 310).

Madison's long speech of June 19 is a logical extension of his argument of June 6 that the "objects" of government at the national level would be many, not least of which would be "providing more effectually for the security of private rights, and the steady dispensation of Justice. Interferences with these were evils which had perhaps more than anything else, produced this convention. Was it to be supposed that republican liberty could long exist under the abuses of it practiced in (some of) the States" (*Records*, vol. 1, p. 134). It was to this fundamental question that Madison again turned on June 19: "Proceeding to the consideration of Mr. Patterson's plan, he stated the object of a proper plan to be twofold. 1. to preserve the Union. 2. to provide a Governmt. that will remedy the evils felt by the States both in their united and individual capacities. Examine Mr. P's plan, & say whether it promises satisfaction in these respects" (ibid., pp. 315–316).

Madison spent the better part of the day going through, point by point for the delegates, his "Vices of the Political System of the United States" and arguing that none of the "Vices" afflicting the current system would adequately be addressed by the New Jersey Plan. Madison addressed six major questions to the delegates; answering each of them in the negative (ibid., pp. 316–319):

1. Will it prevent those violations of the law of nations & of Treaties which if not prevented must involve us in the calamities of foreign wars? No.

2. Will it prevent encroachments on the federal authority? No.

3. Will it prevent trespasses of the States on each other? No.

4. Will it secure the internal tranquillity of the States themselves? No.

5. Will it secure a good internal legislation & administration to the particular States? . . . Under this head he enumerated and animadverted on 1. the multiplicity of the laws passed by the several States. 2. the mutability of their laws. 3. the injustice of them. 4. the impotence of them: No.

6. Will it secure the Union agst. the influence of foreign powers over its members? No.

Madison concluded his remarks with the observation that "the great difficulty lies in the affair of Representation; and if this could be adjusted, all others would be surmountable" (*Records*, vol. 1, p. 321). Yet, rather than attempting to "adjust" this issue of representation, Madison did no more than advise the smaller states to combine with each other to form larger states if they thought it would bring them some benefit. Following Madison's speech, "On the question (moved by Mr. King) whether the Committee should rise & Mr. Randolphs propositions be re-reported without alteration, which was in fact a question whether Mr. R's should be adhered to as preferable to those of Mr. Patterson" (ibid., p. 322). The states voted in the affirmative 7-3-1, with New York, New Jersey, and Delaware opposing and Maryland divided. More surprising than the outcome of this direct comparison of the two plans is the fact that virtually no one spoke in favor of the New Jersey Plan. Once Paterson had introduced the plan, the strong nationalists almost totally dominated the debate: Wilson contrasted the two plans on June 17; Hamilton used virtually all of June 18 to present his plan; and Madison spoke at length on the June 19. As soon as Madison finished speaking, the vote by which the Virginia Plan was resubmitted to the Convention was taken.

When the Convention reconvened on June 20 the Virginia Plan was again before it, and the first resolution came immediately under discussion as the Convention began its second full scale consideration of that plan. The first resolution read: "'Resolved . . . that a national government ought to be established consisting of a Supreme Legislative, Judiciary, and Executive'" (*Records*, vol. 1, p. 228). Ellsworth and Gorham sought to remove the word *national* and to substitute the title "the United States," so that the resolution would read: "that the Government of the United States ought to consist of a supreme legislative, Executive, and Judiciary" (*Records*, vol. 1, p. 335). Ellsworth and Gorham argued that removal of the word "national" would leave the changes under discussion on a "federal" footing and that "under this idea the authority of the Legislatures could ratify it" (ibid.). The New

England delegates, Shay's Rebellion still fresh in their minds, wished to avoid conventions or other forms of popular involvement in the ratification process, Ellsworth observing that "he did not like these conventions. They were better fitted to pull down than to build up Constitutions" (ibid.). Ellsworth's proposal was approved without opposition, though not before Randolph had spoken in defense of popular ratification.

The second resolution, "'that the national Legislature ought to consist of two branches,'" was taken up in turn. The word national was again struck out without dispute. Lansing, speaking for the federalists, "observed that the true question here was, whether the Convention would adhere to or depart from the foundation of the present Confederacy" (*Records*, vol. 1, p. 336). Therefore, Lansing opposed a bicameral legislature, proposing instead "'that the powers of Legislation be vested (in the U. States) in Congress'" (ibid.). Lansing, and those who stood with him, understood that equality could best be defended in a unicameral legislature in which the states stood as sovereign entities. Luther Martin agreed, arguing that "he saw no necessity for two branches. . . . Congress represented the Legislatures" (*Records*, vol. 1, p. 340). Sherman, seconding Lansing's motion, "admitted two branches to be necessary in the State Legislatures, but saw no necessity for them in a Confederacy of States" (ibid.). Nonetheless, adhering to the established compromise position of his delegation, Sherman observed that "if the difficulty on the subject of representation can not be otherwise got over, he would agree to have two branches, and a proportional representation in one of them, provided each State had an equal voice in the other" (ibid., p. 343).

When the vote was taken on the question of postponing the second resolution in order to take up Lansing's proposal for a unicameral legislature, it lost 4-6-1; with Connecticut, New York, New Jersey, and Delaware in favor and Maryland divided. The six states on factor 1 of Table 5.1 voted no. Delaware then sought and achieved an adjournment before bicameralism could be approved. When debate opened on June 21, William Samuel Johnson offered a very calm and lucid description of the Convention's dilemma. Johnson observed that:

On a comparison of the two plans which had been proposed from Virginia & N. Jersey, it appeared that the peculiarity which characterized the latter was its being calculated to preserve the individuality of the States. . . . He wished it therefore to be well considered whether in case the States, as was proposed, shd. retain some portion of sovereignty at least, this portion could be preserved, without allowing them to participate effectually in the Genl. Govt., without giving them each a distinct and equal vote or the purpose of defending themselves in the general Councils. (*Records*, vol. 1, pp. 354–355)

First Wilson and then Madison sought to assure Johnson and the federalists that the national government posed no threat to the states. In fact, both argued, in Wilson's words, that "in spite of every precaution the General Govt. would be in perpetual danger of encroachments from the State Govts." Madison agreed, declaring, rather than arguing, that there was "less danger of encroachment from the Genl. Govt. than from the State Govts." (*Records*, vol. 1, p. 356). When the vote on the bicameralism provision of resolution two was taken, it was approved 7-3-1. With Maryland still divided between Jenifer and Martin, Connecticut pursued its compromise position by voting with the six states of factor 1 against New York, New Jersey, and Delaware. Though this vote clearly rejected the unicameral logic of the Confederation, it did so without the convincing explanation requested by Johnson on how the states, particularly the small states, could be safe in the face of national power.

The third resolution, calling for popular election of the lower house of the national legislature, came before the Convention in its turn. The idea of popular election to offices of the national government was vexing to many of the delegates. The small state delegates were concerned that this suggested that the national government was based on the people rather than on the thirteen sovereign and equal states. Some of the delegates from Massachusetts and the lower South simply questioned the people's fitness, when compared with the state legislatures, to select the members to the national legislature, even its lower branch. South Carolina's General C. C. Pinckney moved "'that the 1st. branch, instead of being elected by the people, shd. be elected in such manner as the Legislature of each State should direct'" (*Records*, vol. 1, p. 358). Pinckney assured his colleagues that this change would allow the state legislatures better to "accommodate the mode to the conveniency & opinions of the people," but Hamilton saw other motives, regarding "the motion as intended manifestly to transfer the election from the people to the State Legislatures, which would essentially vitiate the plan" (ibid.). John Rutledge, at least as committed to the defense of the South Carolina aristocracy as General Pinckney, supported his colleague with the argument that the distinction between popular and legislative selection was specious: "Mr. Rutledge could not admit the solidity of the distinction between a mediate & immediate election by the people. It was the same thing to act by oneself, and to act by another." This very questionable argument aside, Rutledge then went on to make the point consistently recurred to by the Carolina delegates in similar instances. Rutledge argued that "an election by the

Legislature would be more refined than an election immediately by the people" (*Records*, vol. 1, p. 359).

James Wilson, perhaps the single delegate attending the Convention most clear on the logic of democratic politics, as opposed to a British or Hamiltonian conception of balancing classes or estates in government, derided Rutledge's comments. Wilson "considered the election of the 1st. branch by the people not only as the corner Stone, but as the foundation of the fabric: and that the difference between a mediate and immediate election was immense" (*Records*, vol. 1, p. 359). General Pinckney assured his colleagues that his real concern was to leave a large role for the states. He "was for making the State Govts. a part of the General System." He was convinced, as were several of his colleagues, not only from South Carolina but from New England as well, that "If they were to be abolished, or lose their agency, S. Carolina & other States would have but a small share of the benefits of Govt." (ibid., p. 360). When General Pinckney's proposal was put to a vote it was defeated, but a very interesting alignment appeared. The vote was 4-6-1; South Carolina secured the support of three of the small states, Connecticut, New Jersey, and Delaware, with Maryland again divided, against the remaining states on factor 1 and New York. Election of the first branch by "the people" then passed 9-1-1, with New Jersey opposing and Maryland divided. Nonetheless, as the previous vote suggested, and as would become increasingly clear, the concern of some of the larger states, particularly Massachusetts and South Carolina, about the role of the states in the new system was the Achilles' heel of the large state coalition.

June 22 opened four days of debate devoted almost exclusively to the relationships to pertain between the state legislatures and the delegates to the national House and Senate, with particular interest in the Senate. These issues came to the fore when the clause of the third resolution calling for members of the House "to receive fixed stipends to be paid out of the Nationl. Treasury" came under consideration on the twenty-second. Ellsworth immediately "moved to substitute payment by the States out of their own Treasurys" (*Records*, vol. 1, p. 371). Ellsworth pointed to the different levels of wealth and styles of life in the different parts of the country as the reason for assigning this responsibility to the individual states. Roger Sherman and North Carolina's Hugh Williamson "favored the idea. He (Williamson) reminded the House of the prospect of new States to the Westward. They would be poor . . . and would have a different interest from the old States. He did not think therefore that the latter ought to pay the expenses of men who would be employed in thwarting their measures & interests" (ibid., p. 372).

Opposition to the idea of making House members financially dependent upon the states rose to a chorus from very familiar sources. Randolph argued that "if the States were to pay the members of the Natl. Legislature, a dependence would be created that would vitiate the whole System. The whole nation has an interest in the attendance & services of the members. The Nationl. Treasury therefore is the proper fund for supporting them" (*Records*, vol. 1, p. 372). Wilson "thought it of great moment that the members of the Natl. Govt. should be left as independent (as possible) of the State Govts. in all respects. . . . Madison concurred in the necessity of preserving the compensations for the Natl. Govt. independent on the State Govts" while Hamilton declared that "those who pay are the masters of those who are paid" (ibid., p. 373).

The vote on Ellsworth's motion to strike out "National Treasury" failed by the narrow margin of 4-5-2. Both New England and the lower South favored compensation of House members by the states. In New England, both Massachusetts and Connecticut voted in favor, while the New York vote was divided; in the South, the Carolinas voted in favor, and the Georgia vote was divided. Five Middle Atlantic states, ranging from New Jersey through Virginia, favored payment out of the National Treasury and defeated the motion.

On June 25, the focus shifted to the selection of Senators. The Virginia Plan, since its amendment on June 7, called for direct selection of Senators by the state legislatures. Wilson opened argument on this issue with a very long and articulate speech based on the premise that America was a new nation in the world to which old examples, whether British or Roman, did not apply. He saw America as a "great & equal body of citizens . . . among whom there are no distinctions of rank, and very few or none of fortune" (*Records*, vol. 1, p. 403). Wilson concluded from this that both houses of the national legislature, Senate as well as House, should be selected by the people.

Gorham, however, was not so sure. Massachusetts had supported proportional representation in both houses from the beginning. But she had also worked closely with the Connecticut delegation to secure a role for the states in the new system. By now it had become clear that some of the delegates most strongly in support of p. r., Wilson, Hamilton, and Madison among them, wished dramatically to limit the role of the states in the new system. It slowly became clear to Gorham and to a number of delegates from North and South Carolina that a strong role for the states could best be preserved by fastening the states firmly to the Senate. Gorham listened to Wilson's defense of the popular selection of both houses but remained unconvinced. He was now "inclined to a compromise as to the rule of proportion. He thought there was some weight in the objections of the small States" (*Records*, vol. 1, p. 404). North Carolina's Williamson also "professed himself a friend to such a system as would secure the existence of the State Govts. The happiness of the people depend on it" (ibid., p. 407).

Pierce Butler of South Carolina agreed that little could be done until this critical issue was resolved, "observing that we were put to difficulties at every step by the uncertainty whether an equality or a ratio of representation wd. prevail in the 2d. branch" (ibid.). Butler therefore moved and Madison seconded a proposal to postpone the fourth resolution and move to a discussion of this issue immediately, but the Convention refused. A vote was then taken on the clause "'that the members of the 2d. branch be chosen by the indivl. Legislatures'" (*Records*, vol. 1, p. 408). The vote was 9-2 in favor, only Pennsylvania and Virginia opposing. Madison appended an explanatory footnote to the vote which indicates that he understood quite clearly the nature of the coalition that Pennsylvania and Virginia faced on this issue. Madison noted that:

> it must be kept in view that the largest States particularly Pennsylvania & Virginia always considered the choice of the 2d. Branch by the State Legislatures as opposed to a proportional Representation to which they were attached as a fundamental principle of just Government. The smaller States who had opposite views, were reenforced by the members from the large States most anxious to secure the importance of the State Governments. (ibid.)

Madison made at least two critical points in his brief analysis of this vote. The first was that adoption of a prominent role for the states in the Senate, even if only in selecting its members at this point, mediated against a later decision in favor of a proportional distribution of Senate seats. Equal representation of the states in the Senate was not decided by this vote, but such a decision at a later date was made more likely by this vote. Second, Madison pointed to the Achilles' heel of the large-state coalition when he noted that some "members from the large States" were "anxious to secure the importance of the State Governments" (*Records*, vol. 1, p. 408). Further, notes taken by Yates also show quite clearly that Madison saw this vote as a watershed decision militating against a complete adoption of the Virginia Plan's approach to a powerful national government unconstrained by the states. Madison warned his colleagues that they were "preceeding in the same manner that was done when the confederation was first formed—Its original draft was excellent, but in its progress and completion it became so insufficient as to give rise to the present convention. By the vote already taken, will not the temper of the state legislatures transfuse itself into the senate?" (ibid., p. 416).

Madison's concerns and doubts about the strength of the large-state coalition when it came to defending the integrity and independence of the Senate were undoubtedly sharpened by the debates and decisions of June 26. The issue, once again, was who, the states or the national treasury, would pay the members of the Senate. Ellsworth moved to strike out the national treasury in favor of the phrase "'to be paid by their respective States'" (*Records*, vol. 1, p. 427). Madison and Dayton opposed, and Ellsworth's motion was barely defeated by a vote of 5-6. The delegations voting in favor of state payment of national Senators were Connecticut, New York, and New Jersey, joined by South Carolina and Georgia. From Madison's perspective, this was a tenuous victory indeed, as either Delaware or Maryland could reverse the decision simply by returning to the small state coalition. The next vote, on the question "'to be paid out of the public treasury,'" was of equal concern to Madison because it was unexpectedly lost by a 5-6 margin (ibid., p. 428). Once again, South Carolina and Georgia joined Connecticut, New York, and New Jersey to oppose the nationalists, but this time, North Carolina joined them, too. This put all three states of the deep South firmly on record in favor of a strong state presence in the national Senate. Clearly, the main threat to Madison's general program was that the five small states might be able to turn the concern of the deep South about state control of the Senate into support for equality of the states in the Senate. The small states worked with increasing determination over the next week to achieve precisely that goal.

In order to bring the critical question before the Convention to a point, Rutledge moved on the morning of June 27 to postpone consideration of resolution six, dealing with the powers of the Congress, in order to take up resolutions seven and eight, dealing with the distribution of suffrage in the House and the Senate, respectively. The seventh resolution was taken up first. When debate began, Luther Martin took the floor to argue "that an equal vote in each State was essential to the federal idea" and, to the general disgust of his colleagues, held the floor throughout the entire day and for half of the following day (*Records*, vol. 1, p. 437). When Martin finally finished, Lansing and Dayton "moved to strike out 'not.' so that the 7 art: might read that the rights of suffrage in the 1st branch ought to be according to the rule established by the Confederation" (ibid., p. 445). Knowing that this was a critical issue and that the vote would be excruciatingly close, "Dayton expressed great anxiety that the question might not be put till tomorrow; Governr. Livingston being kept away by indisposition, and the representation of N. Jersey thereby suspended" (ibid.).

The Convention eventually agreed to postpone the decision on this question until Livingston could fill out the New Jersey representation on the June 29, but in the meantime, Madison sought both to placate his opponents and to inform them that no compromise was to be expected on this fundamental issue. Madison assured Lansing and Dayton that "he was much disposed to concur in any expedient not inconsistent with fundamental principles, that could remove the difficulty concerning the rule of representation. But he could neither be convinced that the rule contended for was just, nor necessary for the safety of the small States agst. the large States" (*Records*, vol. 1, p. 446).

The opposing coalitions had held firm on the issues of congressional representation, selection, and tenure through all of June. On June 29, the Connecticut delegates again proposed the compromise that had been before the Convention formally on June 11 and again on June 20. Presenting Connecticut's case, Ellsworth declared, "We were partly national; partly federal. The proportional representation in the first branch was conformable to the national principle & would secure the large States agst. the small. An equality of voices was conformable to the federal principle and was necessary to secure the Small States agst. the large. He trusted that on this middle ground a compromise would take place. He did not see that it could on any other" (*Records*, vol. 1, pp. 468–469).

Madison and the larger states still vigorously opposed this solution, arguing that "if the old fabric of the confederation must be the ground-work of the new, we must fail." Further, he contended that the fundamental opposition within the nation did not arise from tension between the large states and the small. Instead, "the great danger to our general government [and to the factor 1 coalition, as events would prove] *is the great southern and northern interests of the continent, being opposed to each other*" (*Records*, vol. 1, p. 476). Madison again reiterated this conception of the country's true division the following day, June 30, but he was vastly overshadowed by one of the most vituperative exchanges of the Convention, as the conflict between the large states and the small threatened to bring the debates to a grinding halt.

James Wilson, arguing against any compromise by the large states on this crucial issue, said he hoped the small states "would not abandon a Country to which they were bound by so many strong and endearing ties, . . . [but] if a separation must take place, it could never happen on better grounds" (*Records*, vol. 1, p. 482). Against this threatening display of determination on the part of Wilson and his colleagues, young Gunning Bedford of Delaware answered for the small states, saying "*I do not, gentlemen, trust you. If you possess the power, the abuse of it could not be checked; and what then would prevent you from exercising it to our destruction?*" (ibid., p. 500). Though Bedford was angry, he spoke with great insight into the realities that had dominated the recent weeks of the Convention's business, so his remarks deserve to be quoted at some length. His comments demonstrate that the precise voting alignments that we identified in Table 5.1 and that Madison anticipated some weeks before the Convention opened, were quite clearly before the eyes of the delegates as they worked. Being consistently in the minority was hard on the nerves, and sometimes tempers flared. Bedford accused his colleagues in the following words:

> If political Societies possess ambition avarice, and all the other passions which render them formidable to each other, ought we not to view them in this light here? If any gentleman doubts it let him look at the votes. Have they not been dictated by interest, by ambition? Are not the large States evidently seeking to aggrandize themselves at the expense of the small? They think no doubt that they have right on their side, but interest had blinded their eyes. Look at Georgia. Though a small state at present, she is actuated by the prospect of soon being a great one. S. Carolina is actuated both by present interest & future prospects. She hopes to see other States cut down to her own dimensions. N. Carolina has the same motives of present & future interest. Virga. follows. Maryd. is not on that side of the Question. Pena. has a direct and future interest. Massts. has a decided and palpable interest in the part she takes. Can it be expected that the small states will act from pure disinterestedness." (*Records*, vol. 1, p. 491)

Obviously the members of the Convention knew where the votes were on this matter because Bedford named the entire large state coalition, scourging its members for acting an interested part, characterized by ambition and avarice, in the service of both present and future gain.

On July 2, Ellsworth's motion was put to a vote. Even after the previous two days of sometimes raucous debate, the result was the familiar large state versus small state split, but with one key variation. Georgia's vote was divided, causing a 5-5-1 tie. This denied equality of representation in the Senate again, but the mood of the Convention seemed to be changing as southern support for p. r. continued to erode.

A Resort to Compromise Committees: Large versus Small

With the proceedings seemingly at another impasse, C. C. Pinckney of South Carolina proposed that a committee of one member from each state be appointed to study the mode of representation in both branches. Only Wilson and Madison, who could now feel the tide of the Convention beginning to flow strongly against them, opposed the formation of a compromise committee, while ten delegates from both voting groups spoke in favor of it. Sherman said, "We are now at a full stop, and nobody . . . meant that we shd. break up without doing something" (*Records*, vol. 1, p. 511). Williamson of North Carolina hoped that "as the Come. wd. be a smaller body, a compromise would be pursued with more coolness" (ibid., p. 515). Not surprisingly, given the men who were selected to serve, the hopes of Sherman and Williamson, as well as the fears of Wilson and Madison, were borne out by the work of the committee.

The compromise committee not only failed to include Wilson and Madison, but omitted every one of the strong spokesmen for proportional representation (Bancroft, 1882, p. 245; McLaughlin, 1905, p. 234; Farrand, 1913, p. 97; Roche, 1961, p. 809). The three large states were represented by Mason, Franklin, and Gerry (compromisers all); the South, by Davie, Rutledge, and Baldwin (the very man who had divided the Georgia vote on July 2); and the small states, by an effective mix of their most persuasive and intransigent spokesmen. The early replacement of Connecticut's Ellsworth by Sherman made little difference because both had presented their state's compromise position several times. William Paterson, who three weeks earlier had been selected by his colleagues opposing the Virginia Plan to present the small state plan, or New Jersey Plan, represented his state. Yates, Bedford, and Luther Martin completed the committee. Gerry was selected as chairman. From the makeup of this committee, it is hardly conceivable that the outcome was still in doubt.

After six weeks of intense debate, almost four weeks concentrating on this issue alone, Madison's pre-Convention prediction that "the smaller states will ultimately yield to the predominate will" began to look less prescient (Hunt, 1901, vol. 2, p. 340). According to Gerry, the small states, rather than bend to the will of the slim 6-5 large state majority held "a separate meeting . . . of most of the delegates of those five States [Factor 2], the result of which was, a firm determination on their part not to relinquish the right of equal representation in the Senate" (*Records*, vol. 3, p. 264). No course was left but compromise, and with this in mind, the Convention had selected its committee.

On July 5, Gerry delivered the report of his committee to the Convention. It was in two parts: "1st That in the first branch of the Legislature each of the States now in the Union be allowed one Member for every forty thousand inhabitants . . . and that no money shall be drawn from the public Treasury but in pursuance of appropriations to be originated by the first Branch. 2ndly That in the second Branch of the Legislature each State shall have an equal Vote" (*Records*, vol. 1, p. 524).

With the twin blows of the tie vote of July 2 and the July 5 committee report of equality in the Senate, the raison d'etre of the large-state–deep-South coalition, organized for the pursuit of proportional representation in both houses, began to fade. With this loss of purpose, the compelling rationale behind the old lines of cleavage began to shift. Although it was still necessary for the small states to protect their recent victory, the compromise brought the sectional stress within the large state coalition to the fore. For the next two weeks, the large northern and southern states battled over the allocation of seats in the first House of Representatives (Warren, 1928, pp. 293–294; Lynd, 1967, pp. 243, 239).

The Conflict between North and South over Representation

The large northern states maintained the early initiative over their southern colleagues with G. Morris' objection to the clause in the compromise proposal that called for one representative for every 40,000 inhabitants. Morris "thought property ought to be taken into the estimate as well as the number of inhabitants," and urged that representation be constitutionally fixed for existing states. This would "secure to the Atlantic States a prevalence in the National Councils" over the new states that would soon be formed in the West (*Records*, vol. 1, p. 533). Members of the Convention recognized two important but separable questions here. First, should the representation of each state be fixed, with the Legislature at liberty, though not bound, to make changes as the states changed in relative weight and importance? Second, should relative importance be gauged by population, or by population and wealth combined?

Morris' motion for a new committee to consider these questions was enthusiastically seconded by the delegates from Massachusetts. Gerry supported "the Commitment and thought that Representation ought to be in the Combined ratio of numbers of Inhabitants and of wealth, and not of either singly." King, also of Massachusetts, agreed, as in his view "property was the primary object of Society," and Butler of South Carolina also weighed in calling property the "only just measure of representation" (*Records*, vol. 1, p. 541–542). With these sentiments on the floor, Morris' motion was approved 7-3-1. The small states of New York, New Jersey, and Delaware, fearing any reconsideration, voted no. Maryland divided. The new committee was made up of Gouverneur Morris, Gorham, Randolph, Rutledge, and King, all large state men, indicating quite clearly that the Convention was fully aware that the dispute was now internal to the large state coalition. Further, the composition of the committee implied general support for the idea of using both wealth and population as factors in determining the allocation of representatives. At least Morris, Rutledge and King are recorded as having spoken directly in favor of this idea. Morris was named committee chairman.

On July 9, the Morris committee reported back, the key section of its proposal reading: "as the present situation of the States may probably alter as well in point of *wealth* as in the number of their *inhabitants* that the Legislature be authorized from time to time to augment the number of representatives" (*Records*, vol. 1, pp. 557–558). Madison recorded that the question was "taken without any debate," with nine in favor and only New York and New Jersey opposed. Morris, and through him the large states of the North, had been given very much their own way on both questions: wealth and population would both carry weight in the first branch, and the Legislature had been authorized, rather than required, to reapportion as population and wealth changed.

Nonetheless, the ease with which the Morris committee's recommendations were accepted is deceptive. Opposition soon arose from several sources as the sectional lines of cleavage continued to shift decisively away from the large-state–deep-South coalition. Increasingly, delegates from the four states of the deep South, joined by uneasy Massachusetts men, stood in opposition to a solid bloc of central and northern states (as shown by the 2b solution). There had always been stress within the large state alliance, especially over the counting of slaves for representation, but its members had been willing to work together when the prize was control of both houses. Now, with the basic decisions adopting proportional representation in one house and equality in the other completed, a more natural set of sectional interests began to fight for special advantages. Slavery and commerce, initially adjuncts to the representation controversy, soon became overriding concerns in their own right.

As the new alignments took hold, Randolph (a Virginian) conducted the first raid on Morris' (a Pennsylvanian) position by complaining that "as the number was not to be changed till the Natl. Legislature should please, a pretext would never be wanting to postpone alterations, and keep the power in the hands of those possessed of it" (*Records*, vol. 1, p. 561). It was obvious to Randolph and other southerners that leaving reapportionment to the discretion of the legislature, with its initial northern majority, might work to the detriment of a growing South, despite Morris' claim that this defense was aimed at a burgeoning West on behalf of all the Atlantic states. Randolph called for yet another committee to examine this problem. Before Randolph's suggestion could be put to a vote, opposition to Morris' plan appeared from another formidable corner when Paterson of New Jersey rose to condemn the rule of wealth and numbers as "too vague." Paterson went on to broach a subject that had been scrupulously avoided while the small states worked to elicit the support of the South for equal voting rights for the states in the Senate. Now, with the question solely one of power distribution within the first House of Representatives, the issue of slavery and the counting of slaves for representation (which would obviously increase the strength of the South in relation to the North) took on new importance. Paterson's position was simply that "He could regard negroes slaves in no light but as property, . . . would the slaves vote? they would not. Why then shd. they be represented?" (ibid.).

With these sentiments in the air, the Convention charged yet another committee to adjust between the jealous regions an acceptable distribution of power in the first House of Representatives. The committee, headed by King, reported the next morning, July 10. Its recommendation sparked one of the clearest North-South confrontations in the Convention. The opening salvo, fired by Rutledge of South Carolina, proposed that "N. Hampshire be reduced from 3 to 2. members." King quickly opposed this move to disturb the sectional interests that his committee had sought so carefully to balance. Echoing Madison's earlier assessment, King argued that "the question concerning a difference of interests did not lie where it had hitherto been discussed, between the great & small States; but between the Southern & Eastern. For this reason he had been ready to yield something in the proportion of representatives for the security of the Southern. No principle would justify the giving them a majority" (*Records*, vol. 1, p. 566). Gouverneur Morris, who saw his position slipping away in the friction between sectionally minded delegates, "regretted the turn of the debate. . . . He thought the Southern States have by the report more than their share of representation" (ibid., p. 567). The wealth of the South and its solicitude in the matter of counting its slaves for representation was beginning to convince Morris and other northerners that there was a hidden danger in their earlier desire to have wealth enter into the calculation for representation. The counting of wealth might render the South, always acknowledged as the new nation's wealthiest region, too powerful. This would be particularly harmful to the commercially oriented Middle Atlantic states. Understanding this, Pennsylvania began to gravitate toward their position in early July (as the 2b solution shows).

When the debate became predominantly one of slaves and commerce, Massachusetts and the South, to which these issues were of vital importance, drew closer together, while Pennsylvania, one of the most intense adherents of the large state coalition up to this point, moved toward its more natural regional allies (see factor 2 of Table 5.4). Only South Carolina and Georgia supported Rutledge's motion to reduce New Hampshire's representation. The reduction of northern representation having failed, three attempts were made to increase by one each the representation of the three states of the deep South. The last of these votes saw the South reach a high-water mark at 4-7, with Virginia, North Carolina, South Carolina, and Georgia opposed by a solid northern bloc. The division on this series of votes indicates an apprehension on the part of all the northern and Middle Atlantic states, large and small, that the South was close to getting more than its due. The delegates were practical men. They understood that some closely held interests had to be specifically provided for, but by its very logic, sectionalism demanded a balancing of interests, not a predominance on one side.

When the vote was finally taken on the representation assigned by the King committee, it was accepted by a vote of 9-2, with only South Carolina and Georgia still adamantly opposed. Finding the door to increased representation in the first session of the Legislature closed, the southern states sought to insure that their minority status would not be continued after demographic shifts had given them a majority of the population. To insure mandatory reapportionment, Williamson moved as a substitute to an earlier census proposal by Randolph, which had not mentioned slaves, "'that in order to ascertain the alterations that may happen in the population & wealth of the several States, a census shall be taken of the free white inhabitants and three-fifths of those of other descriptions . . . and that the Representation be regulated accordingly'" (*Records*, vol. 1, p. 579).

King sought to defend what remained of Morris' northern position by declaring that he was "much opposed to fixing numbers as the rule of representation, . . . particularly . . . on account of the blacks" (*Records*, vol. 1, p. 586). Wilson also complained that he could not "see on what principle the admission of blacks in the proportion of three-fifths could be explained" (ibid., p. 587), and his colleague, G. Morris, "was compelled to declare himself reduced to the dilemma of doing injustice to the Southern States or to human nature, and he must therefore do it to the former" (ibid., p. 588). With this aggressively defensive mood in the northern delegations, led by those of Massachusetts and Pennsylvania, the vote on whether to include three-fifths of the blacks in the computation for representation was taken. It failed by a vote of 4-6. This vote to exclude slaves from the computation reflected the severe tension among the delegates over the initial distribution and the future methods for reallocating representation in the House. This was not the final word of the Convention on this matter. In fact, when the vote was taken on all of the Williamson motion as amended (including the exclusion of the representation for slaves), all states voted in the negative, acknowledging that the plan was as yet unworkable.

On July 12, Randolph offered a proposal very similar to Williamson's, with the formula of a mandatory census to serve as the basis for mandatory reallocation and with slaves being rated at three-fifths. This time, the Pennsylvanians agreed to the proposal, if it could be attached to a suggestion made earlier by G. Morris cautioning that the measure could be made more acceptable to opinion in the North through including slaves indirectly, "by saying that they should enter into the rule of taxation" (*Records*, vol. 1, p. 595). The Pennsylvania delegates were willing to see the South's representation increased only if those states were also prepared to shoulder an increased share of the tax burden that the new central government was certain to create. Randolph's motion was suitably altered and brought to a vote, passing in the affirmative, 6-2-2. New Jersey and Delaware voted no and Massachusetts divided, as did South Carolina, but only because its delegates were still holding out for full representation of slaves. Moderate southern interests had thus been served, and Morris' triumphs of a few days earlier on behalf of the northern perspective had been substantially rolled back. Nonetheless, the real hammer blow was yet to come.

Randolph delivered this blow by moving to reconsider the vote that had authorized the "Legislre. to adjust from time to time, the representation upon the principles of *wealth* & *numbers* of inhabitants . . . in order to strike out '*Wealth*' and adjust the resolution to that requiring periodical revisions according to the number of whites & three fifths of the blacks" (*Records*, vol. 1, p. 603). It is difficult to imagine that Morris and the Massachusetts delegates (Gerry and King) did not see the fundamental nature of this attack on their earlier position that property generally, and not just property in slaves, was entitled to a share of representation in government. But there is no question that they were wholly alive to its impact on the regional balance of power. Morris warned his colleagues that "The train of business & the late turn which it had taken" had led him to believe "that the Southn. Gentlemen will not be satisfied unless they see the way open to gaining a majority in the public Councils" (ibid., p. 604). Despite the isolated misgivings of Morris and a few others, the vote went decisively (9-0-1) in favor of Randolph's motion to strike out wealth, largely because the delegates deemed it impossible to calculate accurately the relative values of, or exchange rates between, slaves, landholdings, commercial properties, and industrial wealth. The southern states, after winning the right to count three-fifths of their wealth in slaves by the indirect route of linking representation to taxation, had no further desire to see northern forms of wealth represented. As a result of this and previous sectional strategies, some of the delegates from the northern and Middle Atlantic states began to believe that they had to fall back to an undesirable, but at least more defensible, position. Morris captured this feeling by saying that he would be "obliged to vote for ye vicious principle of equality in the 2d. branch (Senate) in order to provide some defence for the N. States" (ibid.).

On July 16, the penultimate vote was taken "On the question of agreeing to the whole (Report as amended &) including the equality of votes in the 2d. branch" (*Records*, vol. 2, p. 15). It passed in the affirmative by a vote of 5-4-1. Massachusetts and North Carolina, seeing compromise as the only way to break the stalemate, provided the margin of victory. The Massachusetts vote divided, while North Carolina joined the four smaller states of Connecticut, New Jersey, Delaware, and Maryland to carry the day against Pennsylvania, Virginia, South Carolina, and Georgia. With this vote, the small states finally achieved the equal suffrage in the upper house for which they had contended so long and risked so much, and the South secured a mandatory reallocation process that all assumed would give it a majority in the national councils within a few years.

Only a few diehards, primarily northerners, remained totally opposed to the compromise, some as a result of the solution that gave the small states an equal vote in the Senate, and others as a result of what they saw as inordinate southern gains in the counting of slaves for representation. Some obviously opposed on both counts. Madison was quite distraught. He found it curious and frightening that some members of the large state coalition seemed to have lost their fighting spirit. Madison recorded that immediately after the decisive vote: "a number of the members from the larger States, by common agreement met for the purpose of consulting on the proper steps to be taken in consequence of the vote in favor of an equal Representation in the 2d. branch, and the apparent inflexibility of the smaller States on that point." Unlike the meeting held among the small state delegates in early July, in which they had displayed "a firm determination . . . not to relinquish the right of equal representation in the Senate," there seemed to be two divergent perspectives among the delegates attending the large state meeting: "Several of them supposing that no good Governnt could or would be built on that foundation, . . . would have concurred in a firm opposition to the smaller States, . . . Others seemed inclined to yield to the smaller States. . . . It is probable," Madison concluded, "that the result of this consultation satisfied the smaller States that they had nothing to apprehend from a Union of the larger, in any plan whatever agst. the equality of votes in the 2d. branch" (*Records*, vol. 2, pp. 19–20).

Madison was quite correct. The small states had very little to fear from the large states concerning their equality in the Senate. But this was not even mainly because the larger states no longer opposed equality for their smaller neighbors; rather, it was because a subsequent battle had been decided in favor of the southern wing of the large state coalition. Therefore, both the small states and the deep South had separate reasons for finding the compromise solution to the representation issue acceptable and for opposing any attempt to reopen this divisive issue.

CHAPTER 6

The Role of the Executive in Republican Government

The coalitions of the periphery and the center that had aligned behind conflicting views of republican government during the Convention's first two weeks resurfaced immediately following the Connecticut Compromise as the Convention's focus turned once again to questions at the "higher" level of constitutional choice. For the five weeks during which the representation issue had been at the fore, these philosophically based coalitions had been submerged, though the delegates from the peripheral states consistently expressed concern over the implications for the states of Madison's call for a powerful and unconstrained national government. Following the Connecticut Compromise, these familiar coalitions, still divided by philosophical differences concerning the nature of republican government, controlled the Convention's business for the next five weeks, well into late August (McDonald, 1985, p. 240).

As we have seen, Madison's pre-Convention strategy hinged on winning the representation issue behind a coalition of powerful and populous states in cooperation with the fast rising, but presently less populous, states of the deep South. He anticipated that a resolution favorable to the large states on the control question (Who will dominate the new government?) would encourage the transfer of substantial new powers to the central government. Nonetheless, much of the early momentum enjoyed by the Pennsylvania and Virginia nationalists, securing a government "national" and "supreme" with a negative on all state legislation and the power to displace state action altogether where it might prove inconvenient, came not on the votes of the large states, but on the strength of nationalist votes from the small Middle Atlantic states. Yet, these states, as early as June 11, were forced, by Madison's demand for proportional representation in both houses, to abandon the quest for a strong national government in order to defend the power and status of the smaller states in the proposed new system.

In the end, proportional representation was lost to an unyielding small state opposition and to a fatal northern-free versus southern-slave division within the ranks of the large state coalition itself. Perhaps more importantly, the defense of proportional representation was weakened by the desire of key large states—Massachusetts and South Carolina in particular—to defend a strong role for the states. This desire made them more willing to allow equal representation for the states in the Senate, a critical issue for the small Middle Atlantic states, than they might otherwise have been and than Madison, Wilson, and Morris initially had expected them to be.

Despite the tenacity with which the opposing positions on representation were held while the battle raged, acceptance of the Connecticut Compromise rapidly eroded both this issue's salience and its ability to divide the delegates and their states along the lines that had persisted in the Convention for the five weeks between June 11 and July 16. When it became obvious in early July that the small states' intransigence would make it impossible to deny them an equal vote in the Senate, the latent question of the distribution of voting power between the North and the South became the new battleground. The agitation of this long antici-pated division within the large-state–deep-South coalition drastically reduced the range of issues on which the members held similar interests. With complete control of the legislative branch no longer possible, the allocation of broad authority to the federal government began to look less advisable, perhaps even dangerous, to the localist delegates from Massachusetts and the deep South: How would these powers be used? To accomplish what? And against whom? As soon as the possibility of dominating the new government was lost, the rationale for the voting coalitions based on state size quite simply evaporated. Madison's descrip-tion of the early morning meeting of July 17 stressed his disappointment that the representation issue was no longer able to mobilize the large-state–deep-South coalition. Almost overnight, new interests and new ideas, linking new partners into new patterns of cooperation and opposition, came to characterize the Convention's business.

The Origins of a New Cleavage Structure

As Figure 2.3, the summary graph on coalition realignment, indicates, the decline of the coalitions based on state size occurred almost imme-diately following the compromise resolution of the thorny legislative representation question. The opposition pattern of the large states and the deep South against the small states of the Middle Atlantic region was rapidly replaced by the original alignment of forces that, early in the Convention, had pitted the wings of the new nation, the Northeast and

TABLE 6.1.   Localist Periphery versus Nationalist Middle States;
Two-Factor Solution to Roll-Call Votes 157–231, July 17–July 26,
Varimax Rotation (Ortho)

	1 Peripheral States	2 Middle Atlantic States	h^2
New Hampshire	(.86)	.17	.77
Massachusetts	(.72)	.29	.61
Connecticut	.24	(.52)	.33
New York	absent	absent	absent
New Jersey	.09	(.69)	.48
Pennsylvania	.01	(.70)	.49
Delaware	.17	(.61)	.41
Maryland	.06	(.69)	.47
Virginia	.30	(.62)	.47
North Carolina	(.71)	.13	.52
South Carolina	(.87)	.01	.76
Georgia	(.75)	.19	.59
Sum of squares	3.27	2.63	5.90
% variance explained	29.70	23.80	53.60

deep South, against its solid middle in a periphery versus middle states coalition pattern (see Table 6.1).

Why did the center-periphery alignment replace the alignments based on state size and region so quickly and forcefully? Quite clearly, because a new cluster of issues at the "higher" level of constitutional choice, which during the Convention's early days had divided the states along philosophical lines, quickly resurfaced to fill the void left by the compromise solution to the "lower" level questions of state and regional power that were central to the issue of legislative representation. These new issues, centering squarely on the nature, composition, and powers of the executive branch, and particularly of the President, dominated the Convention's agenda for the ten day period from July 17 to July 26. The behavior of the Convention in response to the displacement of the representation issues by the executive questions further demonstrates how coalitions in the Convention realigned as old issues were decided and new issues arose to provoke new battles.

As the salience of issues changes over time, the primary cleavage lines that define the principal cooperation-opposition patterns active in the system may change as well (Schattschneider, 1960, pp. 64–68). This is precisely what happened in the days around June 11 and again immediately following the Connecticut Compromise on July 17. Table 4.1 clearly indicates that the dominant coalition alignment during the Convention's first two weeks was the periphery versus the center, an alignment based on ideology, while Table 5.1 demonstrates that the next five weeks saw the pattern of the large states and the deep South versus the small middle Atlantic states dominate the Convention's business as the struggle over representation was waged. Although the conflicting views on representation, and the coalitions that arose in support of them, almost completely dominated the Convention's proceedings from June 11 to July 17, the important executive branch issues had been canvased before June 11. During the initial debates on the organization of and the control over the executive branch, the states divided according to ideology rather than state size or region (see Figure 6.1). Following the Connecticut Compromise, the executive issues once again divided the states according to ideology: localists versus nationalists.

In each diagram, the solid line represents the dominant cleavage, while the broken line represents an alternative and competing cleavage that had the clear potential to realign or disrupt the dominant voting coalitions, should the issues from which they sprang once again be activated (Sundquist, 1973, p. 10). Just as the influence of the ideological division between the states was not totally erased by the rise of the representation issue, the alignment based on state size was not, as we shall see below, totally and irrevocably expunged by the compromise resolution of the representation issue. It could, and in fact did, arise on later issues, but it never dominated the Convention's business again as it had between June 11 and July 17. With the Connecticut Compromise solution, the representation issue faded from its position of central importance and lost its ability to define the lines along which the Convention's battles would be waged. The executive issues, and the ideologically based periphery versus center cleavage which contested them, quickly filled this void and dominated the ten-day period between the Connecticut Compromise (July 17) and the adjournment of the Convention in favor of the Committee of Detail (July 26).

The Problem Posed: An Independent Executive in a Republican Government

The place of the executive in republican government was by far the most persistently challenging problem faced by the Convention (Thach, 1923, p. 76; Warren, 1928, p. 173). It involved a paradox not yet solved

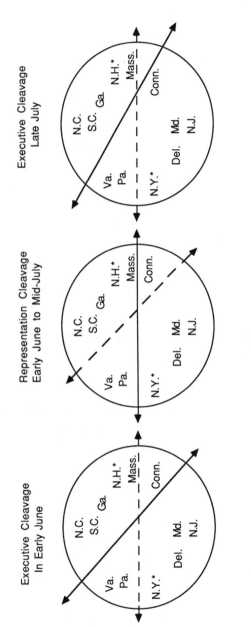

Figure 6.1. Comparison of cleavage structures between representation and executive issues.
*New York abandoned the Convention on July 11 at vote #132. New Hampshire did not arrive until July 23 at vote #203.

by eighteenth century political thought: how to construct and empower an efficient and responsible executive without setting the country on a slide toward monarchy. The republican tradition seemed to provide no positive guidance at all concerning the executive branch. History, recent experience, and the best political science of the day seemed to be unanimous in telling the delegates that vigor, efficiency, and responsibility in an extended republic demanded a powerful unitary executive. But, as Pierce Butler reminded his colleagues, these same sources seemed to stress "that in all countries the Executive power is in a constant course of increase." He cautioned that some "Gentlemen seemed to think that we had nothing to apprehend from an abuse of Executive power. But why not a Cataline or a Cromwell arise in this Country as well as in others?" (*Records*, vol. 1, p. 100)

When a dubious Convention turned, during its opening days in early June, to consider the balance between efficiency and responsibility in the executive branch, two preliminary questions were decided quickly. First, should there be an executive? Still vivid memories of George III and the colonial governors had led to a substantial weakening of the executive powers in the state constitutions, while at the national level, the Articles of Confederation provided for no executive at all. However, experience with uncontrolled legislatures during the previous decade had indicated a need for some check on those volatile bodies, so the Virginia Plan included a separate executive branch (Bailyn, 1967, pp. 68–80; Main, 1973, pp. 188–194; Wood, 1969, pp. 132–150, 432–453). Second, should the executive be composed of one man or several? Bluntly posed, this question inevitably raised the spectre of monarchy in the eighteenth century mind. When James Wilson moved, on the morning of June 1, "that the Executive consist of a single person," the delegates were so reticent that Benjamin Franklin had to prompt them to "deliver their sentiments on it" (*Records*, vol. 1, p. 65). John Rutledge and Wilson gave clarifying arguments, but final approval of the motion was not secured until June 3.

A third important question, and the one that was to resist solution for over three months, was how the Chief Executive and his executive department should be related to the legislative branch. Should the President be dependent or independent? Should he be an agent carrying out the policies of the legislature, or should he have the power to shape policy (Vile, 1967, pp. 132–142; Wood, 1969, p. 138)? Expressing the old Whig or small republic doctrine that had informed the Revolution, the early state constitutions, and the creation of the Articles themselves, Connecticut's Roger Sherman spoke for New England when he said that "he considered the Executive magistracy as nothing more than an institution for carrying the will of the legislature into effect," concluding that the legislature "should be at liberty to appoint one or more as experience might dictate" (*Records*, vol. 1, p. 65). This statement was an endorsement of the practice of the Continental Congresses, not an indication that Sherman understood the idea of a parliamentary system. Yet the practice was known to all, and the bitter experience of the Congress with John Jay and Robert Morris as congressionally appointed executives who became overly powerful and independent lay behind Sherman's observations on legislative-executive relations (Jensen, 1950, pp. 55–57, 360–374). But as events unfolded, Sherman's view was challenged almost immediately and was eventually superceded by another held by the extended republic men. They contended that concentrated power anywhere in the proposed government needed restraining, legislative at least as much as executive, and that the executive could be used to restrain an overly democratic legislature if it were established as a powerful and independent force (Bailyn, 1967, pp. 55–93; Wood, 1969, pp. 430–438). Wilson, G. Morris, and their convert, James Madison, championed the independent executive position.

The Convention took only two days to sort these concerns into three major elements, all revolving around the question of the executive's relationship to the legislature, and to discover that the delegates were sharply divided on each (see Table 6.2). Moreover, it became apparent that the three elements were themselves interrelated, so that two competing packages of options, combining the elements in different ways, gained broad and tenacious support. The three elements were: (1) the mode of appointment; (2) the length of the term (tenure); and (3) reeligibility (see Figure 6.2). The pivotal nature of these three issues and their interdependence has been noticed by several scholars, most clearly by Charles Warren, who pointed out that "in almost all the votes a long term with no re-election was favored, if the choice of Executive was to be by the Legislature; and a short term with possibility of re-election, if the choice was to be otherwise than by the Legislature. In other words, the views of most of the delegates as to length of term and as to re-election were dependent on the *mode* of election" (Warren, 1928, pp. 364–365; see also Thach, 1923, pp. 97–98). Therefore, one would expect to find fairly stable voting patterns, because a vote on any one of the three issues making up a package took cognizance of the other two (see Riker, 1984, for another version).

Although the internal coherence of the packages was evident to the delegates, each package seemed to contain aspects that rendered it suspect. The reeligibility of an excellent President obviously would be

TABLE 6.2. Two-Factor Solution to 16 Executive-Issue Votes prior to the Connecticut Compromise, Varimax Rotation (Ortho)[a]

	1 Peripheral States (Package 1)	2 Middle Atlantic States (Package 2)	h^2
New Hampshire	absent	absent	absent
Massachusetts	(.87)	.45	.96
Connecticut	(.60)	)−.52(	.63
New York	.35	(.70)	.60
New Jersey[b]	absent	absent	absent
Pennsylvania	.08	(.78)	.61
Delaware	.18	(.60)	.39
Maryland	−.31	(.77)	.68
Virginia	.48	(.52)	.50
North Carolina	(.85)	.14	.75
South Carolina	(.92)	.15	.86
Georgia	(.88)	−.05	.78
Sum of squares	3.95	2.82	6.73
% Total variance	39.50	28.20	67.70

[a]The 16 roll-call votes dealing with the executive branch taken prior to the Connecticut Compromise were 9–21, 30, 35, and 36.
[b]New Jersey was present for only 4 of 16 votes. In every case N.J. aligned with the majority of the Middle Atlantic states coalition of factor 2.

advantageous, but not all would be excellent. If selection was to be by the national legislature, as in package 1, it was thought that the possibility of a second term would be dangerous, allowing the executive to enter into corrupt bargains with the legislature in the hopes of securing a reappointment. Therefore, his single term could be the relatively long but risky one of seven years. Selection by an electoral college would reduce the likelihood of "cabal and corruption" because the electors would not be a permanent body. This opened the possibility of rewarding good behavior with a reappointment, but required the shorter term to insure accountability. But several of the delegates questioned whether citizens of the first rank would travel long distances to the national capital solely for the purpose of selecting the Chief Executive. And if not, would citizens of a lower order choose wisely? Within the parameters of a republican solution to the problems of republican government, these seemed to be the choices open to the delegates. It is also important to note that the two packages could not be mixed without destroying the internal coherence of each. For instance, the introduction of a short

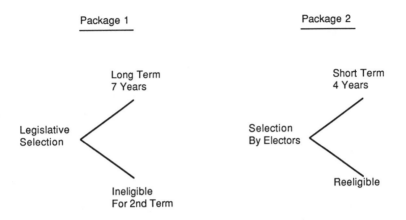

Figure 6.2. Two positions on the structure of the executive branch.

term into package 1 would mean a revolving door executive, barely in office before constitutionally required to step down. The introduction of an ineligibility into package 2 would negate the very rationale for a separate body of electors because the incumbent would be constitutionally forbidden to approach the legislature for a second term.

Now that two competing voting coalitions and two competing solution packages have been identified, the relationship between the general coalitions, the smaller voting groups of which they were composed, and the alternative approaches to executive selection must be demonstrated. Further, we will want to know how the general coalitions and the smaller blocs of which they were composed operated to structure and determine the debate.

The Initial Decision: A Creature of the Legislature

The influence exerted by the Virginia Plan was decisive in the early discussions of the executive branch. Reflecting Madison's own uncertainty over the proper design of a republican executive, the Virginia Plan envisioned a subordinate executive to be selected by the national legislature, for a term of unspecified length, to be ineligible thereafter. What minimal independence the executive was to have was to be insured by the entirely negative vehicle of barring him from a second term (Thach, 1923, p. 84). This expedient was designed to forestall the seemingly endless possibilities for vote trading and factional meddling if an incumbent executive was allowed to connive with the legislature for a reappointment.

James Wilson of Pennsylvania, speaking for only a few of the most forward looking of the Middle Atlantic state nationalists on June 2, initially countered with the alternative of "an election by the people," as the only proper foundation for a strong independent executive magistrate. Rather than the executive subordination envisioned by the Virginia Plan and supported by the periphery, Wilson's plan sought to "place the executive in a relation of equality to the legislature, since they both would derive their powers from the same source and on the same terms, and both would be responsible alike to the voters" (Thach, 1923, p. 87). Nonetheless, Wilson was soon convinced that direct election was fundamentally unacceptable to his colleagues. Wilson then reformulated his motion to call for selection by an electoral college. Only Pennsylvania and Maryland followed him in opposing the Virginia Plan's suggestion of legislative selection, while eight states supported it. All eight immediately proceeded to vote in favor of "electing the Executive by the national legislature (for the term of seven years)" (Records, vol. 1, p. 81). The Convention then decided, in view of the long term and the selection by the national legislature, to complete the package originally presented in the Virginia Plan, though its principal support now came from the peripheral states, by making "ye. Executive ineligible after seven years" (Records, vol. 1, p. 88).

Though several proposals were made to amend or revise part or all of this package, such as Gerry's state oriented proposal of June 9, in which he moved "'that the National Executive should be elected by the Executives of the States,'" none were successful (Records, vol. 1, p. 175). This relatively easy initial acceptance of executive selection by the legislature (package 1) can, at least in part, be accounted for by the fact that many of the delegates were looking past the executive question to the more threateningly divisive issue of representation (Thach, 1923, pp. 91, 97). It was universally understood that the Convention might well founder over the question of suffrage in the legislative branch. Not until the small states of Connecticut, New York, New Jersey, Delaware, and Maryland brought the Convention to the brink of dissolution in their determination to retain equality in at least one branch of the legislature was a solution found. In the face of such unbending opposition, some members of the majority coalition, Massachusetts and the lower South in particular, finally relented, allowing equality in the Senate (Jillson, 1981b, p. 22).

Decision Reconsidered: An Independent Executive

With the final decision on the structure of the legislative branch taken, the debates of July 17, the day after the Connecticut Compromise, saw the reopening of all that had been hastily decided concerning the executive in early June. Again, the three interdependent issues of mode of election, tenure, and reeligibility provided the parameters of the battlefield. These issues dominated the Convention's next ten days, until the Virginia Plan was completed and the Convention adjourned so that the Committee of Detail could put together a draft constitution from the results of the debates to that time. As in early June, the peripheral states worked for appointment of the executive by the legislature, for the relatively long term of six years, with no possibility of a reappointment; while the delegates from the states of the Middle Atlantic region sought election or appointment by the people or a specially appointed electoral college, for a shorter term of four years, and with the possibility that excellent service could be rewarded by a reappointment.

Table 6.3 serves to highlight the voting coalitions that confronted one another on the executive issue between the July 17 resolution of the representation issue and the Convention's adjournment in favor of the Committee of Detail on July 26. During that time, seventy-five roll-call votes were taken, and fully thirty-nine of them dealt directly with the executive branch in all three of the aspects delineated above: mode of election, tenure, and reeligibility.

This distribution of the states and the accompanying list of critical issues identified by high factor scores (Table 6.4) support the impression that essentially the same two stable groups of states opposed one another on the executive issues after the Connecticut Compromise as had opposed each other during the Convention's first two weeks. If anything, the pattern of peripheral versus Middle Atlantic states was even more clear than it had been during the early days of the Convention. New Hampshire had joined Massachusetts in forming the northern wing of the peripheral coalition, while the three states of the deep South still formed its southern wing. Connecticut, the only state unambiguously to change coalitions as a result of the compromise solution on representation, had joined the coalition of large and small Middle Atlantic states backing a powerful national government. As a result, a coalition of five peripheral states stood against a countercoalition of five Middle Atlantic states, with Delaware now seemingly hesitant, but potentially leaning toward its Middle Atlantic state colleagues. Nonetheless, these coalitions were not of equal strength. Though the Middle Atlantic states would seem to have had at least a 5-5 standoff, their coalition was much less cohesive than was that of the periphery. Each state in the coalition of the periphery was strongly committed to its voting group for between 53% and 81% of the variance in its voting. The coalition of Middle Atlantic states, on the other hand, sustained levels of commitment ranging from

TABLE 6.3.   Two-Factor Solution to 39 Executive-Issue Votes between 157 and 231, July 16–July 26, Varimax Rotation (Ortho)[a]

	1 Peripheral States (Package 1)	2 Middle Atlantic States (Package 2)	h^2
New Hampshire	(.90)	−.48	1.04
Massachusetts	(.73)	.13	.56
Connecticut	.05	(.70)	.50
New York	absent	absent	absent
New Jersey	.34	(.64)	.52
Pennsylvania	−.31	(.70)	.59
Delaware	.35	.41	.29
Maryland	−.03	(.75)	.56
Virginia	−.02	(.75)	.56
North Carolina	(.80)	.05	.65
South Carolina	(.78)	−.12	.62
Georgia	(.80)	.21	.69
Sum of squares	3.57	2.98	6.58
% Total variance	32.45	27.09	59.54

[a]The 39 executive-branch votes taken between the Connecticut Compromise and adjournment in favor of the committee of detail, or between Votes 157–231 were 164–173, 181–194, 196, 198–201, 208, 209, 215–220, 224, and 225.
[b]The New Hampshire delegates, Gilman and Langdon, did not arrive in Philadelphia and begin attending the Convention until July 23.

a high of 56% down to only 41%. As we shall see shortly, Delaware's dissociation from its natural allies forecast a broader weakness in this coalition.

The cohesiveness of the peripheral coalition suggests that it would be more likely to muster all of its votes on any given question, while the less cohesive Middle Atlantic state coalition would face relatively frequent defections. This alignment and the distribution of strength between the coalitions suggest an explanation for the Convention's three-month vacillation on the executive issue. Although the periphery was clearly the stronger coalition, it was not a majority, while the coalition of the Middle Atlantic states, which was at least potentially a majority, could not consistently bring its members into line.

This reading of the situation can be clarified by analyzing a four-factor solution, which will allow each coalition to reveal an internal division if one existed (see Table 6.5). The great disparity of geography and customs between the northern and southern wings of the peripheral coalition might be expected to divide it; and the great differences in the

TABLE 6.4.   Nine Critical Votes between 157 and 231 Identified by Factor Scores 1.25 on One Factor or 1.0 on Both Factors of the Two-Factor Varimax Solution in Table 6.1

Vote No.	Factor Score	Factor No.	Voting Split	Issue	Date	*Records,* v.2, p.
182	1.12 −1.60	1, 2	6-3-1	To be chosen by electors selected for that purpose.	July 19	51
185	1.47	2	3-5-2	Seven-year term for the exec.	19	51
190	1.51	2	3-7	To add one elector to New Hampshire and Georgia.	20	62
203	1.46	1	3-7	Constitution to be submitted to the state legislatures for ratification.	23	86
208	1.52	1	7-3	To reconsider the executive clause.	23	86
215	−1.44 1.09	1, 2	7-4	Strike out *electors* in favor of *national legislature.*	24	98
216	1.56	1	4-6-1	To postpone the executive resolution.	24	98
219	1.65 −1.22	1, 2	5-6	To postpone clause that says executive cannot serve more than six in any twelve years.	25	108
220	−1.61 2.10	1, 2	5-6	Agree to vote 219 above.	25	108.

size of the states in the Middle Atlantic coalition might explain its relatively low cohesion. In fact, the complex interaction of forces operating to influence decisions on the structure of the executive branch was a major concern of Charles C. Thach in his classic study, *The Creation of the Presidency, 1775–1789.* Thach, though only implicitly, uses the circular model analogy that has been employed throughout the present study to argue that:

It is not very easy to differentiate the delegates into classes solely on the basis of their adherence to a strong executive or a weak. There were other divisions, frequently more fundamental, whose lines cut across those which concern our investigation. Chief of these was that which separated the members into small state and large state groups. There was a further division, based on social and

TABLE 6.5.   Four-Factor Solution to 39 Executive-Issue Votes between 157 and 231, July 16 and July 26, Varimax Rotation (Ortho)

	1 Peripheral States (Package 1)	2 Large States (Package 2)	3 Small States (Package 2)	4 Connecticut Position (Package 2)	h^2
New Hampshire	(.76)	−.45	.16	−.56	1.13
Massachusetts	(.70)	.33	.22	−.44	.84
Connecticut	.15	.30	.19	(.81)	.81
New York	absent	absent	absent	absent	absent
New Jersey	.23	.21	(.69)	.22	.62
Pennsylvania	−.22	(.89)	.12	.08	.87
Delaware	.10	.00	(.87)	.18	.81
Maryland	−.15	.19	(.71)	.45	.76
Virginia	.08	(.84)	.15	.21	.78
North Carolina	(.80)	−.01	.14	−.05	.66
South Carolina	(.88)	−.10	−.19	.12	.83
Georgia	(.83)	−.09	.19	.33	.84
Sum of squares	3.32	2.00	1.99	1.61	8.95
% Total variance	30.18	18.18	18.09	14.64	81.09

economic grounds, between the North and the South, and especially between the North and the three southernmost states. . . . The executive was wholly the product of no one of these influences, but rather of the checking of one interest by another, the counterchecking of each by a third. (Thach, 1923, p. 78)

The four-factor solution reveals the surprising strength of the peripheral group and clearly identifies the source of the Middle Atlantic state coalition's vulnerability. The peripheral coalition loses little of its cohesion. Factor 1 still defines over 30% of the variance in the voting on the executive question. The Middle Atlantic state coalition suffered a much different fate. Its members are distributed in smaller voting groups, primarily on the basis of state size, across the three remaining factors. Factor 2 becomes a large state group composed of Pennsylvania and Virginia, two of the three largest, wealthiest, and most populous states. These states formed the core of the large state group that stood unwaveringly against a countercoalition of small, equality oriented states throughout the recent debates over representation. Factor 3 is made up of precisely those small states of the Middle Atlantic (New Jersey,

Delaware, and Maryland) that supplied such a formidable opposition to the large states in the early battles over representation (Jillson and Anderson, 1978, pp. 535–547). The fourth factor again highlights Connecticut's independent behavior. As on the representation issue, so on the executive questions, Connecticut mediated between the large states and the small, the nationalists and the federalists.

Table 6.5 also indicates that Thach was properly sensitive to the importance of secondary cleavages that might complicate and disrupt the periphery versus middle alignment. It is equally clear that the crosscutting cleavages to which Thach pointed, large states versus small and North versus South, were not equally important at this stage of the executive debate. The strength of the peripheral coalition argues that the very destructive regional cleavage that defined the coalitions confronting each other during the final days of the struggle over suffrage in the House did not directly influence the outcome of the debates over the executive branch during the ten days immediately following the Connecticut Compromise. On the other hand, the interaction of the cleavage based on state size with the executive issue was sufficiently disruptive of the coalition of Middle Atlantic states to give the early victory to the more cohesive periphery.

Obviously, these are the same groups—the deep South, the small Middle Atlantic states, the large states, and with New Hampshire's arrival on July 23, a new northeastern group of New Hampshire and Massachusetts, with Connecticut hewing an independent line—that had dominated the representation issue. But on the executive question, they were aligned differently, re-forming the old coalition patterns of the Convention's early days.

The fray was again joined on July 17 over the clause "to be chosen by the National Legislature," which, after two challenging proposals from the Middle Atlantic states for popular election and selection by electors were soundly rejected, won unanimous approval. When the question "to be chosen by the National Legisl: "came up for debate, Gouverneur Morris objected for the Middle Atlantic states. Morris warned that the executive "will be the mere creature of the Legisl: if appointed & impeachable by that body. He ought to be elected by the people at large, by the freeholders of the Country" (*Records*, vol. 2, p. 29). South Carolina's Pinckney rejected Morris' argument, with the description of "an Election by the people being liable to the most obvious & striking objections. They will be led by a few active & designing men" (*Records*, vol. 2, p. 30). Mason supported Pinckney by arguing that "it would be as unnatural to refer the choice of a proper character for chief Magistrate to the people, as it would, to refer a trial of colours to a blind man"

(*Records*, vol. 2, p. 31). The Convention, at this early stage in its business, obviously agreed with Pinckney and Mason, as it defeated popular election by a vote of 9-1, only Pennsylvania voting in favor. The debate over selection by electors was brief indeed. Luther Martin moved electoral selection, with the electors to be chosen by the state legislatures; Broome of Delaware seconded; and the measure was immediately defeated 8-2 with only Delaware and Maryland voting in favor.

To counter the peripheral states' achievement of selection by the national legislature, the Middle Atlantic states, behind Gouverneur Morris of Pennsylvania, successfully moved to strike out "to be ineligible a second time," arguing that to do otherwise would be to institutionalize inexperience at the helm of the national government. When a motion was defeated to strike out the seven-year term as well, the Convention was left with a mixed package of legislative selection and a long term of seven years, but with reeligibility, thus virtually assuring in the minds of many that, in Madison's words, "the Executive could not be independent of the Legislure, if dependent on the pleasure of that branch for a re-appointment" (*Records*, vol. 2, p. 34). George Mason raised the even more ominous possibility that if reappointment by the legislature was allowed, "the next would be an easy step to hereditary Monarchy" (*Records*, vol. 2, p. 35). Even the advocates of a strongly empowered national executive hesitated at the prospect of an unrestricted eligibility for long terms of office.

With the periphery's package 1 stalled, these questions reappeared on July 19, allowing Ellsworth of Connecticut to introduce package 2 on behalf of the Middle Atlantic states. His motion, rendered as the general question "shall ye. Natl. Executive be appointed by Electors?" was ultimately approved 6-3-1 (*Records*, vol. 2, p. 58). Wilson summarized the discussion to this point, observing that "it seems to be the unanimous sense that the Executive should not be appointed by the Legislature, unless he be rendered in-eligible a 2d. time: he perceived with pleasure that the idea was gaining ground, of an election mediately or immediately by the people" (*Records*, vol. 2, p. 56). Madison then followed immediately with the observation; "if it be a fundamental principle of free Govt. that the Legislative, Executive & Judiciary powers should be *separately* exercised; it is equally so that they be *independently* exercised. . . . It is essential then that the appointment of the Executive should either be drawn from some source, or held by some tenure, that will give him a free agency with regard to the Legislature" (*Records*, vol. 2, p. 56). The delegates from the peripheral states rejected this logic out of hand. Gerry again noted that "he was agst. a popular election. The people are uninformed, and would be misled by a few designing men"

(*Records*, vol. 2, p. 57). Rutledge simply declared that he "was opposed to all the modes except appointmt. by the Natl. Legislature. He will be sufficiently independent, if he be not re-eligible" (*Records*, vol. 2, p. 57).

The six Middle Atlantic states on factor 2 of Table 6.1, ranging in a phalanx from Connecticut to Virginia, were solidly in favor of electors, with the three states of the deep South opposed and Massachusetts divided (recall that New Hampshire was not yet present). Reeligibility was then passed as being compatible with electors, over the objections of only North and South Carolina. At this point, for the Middle Atlantic states to complete a consistent package, a short term of four years was needed to insure executive responsibility. To block the shorter term, the periphery proposed that "the Executive continue for 7 years," but the cohesion of the Middle Atlantic states held from New Jersey to Virginia in the negative, with the periphery again indecisive. Connecticut, South Carolina, and Georgia voted yes, but both Massachusetts and North Carolina divided their votes (*Records*, vol. 2, p. 58). Then, instead of the short term of four years, the Convention voted 9-1, overruling Delaware, to establish a longer term of six years. The six-year term was designed to prevent the additional expense and bother of more frequent meetings of the electors, who, it was still assumed, would gather at the national capital to select the Chief Executive. Rather than achieving logical closure of the package characterized by electoral selection, this longer term introduced an incompatibility that invited the reopening of the entire question.

Beyond this minor incompatibility lay the major flaw in the coalition of the Middle Atlantic states: state size. Although selection by electors had been temporarily achieved by a united coalition of the Middle Atlantic states, the issue was not yet fully settled. Charles Thach touched the critical point directly when he noted that "it was on the rock of apportionment of electors that the tentative scheme was wrecked" (Thach, 1923, p. 102). Though the principle of electoral selection now seemed to enjoy majority support in the Convention, the practical question of distributing power among the states as they participated in that process continued to defy resolution.

This problem in "lower" level constitutional design (the allocation of presidential electors among the states), calling forth interests based on state size, was directly confronted on July 19 when Oliver Ellsworth, speaking for the small Middle Atlantic states on factors 3 and 4 of Table 6.5, proposed "the following ratio; towit—one for each State not exceeding 200,000 inhabts. two for each above yt. number & not exceeding 300,000. and, three for each State exceeding 300,000" (*Records*, vol. 2, p. 57). This distribution would have been advantageous to the small states because it would have given them a much larger impact on executive selection than their population would directly justify. Madison, always the advocate and defender of proportional representation, observed on the following day "that this would make in time all or nearly all the States equal. Since there were few that would not in time contain the number of inhabitants entitling them to 3 Electors" (*Records*, vol. 2, p. 63). Madison was voicing the concern of his large state brothers on factor 2 of Table 6.5 that their full weight be reflected by the proposed selection mechanism. To make this point very directly Williamson proposed that "the number of Electors . . . shall be regulated by their respective numbers of Representatives in the 1st. branch" (*Records*, vol. 2, p. 64). With this demand for proportional representation again dominating the large state delegations, the decision confronting the smaller members of the Middle Atlantic coalition was quite simple. Their equality in the Senate gave them more leverage in a system of legislative selection than they would have under the system of electors being proposed by the larger members of their coalition. Therefore, when the larger members of the Middle Atlantic coalition (Pennsylvania and Virginia on factor 2) balked at the small members' (New Jersey, Delaware, and Maryland on factor 3) proposed allocation scheme, as enunciated by Ellsworth, the small states responded by abandoning electoral selection altogether. New Jersey and Delaware joined the five members of the peripheral coalition in reinstating the package characterized by legislative selection, not because they now wanted it, but because "the large ones [factor 2 of Table 6.5] were not yet ready to pay their price" (Thach, 1923, p. 103).

Again, just as in the earlier case of legislative representation, once the general principle governing executive selection was determined (selection by electors), the question was immediately reduced to one of state power or control. If the chief magistrate was to be chosen by electors, how would these electors be distributed among the states? The old representation question, decided only a week earlier as it related to the legislative branch, resurfaced with a vengeance to plague discussion of the executive branch and to overturn the tentative decision in favor of an independent executive. When the question became one of apportioning electors among the states, the determination of each state to be well positioned in the new system severely strained the coalition of the Middle Atlantic states' general interest in an independent executive. As Thach argued, and as the alignment in Table 6.5 very clearly suggests, "the small States were willing to accept the principle of the independent representative executive, if properly recompensed. When . . . they were satisfied on the score of representation, they were willing to join the two large States . . . for the independent executive" (Thach, 1923, pp. 102–103). But until they were properly recompensed, they would be as uncompromising and demanding as they had been on the question of legislative suffrage.

Decision Reconsidered: A Creature of the Legislature

Reconsideration of these issues was again undertaken on July 23, a pivotal day for the development of the new coalitions, as it saw the long delayed arrival of New Hampshire's John Langdon and Nicholas Gilman. These men immediately aligned their state with the peripheral group on factor 1, bringing that coalition's voting strength to its full five, as against the six Middle Atlantic states. With this infusion of new strength, the peripheral states returned to the offensive, with Houstoun and Spaight, of Georgia and North Carolina, respectively, moving "'that the appointment of the Executive by Electors chosen by the Legislatures of the States, be reconsidered'" (*Records*, vol. 2, p. 95). They were successful by a 7-3 margin, with the five peripheral states of New Hampshire, Massachusetts, North Carolina, South Carolina, and Georgia joining Connecticut and Delaware to defeat the contiguous Middle Atlantic states of Pennsylvania, Maryland and Virginia.

Immediately, the well-worn arguments about what were and were not compatible packages arose, Gerry arguing that "if the motion (Houstoun's) should be agreed to (to go back to Legislative selection), it will be necessary to make the Executive ineligible a 2d. time, in order to render him independent of the Legislature" (*Records*, vol. 2, p. 100). Nonetheless, when the vote on Houstoun's motion was taken, the peripheral five were again solid and were joined by two defectors from the Middle Atlantic group, New Jersey and Delaware, against the remainder of that group, Connecticut, Pennsylvania, Maryland, and Virginia.

Although the tide had clearly turned again, the coalition of the Middle Atlantic was able to maintain the deadlock for nearly two more days, as the delegates became increasingly skeptical of a satisfactory resolution. Madison observed on July 25 that "there are objections agst. every mode that has been, or perhaps can be proposed" (*Records*, vol. 2, p. 109). Colonel Mason obviously shared Madison's opinion, because on the following day, he offered the dejected assessment that "in every Stage of the Question relative to the Executive, the difficulty of the subject and the diversity of opinions concerning it have appeared. Nor have any of the modes of constituting that department been satisfactory" (*Records*, vol. 2, p. 118).

Even in this atmosphere of deadlock and resignation, what remains significant about the voting during these days is that the coalitions we have identified stabilized and held firm, with the periphery winning when it could entice Connecticut, New Jersey, or Delaware over to its side and losing when the Middle Atlantic states held against it. In such circumstances, it is not surprising that the more cohesive peripheral coalition was able to reimpose its package of legislative selection, a long term and ineligibility, sending this version to the Committee of Detail, on a vote of 6-3-1-1. With Massachusetts off the floor, the periphery mustered the votes of New Hampshire, Connecticut, and New Jersey in the North, and North Carolina, South Carolina, and Georgia in the South, against the contiguous Middle Atlantic states of Pennsylvania, Delaware, and Maryland, with Virginia divided (*Records*, vol. 2, p. 121).

With these decisions on the executive finally made, the Convention adjourned for ten days to give the Committee of Detail "time to prepare and report the Constitution." After nine weeks of intense debate, the Convention had gone entirely through the Virginia Plan three times, making decisions, some of them admittedly provisional, on all of its major points. Now the delegates wanted these decisions cast in the form of a draft constitution, so that they could better gauge the symmetry and balance of the separately considered parts (see the Committee of Detail Report in Appendix D).

CHAPTER 7

Localist Periphery and Nationalist Center: On Restraining Government

The first major realignment of the voting coalitions in the Convention occurred when the representation issue came to occupy a position of central importance around June 11, and the second major realignment occurred when this issue was resolved with the adoption of the Connecticut Compromise on July 16. The executive issues and the new cleavage to which they appealed quickly filled the void left by the resolution of the representation question; the result was a reestablishment of the coalition patterns that had dominated the Convention's first two weeks, pitting the Northeast and the deep South against a solid phalanx of Middle Atlantic states. This new coalition alignment was severely disrupted by the continuing salience of distributional or control questions that tapped divisions similar to those active on the issue of legislative representation. The ten days following the Connecticut Compromise were characterized by the interdependent operation of the new scope and independence of government coalition patterns as cross-cut and disrupted by the now secondary but still active power and control alignment. In the end, the consensus among the Middle Atlantic states in favor of a strong executive chosen by independent electors was temporarily disrupted by that coalition's inability to allocate between the states this new type of representative (the presidential elector).

Scope, Meaning, and Mission: The New American Nation

Analyzing just the executive questions as those were debated in late July provides only partial insight into the "rationale" behind the Periphery versus Middle Atlantic states coalition alignment. This confrontation was more than a fight between the proponents of a strong independent executive and those favoring an executive cut in the mold of a legislative messenger boy. Figure 2.3, the dynamic realignment graph, indicates that the new opposition alignment of the Periphery versus Middle replaced the old representation alignment soon after the Connecticut Compromise (July 17) and controlled the Convention's proceedings for the next six weeks (until August 29). The several discrete issues that this alignment of forces in the Convention addressed concerned not only the position of the executive in republican government, but also the nature of and the possible restrictions on citizenship, citizen participation, officeholding, and the origin of money bills. All of these issues generally related to the very broad but centrally important philosophical question of the scope, meaning, and mission of the new American nation. These critical questions provided the grounds for heated debate under the auspices of the coalitions that had initially formed around the executive issues. Not until late August would the very divisive "lower" level issues of control over commerce, slavery, and the western lands disrupt the coalitions displayed below.

Eleven states were generally present during this period; New York was officially unrepresented after July 10, and New Hampshire's delegates did not arrive and take their seats until July 23. An initial glance at Table 7.1 would still seem to indicate that the six-member coalition of contiguous Middle Atlantic states, ranging from Connecticut to Virginia, overbalanced by one the five-member coalition of the peripheral states, made up of New Hampshire and Massachusetts in the North, together with the Carolinas and Georgia from the deep South. On closer analysis, the match once again begins to look more even, if not positively skewed in favor of the peripheral group. Every state associated with the peripheral coalition sustains a loading on factor 1 that accounts for between 49% and 62% of the variance in its voting behavior, while the Middle Atlantic group is much less cohesive, with loadings on factor 2 accounting for a low of 27% and a high of 50%.

On the first factor, the loadings are not only quite strong, but all five are closely clustered between .70 and .79, whereas on the second factor, Connecticut, New Jersey, and Delaware appear to have been somewhat less committed to the coalition than Pennsylvania, Maryland, and Virginia. The likelihood, therefore, in close votes on critical issues, is that the Middle Atlantic state forces would be weakened by relatively frequent defections. In addition, we can anticipate that the strategy of the peripheral coalition would be geared to bargaining or compromising to achieve these defections. The issues around which the major battles between these coalitions were fought can again be identified by an analysis of the factor scores generated on each roll-call vote. High factor scores point to the specific roll-call votes that contributed most heavily to the coalition patterns identified in Table 7.1. These are the roll-call votes upon which the periphery and the center clashed most directly.

As the Convention reconvened to receive the report of the Committee of Detail, the coalitions that had clashed over the executive issues ten

TABLE 7.1. Localist Periphery versus Nationalist Center: On Restraining
Government; Two-Factor Solution to Roll-Call Votes 157–402,
July 17–August 29, Varimax Rotation (Ortho)

	1 Localist Periphery	2 Cosmopolitan Middle	h^2
New Hampshire	(.74)	.16	.57
Massachusetts	(.70)	.13	.51
Connecticut	.24	(.53)	.33
New York	absent	absent	absent
New Jersey	.09	(.59)	.35
Pennsylvania	.18	(.71)	.54
Delaware	.19	(.55)	.34
Maryland	−.05	(.67)	.45
Virginia	.18	(.62)	.42
North Carolina	(.71)	.21	.55
South Carolina	(.80)	.06	.64
Georgia	(.70)	.18	.53
Sum of squares	2.84	2.39	5.23
% Total variance	25.82	21.73	47.55

days earlier resurfaced immediately to do battle over new and different
issues (see Table 7.2). Once again, a three-factor analysis of the major
coalitions (periphery and Middle Atlantic) indicates the lines along
which the less cohesive Middle Atlantic state coalition was likely to
degenerate (see Table 7.3). On the Executive issues, the Middle Atlantic
states had proven to be quite vulnerable to a reactivation of the old state
size or representation cleavage. When discussion of an appropriate
mechanism for selecting the chief executive moved from a choice
between electoral and legislative selection to the specific apportionment
of the electors, the small states of the Middle Atlantic region immediately began to struggle against the large. When the large states held their
ground, the smaller states defected to the periphery and its favored
mechanism of legislative selection. The power cleavage based on state
size cut across and so weakened the coalition of the Middle Atlantic
states that the periphery was easily able to carry its preference for
legislative selection, a long term, and no reeligibility.

Nonetheless, this three-factor solution shows a somewhat different
division within the coalition of the Middle Atlantic states from the one

TABLE 7.2.   Thirty-One Critical Votes between Roll Calls 232 and 375 as Identified by Factor Scores of 1.25 on Either Factor or 1.0 on Both Factors of the Two-Factor Varimax Solution in Table 7.1[a]

Vote No.	Factor Score	Factor No.	Voting Split	Issue	Date in Aug.	Records, v.2, p.
232	1.36	1	3-5	To adjourn for two days to study the committee-of-detail draft.	6	176
242	1.38 −1.03	1, 2	4-5	To adjourn to avoid losing motion to restrict suffrage to free-holders.	7	195
243	1.27	2	3-5-1	To adjourn until 10 o'clock.	7	195
251	1.39	2	4-7	To give six representatives to South Carolina.	8	215
257	−1.42	2	7-3-1	To demand that money bills be restricted to the House or equality in the Senate would be reconsidered.	9	230
259	1.47	2	4-7	14 years' citizenship to qualify for the Senate.	9	230
260	1.47	2	4-7	13 years' citizenship to qualify for the Senate.	9	230
261	1.47	2	4-7	10 years' citizenship to qualify for the Senate.	9	230
265	1.60	2	3-7	Uniform property qualifications for legislators.	10	247
266	1.07 −1.17	1, 2	6-5	To reconsider qualifications for the House of Representatives.	10	247
281	1.53	1	4-7	To insert "and inhabitant" in "shall have been a citizen of the U.S. for at least 7 years before his election" to qualify for the House.	13	267
282	1.98	2	3-8	To make it "to have been a Citizen 9 years for the House."	13	267
283	1.39	1	3-8	To make it "to have been a Citizen 4 years for the House."	13	267
284	1.66 −1.22	1, 2	5-6	Provided 7 years does not disqualify current citizens.	13	267

TABLE 7.2.   (*Continued*)

Vote No.	Factor Score	Factor No.	Voting Split	Issue	Date in Aug.	*Records,* v.2, p.
285	1.47	1	3-7-1	To strike out 7 years and insert 5.	13	267
286	−1.40	1	8-3	9-year residency requirement for Senate.	13	267
288	1.28	2	4-7	To reinstate exclusive origin of money bills in the House.	13	267
289	1.84	2	4-7	On originating money bills in the House but allowing the Senate to amend.	13	267
294	−1.57 1.54	1, 2	6-5	To postpone question on Senate amending of money bills.	15	296
295	1.45	1	3-8	Acts to be submitted to both the executive and the judiciary before becoming law.	15	296
300	1.54	1	3-7	To adjourn.	15	296
306	−1.39	1	7-3	To appoint a treasurer by joint ballot.	17	314
328	−1.57	2	7-3-1	To add to the treason clause "or on confession in open court."	20	340
334	1.45	1	3-8	To add no tax or duty "for purposes of raising revenue shall be laid by the Legislatures on the exports of any state."	21	355
350	1.43 −1.24	1, 2	5-5	To postpone motion to make treaties binding only when ratified by law.	23	384
353	1.44	2	3-7	To postpone clause on resolving disputes between states and over land questions.	24	399
359	1.47	2	3-7	Executive "to be elected by 'Electors'" rather than by the national legislature.	24	399
360	1.71 −1.51	1, 2	5-5-1	To commit "He shall hold his office for a term of 7 years but shall not be elected a second time."	24	399

TABLE 7.2.   *(Continued)*

Vote No.	Factor Score	Factor No.	Voting Split	Issue	Date in Aug.	*Records,* v.2, p.
361	1.33	1, 2	4-4-2	"To be elected by electors."	24	399
367	−1.40 1.03	1, 2	7-4	To agree to 20 years' (until 1808) unrestricted importation of slaves.	25	412
368	−1.40	1, 2	7-4	To agree to the slavery clause.	25	412

*a*Ten-day (July 26 to August 6) recess for the Committee of Detail to prepare and report the Constitution occurred during this period.

that occurred on the executive questions. This separation, rather than resulting from the activity of a disruptive secondary cleavage, resulted from ideological or philosophical differences within the Middle Atlantic state coalition about how thoroughly national and unrestrained this new government should be. The divisive issue was no longer who would control some branch or department of the proposed government, but how powerful and independent of state and regional control it could safely be. On this general question, the periphery held solidly for local control, while the Middle Atlantic states envisioned a powerful national government with the discretion and flexibility to effectively address the wide range of problems confronting it. It was the nature and scope of this flexibility, as well as the potential dangers that might flow from it, that provoked debate within, and ultimately defections from, the coalition of Middle Atlantic states. Pennsylvania and Delaware, the nationalist center on factor 3, wanted to create a powerful and only loosely constrained national government, whereas Connecticut, New Jersey, Maryland, and Virginia, the moderate center on factor 2, sought to strengthen the central government while maintaining both a sense of appropriate limits and a willingness to bargain and compromise with the periphery on factor 1. Therefore, we can expect to see the coalition of the Middle Atlantic states losing when members from the moderate center defected to the localists of the periphery.

As the roll-call votes listed in Table 7.2 indicate, the important battles on the broad empowerment versus restrictions front were decided in the week between August 9 and 15. There followed a relatively quiet week, during which the implications of these decisions were worked out as they affected several rather tangential questions, and as new and more volatile issues percolated to the surface. Once there, they found coalitions already poised to do battle over such explosive issues as commercial

TABLE 7.3. **Localist Periphery versus a Divided Nationalist Center;
Three-Factor Solution to Roll-Call Votes 157–402, July 17–August 29,
Varimax Rotation (Ortho)**

	1 Localist Periphery	2 Moderate Center	3 Nationalist Center	h^2
New Hampshire	(.69)	−.03	.40	.64
Massachusetts	(.65)	−.10	.45	.63
Connecticut	.24	(.60)	.07	.43
New York	absent	absent	absent	absent
New Jersey	.06	(.50)	.32	.35
Pennsylvania	.10	.37	(.74)	.69
Delaware	.10	.18	(.75)	.60
Maryland	−.05	(.72)	.13	.53
Virginia	.19	(.68)	.12	.51
North Carolina	(.71)	.21	.12	.56
South Carolina	(.81)	.12	−.01	.67
Georgia	(.74)	.35	−.14	.69
Sum of squares	2.67	2.00	1.63	6.30
% Total variance	24.27	18.21	14.82	57.30

regulation, slavery and the trade in slaves, taxation of exports, and money bills. Each of these issues was conceived of as a particular case of the earlier and more general conflict between an expansive Americanism and a restricted regionalism. Before they were finally decided, these questions were destined to convulse the Convention to the extent that neither the coalition of the periphery nor that of the center would survive the contest.

Choice of a Guiding Principle:
Separation of Powers or Checks and Balances

Before the recess in favor of the Committee of Detail (July 26–August 6), the issues that would dominate the Convention's attention when it returned and through the month of August were already on the minds of the delegates. A contest between the traditional understanding of "separation of powers" adopted by the coalition of the periphery and the more dynamic principle of "checks and balances" backed by the Middle Atlantic state group arose as early as July 21 and clearly differentiated the approaches adopted by the opposing coalitions. On that day, James Wilson sought to raise an issue that had been considered and rejected earlier. The motion was "that the (supreme) Natl Judiciary should be associated with the Executive in the Revisionary power," whereby it was hoped that the combined weight of these departments would be able to restrain a powerful and potentially intemperate legislature (*Records*, vol. 2, p. 73).

Madison and his fellow nationalists from the Middle Atlantic states argued that the periphery's fear that such a combination of the executive and the judiciary would dominate the legislature and therefore the new government as a whole was misplaced. Madison contended that it was "much more to be apprehended that notwithstanding this co-operation of the two departments, the Legislature would still be an overmatch for them." Madison's historical research and practical political experience prior to the Convention had convinced him that "the States had evinced a powerful tendency in the Legislature to absorb all power into its vortex. This was the real source of danger to the American Constitutions." The goal then should be to provide for "every defensive authority to the other departments . . . consistent with republican principles" (*Records*, vol. 2, p. 74). The members of the peripheral coalition thought that the "joint negative" involved the unnecessary subordination of the pure principle of "separation of powers" to the much less determinate and perhaps more dangerous principle of "checks and balances." Madison's arguments, as expanded and elaborated by Morris and Wilson, brought an immediate reaction from the champions of the more defensively minded and traditionally oriented peripheral coalition. Two Massachusetts men, Gerry and Strong, contended, in Gerry's words, that "the motion was liable to strong objections. It was combining & mixing together the Legislature & the other departments" in direct violation of the doctrine of separation of powers (ibid., p. 75).

Madison countered with an argument that the Middle Atlantic states considered definitive and to which they frequently recurred. He argued that the measure contained no "violation of the maxim which requires the great departments of power to be kept separate & distinct." Completely to the contrary, adequate "checks and balances" were rightly viewed "as an auxiliary precaution in favor of the maxim." In many cases, mere separation would be insufficient to the absolutely fundamental purpose of holding the "great departments of power" in proper relation to one another and, hence, in proper relation to the liberties of the people. In justifying this purpose, Madison reasoned that:

> If a Constitutional discrimination of the departments on paper were a sufficient security to each agst. encroachments of the others, all further

provisions would indeed be superfluous. But experience had taught us a distrust of that security; and that it is necessary to introduce such a balance of powers and interests, as will guarantee the provisions on paper. Instead therefore of contenting ourselves with laying down the Theory in the Constitution that each department ought to be separate & distinct, it was proposed to add a defensive power to each which should maintain the Theory in practice. In so doing we did not blend the departments together. We erected effectual barriers to keep them separate (*Records*, vol. 2, p. 77; see also Madison in *Federalist*, nos. 46, 48, and 51).

What the nationalists were trying to accomplish by stressing the principle of "checks and balances" as a supplement and buttress to "separation of powers" was to create a governmental structure in which each department was fully capable of and motivated to self-defense. If one could depend on the integrity of the structure and its ability to forestall tyranny by maintaining separate centers of power, one could give great scope and authority to that government in the knowledge that it would not only resist consolidation, but that the right hand would check the potential abuses of the left. Nonetheless, the principle was lost. It was lost because the peripheral coalition, with occasional support from defecting members of the moderate Middle Atlantic state group, sought to anticipate and control potential abuse by means of positive constitutional restraints, always within the parameters of a strict separation of departments and tasks, and of a modest empowerment.

A second aspect of the defensive mindedness and localism characteristic of the peripheral coalition is evidenced in the regional attempts, by both the Northeast and the South, to write into the constitution protections for their most closely held parochial interests: slavery and commerce. Only one comment intervenes in Madison's notes between Gerry's motion to appoint a Committee of Detail and the Convention's agreement to do so. General Pinckney of South Carolina, in the guise of a polite reminder to the committee about to be appointed, threatened that if they "should fail to insert some security to the Southern States agst. an emancipation of slaves, and taxes on exports, he shd. be bound by duty to his State to vote agst. their Report" (*Records*, vol. 2, p. 95). The South was serving notice in no uncertain terms that it would tenaciously defend its local control over both its slaves and its bulk exports.

A last major concern of the periphery was brought to the attention of the committee immediately following its appointment when George Mason moved "that the Committee of detail be instructed to receive a clause requiring certain qualifications of landed property & citizenship (of the U. States) in members of the Legislature" (*Records*, vol. 2, p. 121). Mason was immediately supported by the Pinckneys of South Carolina.

They moved to amend Mason's proposal to include the "Judiciary & Executive so as to extend the qualifications to those departments." Gerry of Massachusetts weighed in for the northern Periphery by observing ominously "that the motion did not go far enough" (ibid., pp. 122–123). Establishing restrictions on citizenship and officeholding were the avowed aims of the peripheral coalition.

Morris and Dickinson carried the burden of the Middle Atlantic states nationalist argument for the unrestrained operation of a properly constituted national government. Morris approvingly observed that "it was a precept of great antiquity as well as of high authority that we should not be . . . wise over much," therefore "he was opposed to such minutious regulations in a Constitution" (*Records*, vol. 2, p. 122). Dickinson further argued that "the best defence lay in the freeholders who were to elect the Legislature," not in the minute anticipatory controls envisioned by Mason, the Pinckneys, Gerry, and their supporters. Dickinson believed that as long as the nation's freeholders remained the base upon which the government rested and "this Source should remain pure, the public interest would be safe. If it ever should be corrupt, no little expedients would repel the danger" (ibid., p. 123).

The more locally oriented delegates from the periphery found it very difficult to believe that the same citizens who had agitated their state and local governments to such mischief during the previous decade would not have a similar influence on a more broadly conceived and powerful national government. Therefore, this new government had to be closely watched, and in the most dangerous instances, constitutionally restrained. With this radical difference in the hopes, fears, and approaches of the opposing groups, but with the objects of their concern not yet fully before the Convention, adjournment was secured in favor of the Committee of Detail on July 26. Five members served on this committee: two southerners, Rutledge and Randolph; Gorham of Massachusetts representing the Northeast; and Ellsworth and Wilson from the Middle Atlantic states.

The Convention Reconvenes: New Issues Come to the Fore

On August 6, the Committee of Detail reported back to the Convention with a series of twenty-three resolutions, laid out and detailed in constitutional form, embodying the progress and agreement achieved to that point. Little discussion was undertaken immediately because, as Luther Martin reported, "many of the members being absent, we adjourned to the next day" (*Records*, vol. 3, p. 189). By August 8, the tardy delegates had trickled in, and the major questions that would

TABLE 7.4. Localist Periphery versus Cosmopolitan Center; Two-Factor
Solution to Roll-Call Votes 232–329, August 6–August 20,
Varimax Rotation (Ortho)

	1 Localist Periphery	2 Cosmopolitan Middle	h^2
New Hampshire	(.77)	.10	.60
Massachusetts	(.67)	.03	.45
Connecticut	.19	(.56)	.35
New York	absent	absent	absent
New Jersey	.23	.36	.18
Pennsylvania	.20	(.77)	.63
Delaware	.22	(.57)	.38
Maryland	−.27	(.76)	.66
Virginia	.04	(.65)	.42
North Carolina	(.56)	.38	.46
South Carolina	(.71)	.12	.52
Georgia	(.71)	.12	.52
Sum of squares	2.60	2.56	5.17
% Total variance	23.64	23.16	46.80

occupy the Convention until the end of August broke the surface and
again divided the Convention. During the remainder of August the
Convention dealt first with a set of questions involving the qualifications
for and the restrictions on service in government and then with the very
divisive issues of commerce and slavery.

The periphery versus Middle Atlantic states alignment described in
Table 7.4 held sway over the Convention's business between August 6
and 20, while the debates dealt almost exclusively with a set of related
issues revolving around residency requirements for citizenship, voting,
and officeholding (see the factor scores in Table 7.2). The locally
oriented periphery attempted to restrict these rights, while the more
cosmopolitan Middle Atlantic state nationalists sought to promote free
and open access to both citizenship and governmental service. The
coalitions contesting these issues were essentially those that dominated
the Convention's business from the Connecticut Compromise (July 17)
to the Commerce and Slave Trade Compromise (August 29), with one
very significant difference. On these general philosophical questions of
access to citizenship and governmental service, New Jersey aligned with

the periphery, rather than with its traditional allies from the small Middle Atlantic states, to give the periphery a decisive 6-5 advantage.

The first question to arise on August 8 concerned eligibility requirements for service in the national House of Representatives. Specifically, the Committee of Detail reported, as requested, a requirement of three years' residency in the United States to qualify for election to the House. Mason's motion to increase the residency requirement from three years to seven was adopted with little resistance. Rutledge of South Carolina sought further to restrict candidacy for the House to persons who had been seven years a citizen of the particular state in which they wished to stand for election. Although no vote was taken on Rutledge's motion, representatives of the Middle Atlantic coalition rose to combat this trend in the business. Read of Delaware reminded Mason "that we were now forming a *Natil* Govt and such a regulation would correspond little with the idea that we were one people." Mercer of Maryland observed that "it would interweave local prejudices & State distinctions in the very Constitution which is meant to cure them" (*Records*, vol. 2, p. 217). Such views were closely and passionately held; the periphery feared much, while the partisans of the Middle Atlantic coalition hoped for much. But this and similar issues of residency and qualifications for voting and officeholding would, after much pulling and hauling, be effectively compromised. The difference between three years and seven, being eminently negotiable, was not likely to break the Convention.

Not so with the next issue: slavery and the continuing trade in black Africans and their descendants in this country. Rufus King, the isolated and increasingly frustrated Massachusetts nationalist, first exposed this very sensitive subject by declaring that "the admission of slaves was a most grating circumstance to his mind." King explained that "he had not made a strenuous opposition to it heretofore because he had hoped that this concession," made on the motion of Wilson in early June to hold the South to the coalition favoring proportional representation in both houses, "would have produced a readiness which had not been manifested, to strengthen the Genl. Govt. and to mark a full confidence in it" (*Records*, vol. 2, p. 220). Not only had proportional representation in both houses been lost, but the additional influence that the counting of slaves had given to the South had not led her to support the strengthening of the government, much less to "mark a full confidence in it." In point of fact, the South stood daily in the path of the Middle Atlantic states as they sought to broadly empower the new government. The issue of slaves and their continued importation revealed powerful emotions on both sides, emotions that would again bring the Convention's dissolution into view.

The third and final critical issue to come briefly to the surface on August 8 was the restriction of the origin of money bills to the House. This resolution had been originally passed as a concession to the large states by way of partial compensation for the loss of proportional representation in the Senate. Even when it was initially approved, many delegates from the large states rejected it as meaningless, if not positively pernicious. Now with the approval of four of the six members of the former large state–deep South coalition, the Convention voted 7-4, over the objections of New Hampshire, Massachusetts, Connecticut, and North Carolina, to strike out this restriction so that both branches would be equally able to originate and amend appropriations bills. Several delegates sought to retain the provision because they saw it as an integral part of the Connecticut Compromise and were apprehensive that to deny this section might be to unhinge the whole structure. Others, particularly the New England delegates, saw it as a tried and traditional component of mixed government and, therefore, as essential. Wilson spoke for his colleagues from the Middle Atlantic states when he simply observed that he "was opposed to it on its merits, without regard to the compromise," while Madison made the important point that beyond being of "no advantage to the large States," it was "fettering the Govt." unnecessarily, and this was, on its face, undesirable (*Records*, vol. 2, p. 224). Each of these questions continued to haunt the Convention throughout the month of August.

Citizenship, Voting, and Officeholding: Openness or Constraints

The debates on residency qualifications for the Senate provide an example of the Middle Atlantic nationalists' aversion to absolute constitutional prohibitions. G. Morris, separating himself from his Middle Atlantic colleagues, proposed a 14 year residency requirement for Senators, urging "the danger of admitting strangers into our public Councils." Not surprisingly, Pinckney agreed when Col. Mason indicated that, if it were not for the fact that many foreigners had served nobly in the Revolution, "he should be for restraining the eligibility into the Senate, to natives" (*Records*, vol. 2, p. 235). Butler of South Carolina supported Mason and Morris, observing that foreigners bring with them "ideas of Govt. so distinct from ours that in every point of view they are dangerous," thereby wholly justifying the requirement for "a long residence" (ibid., p. 236).

Madison and his nationalist supporters in the Middle Atlantic states thought this approach unnecessary, illiberal, and unbecoming to the nation. Madison indicated that although he was "not averse to some restrictions," certainly the length and the mode proposed by Morris were wrong. Madison "thought any restriction (however) in the *Constitution* unnecessary, and improper" (*Records*, vol. 2, p. 235). It was unnecessary because it would constitutionally and forever tie the hands of the legislature, when the same object could be more simply accomplished by ordinary legislative acts controlling naturalization and citizenship. But even more, it would be "improper: because it will give a tincture of illiberality to the Constitution" to bar new citizens from the Senate for fully 14 years, let alone to restrict that high privilege to natives (ibid., p. 236). Benjamin Franklin rose to Madison's support. Franklin also noted the "illiberality" of the proposal as well as the probable adverse impact on European opinion of such an idea permanently ensconced in the Constitution. James Wilson, a Scotsman by birth, but an American since before the Revolution, "said he rose with feelings which were perhaps peculiar; mentioning the circumstance of his not being a native, and the possibility, if the ideas of some gentlemen should be pursued, of his being incapacitated from holding a place under the very Constitution which he had shared in the trust of making." Wilson also joined Madison and Franklin in remarking upon "the illiberal complexion which the motion would give to the System" (ibid., p. 237).

The vote was then taken on Morris' motion for a 14-year residency requirement. The proposition for 14 years, then one for 13 years, and finally another for a 10-year requirement were all defeated by the identical vote of 4-7. The peripheral states of New Hampshire, South Carolina, and Georgia, joined by New Jersey, were, each time, defeated by an otherwise solid bloc of Middle Atlantic states stretching from Massachusetts to North Carolina. Finally, nine years was proposed and approved by a vote of 6-4-1, after Rutledge's argument that a seven-year requirement existed for the House, and that since the Senate was to be more powerful, a longer requirement was justified.

The question of requirements and restrictions carried over into the debates of August 10, and once again, the periphery squared off against the Middle Atlantic states. Charles Pinckney moved to have uniform property qualifications constitutionally established for the major officers in all three branches of the national government. He mentioned $100,000 unencumbered property for the President and half that for the Legislature and the Court. Pinckney's extreme proposal found little favor and was "rejected by so general a *no*, that the States were not called" (*Records*, vol. 2, p. 249). But on the general question of a legislative power "'to establish such uniform qualifications of the members of each House, with regard to property, as to the said Legislature shall seem expedient,'" the vote was 3-7 (ibid., pp. 248–251). The favorable votes came from the extreme northern and southern states of the periphery (New Hampshire, Massachusetts, and Georgia), against a solid Middle Atlantic group extending from Connecticut to South Carolina.

Having stopped the locally oriented delegates of the periphery from attaining their most extreme demands, Wilson sought to turn this advantage into a positive momentum for the Middle Atlantic nationalists by moving to reconsider the citizenship requirement for the House in order to reduce it from seven years back to the original provision for three years. Reconsideration was granted for Monday, August 13, by a vote of 6-5. The five negative votes came from New Hampshire and Massachusetts in the far North, South Carolina and Georgia in the deep South, and New Jersey against an otherwise solid Middle Atlantic tier of states from Connecticut to North Carolina.

By the time the Convention reconvened on the morning of August 13, a full week's consideration and much debate had been expended on this and related questions. Each delegate was familiar with the arguments, had tested the tenacity of the opposition, and knew where the votes were liable to fall. Few appeared to think that additional argument would prove useful, so the questions came quickly. Fully eight of the ten roll-call votes registered on this day are identified by high factor scores as representing issues on which the opposing coalitions clashed directly (See Table 7.2). No other day in the Convention experienced such a concentration of critically divisive votes. The dominant coalitions clashed directly over issues that activated, on the one hand, strains of regionalism and nativism, and on the other, an expansive and confident nationalism and Americanism.

Wilson moved to strike out seven years and insert four, adding the caveat that he disapproved even of the four years, thinking it "very proper the electors should govern themselves by this consideration" in their own voting, "but unnecessary & improper that the Constitution should chain them down to it" (*Records*, vol. 2, p. 268). Gerry immediately juxtaposed to Wilson's view that of the more extreme members of the peripheral group, saying that he "wished that in future the eligibility might be confined to Natives," in order to prevent the possibility of foreign powers' insinuating their paid minions into the national councils. The more moderate peripheral position on the matter was brought forward by Williamson of North Carolina in the form of a proposal to increase the seven years' residency to nine years rather than to reduce it to Wilson's four years. Then, as if to give Wilson's proposal the moderate appearance of a middle ground where compromise might take place,

Hamilton moved that the requirement be reduced to the bare minimum of "Citizenship & inhabitancy." He explained that he "was in general agst. embarrassing the Govt. with minute restrictions" (ibid.). Therefore, the possibilities before the Convention ranged from Gerry's natives, which was never cast as a formal motion, to Williamson's proposed increase to nine years, to Wilson's four years, to Hamilton's "Citizenship & inhabitancy."

After Madison again expressed his hope that a "character of liberality" would be demonstrated, the questions were taken. A united coalition of the Periphery—New Hampshire and Massachusetts in the North, with the Carolinas and Georgia in the South, aided by New Jersey and Delaware—struck down Hamilton's motion to virtually eliminate residency requirements from the Constitution. Nonetheless, the coalition of the periphery failed to get behind Williamson's motion to increase the requirement from seven years to nine. That proposal went down 3-8, supported by only New Hampshire, South Carolina, and Georgia, against a Middle Atlantic group expanded to include every state from Massachusetts to North Carolina. Even with the extreme demands of each coalition thus rejected, Wilson's proposal for a reduction from seven years to four also failed, this time by another vote of 3-8, with Connecticut, Maryland, and Virginia being denied. So when the smoke cleared, the seven-year residency requirement that had been passed on August 8 was left untouched.

Nonetheless, though disappointed in their attempt to reduce the residency requirement for the House, several of the delegates from the Middle Atlantic states were eager to try other means to liberalize and moderate the requirement. A motion was made to attach "a proviso that the limitation (of seven years) should not affect (the rights of) any person now a Citizen" (*Records*, p. 270). A familiar chorus of voices from the periphery sounded to the effect that even this presumption in favor of those immigrants who had attained citizenship under current state laws would constitute a danger. Rutledge observed that "the policy of the precaution was as great with regard to foreigners now Citizens; as to those who are to be naturalized in the future." Sherman supported Rutledge with the very remarkable statement that "the U. States have not invited foreigners nor pledged their faith that they should enjoy equal privileges with native Citizens" (ibid.). Sherman reasoned that only the states, if anyone at all, had made commitments to the foreigners then resident among them. Therefore, the national government that they were in the process of framing was completely "at liberty to make any discriminations they may judge requisite" (ibid.). Pinckney agreed that the Convention "was a sort of recurrance to first principles," in which case, earlier promises made by the states could not be binding (*Records*, vol. 2, p. 271). Madison, Morris, and Wilson presented counterarguments, but when the votes were recorded, a familiar pattern was evident. The peripheral coalition collected the votes of New Hampshire and Massachusetts in the North and of the Carolinas and Georgia in the South, while a defector from the less cohesive coalition of the Middle Atlantic, in this case Delaware, delivered the victory to them.

Two more attempts were quickly made by representatives of the Middle Atlantic states to moderate the residency requirements, first for the House, and then for the Senate. Both proposals were unsuccessful because the less committed members of the Middle Atlantic state coalition continued to drift away in recognition of the fact that a certain acceptable balance had been reached. Carroll of Maryland moved to reduce the requirement for the House from seven years to five only to see the victory again go to a united periphery aided by both New Jersey and Delaware, with Pennsylvania divided. Wilson then asked that the Senate requirement be reduced from nine years to seven. The motion was lost by a vote of 3-8, when even Virginia wearily resigned herself to nine years in the Senate and seven in the House. With these two votes, the question of constitutional requirements for holding national office passed from the scene. Once again, a united coalition of the periphery had successfully exploited the divisions within the more diffuse coalition of Middle Atlantic states to transform its preferences into constitutional provisions.

Money Bills: Access to the Public Purse

Just below the surface lay volatile issues at the "lower" level of constitutional choice that would soon demand resolution. Sensitive regional issues, including the power to set commercial policy, to tax exports, and to continue the importation of slaves, would not fade away in a fuzzy consensus. Knowing this, and given the uncertainty of where tempers might carry them, the delegates were loath to confront these questions head on.

Therefore, these explosive issues came to the fore only slowly and over the space of a week. Meanwhile, both coalitions sought to exert their influence on collateral issues. The peripheral group did so always for the general purpose of maintaining the cherished doctrine of "separation of powers," and where danger still seemed to lurk, of applying positive constitutional restraints. The Middle Atlantic coalition aimed to provide each department, or each combination of departments, with the ability to defend itself. This defensive capability would generally be needed against the legislative branch, which was seen as an ominous vortex into which all power would inevitably drift unless properly anchored. But once the integrity of the structure was guaranteed by a separation of powers supported, though perhaps somewhat blurred, by an adequate system of checks and balances, they sought to avoid minute restrictions on the assumption that future governments, confronting new and unforeseen problems, would need to draw on an unrestricted range of options.

As Randolph had forewarned his colleagues on August 9 and again on August 11, the first such question to be confronted was a review of the Convention's action in striking out the restriction of the origin of money bills to the House. Madison, Wilson, and Morris spoke against the restriction as being an unnecessary encumbrance on the legislative process and as being of no value to the large states, in whose favor it had originally been presented. Dickinson, speaking the minds of many from the peripheral coalition, called upon Madison and his nationalist colleagues to restrain their political imaginations in favor of provisions that had proven effective in the past. He reminded his colleagues that "Experience must be our only guide. Reason may mislead us . . . has not experience verified the utility of restraining money bills to the immediate representatives of the people. Whence the effect may have proceeded he could not say . . . but the effect was visible & could not be doubted" (*Records*, vol. 2, p. 278). The periphery was loath to sacrifice the salutary effect, even if it did not fully understand the means by which it was achieved. Nonetheless, only four states, New Hampshire, Massachusetts, Virginia, and North Carolina, voted in favor of the restriction.

In a related decision, delegates from the Middle Atlantic states sought on August 14 to weaken the provision prohibiting members of the House from holding any other office under the national government during the period for which they were elected. Senators were restricted for an additional year beyond the expiration of their term. The intent of this prohibition, backed strongly by the periphery, was to forestall the possibility of legislators creating lucrative new offices and then having themselves appointed to fill them. The periphery saw this restriction as a demonstrated expedient for heading off corruption in the Legislature. The partisans of the Middle Atlantic states (Madison, Wilson, and Morris spoke against it) saw it as another unnecessary constraint on the political process that would serve simply to disqualify the most qualified: those in whom the people had already shown their confidence by electing them to national office. Williamson of North Carolina used the general approach of the delegates from the periphery to bind together this issue and the earlier question of the appropriate origin of money bills. Williamson deserves to be quoted at some length here because, though obviously employing hyperbole to draw attention to his fears, he pointed directly to one of the central concerns of the peripheral states: "Mr. Williamson; introduced his opposition to the motion by referring to the question concerning 'money bills'. That clause he said was dead. Its ghost he was afraid would notwithstanding haunt us. . . . All that was said on the other side was that the restriction was not *convenient*. We have now got a House of Lords (Senate) which is to originate money-bills. To avoid another *inconveniency*, we are to have a whole Legislature at liberty to cut out offices for one another. He thought a self-denying ordinance for ourselves would be more proper" (*Records*, vol. 2, p. 287).

Williamson saw an obvious connection between the successful attempt to allow the Senate an equal right to generate money bills and the attempt to do away with restrictions on the liberty of legislators "to cut out offices for one another." The representatives of the Middle Atlantic states argued in both cases that *inconveniencies* would be created by reducing the options open to government for dealing with new and unexpected problems. The periphery, on the other hand, was willing to forego this additional streamlining of the system by constitutionally mandating regulations and restrictions—"self-denying ordinances," as Williamson called them—in the hope of avoiding or at least minimizing corruption.

The architects of the Middle Atlantic perspective argued convincingly that such "parchment barriers" or "self-denying ordinances" would be of little service in critical situations. As Madison had observed many times, the need for a governmental structure characterized by both strength and stability over the long haul could only be filled by a proper balance among its component parts and a generous empowerment. On August 15, Madison again sought to achieve this balance by bringing forward a familiar but slightly reformulated proposal to join the executive and the judiciary in a provisional negative. He argued that before an act became law, it should be submitted to both the executive and the judiciary for review. If one branch opposed, two-thirds would be required to override; if both objected, three-fourths would be required. After only listless debate, Gerry simply noting that "this motion comes to the same thing with what has been already negatived" (referring to the July 21 rejection of a joint executive-judicial council), the dominant and increasingly impatient periphery overwhelmed the remnants of the Middle Atlantic state group (*Records*, vol. 2, p. 298).

Several members from the peripheral states, now in full confidence that the Convention had explicitly rejected the program of the extreme nationalists for a broadly empowered and virtually unrestrained national government, began to tire of the extended bickering over what they considered to be settled issues. Gorham declared that he "saw no end to these difficulties." Rutledge "complained much of the tediousness of the proceedings," while "Ellsworth held the same language. We grow more & more skeptical as we proceed" (*Records*, vol. 2, pp. 300–301). If the attention and interest of the members of the peripheral coalition drifted for a moment, it was soon to be riveted fast to their business as the issues of slavery and the trade in slaves and of navigation acts or commercial regulation finally came fully before the Convention.

Slavery, Commerce, the Executive, and the West: State and Regional Interest

As the Convention moved into late August, several critical issues at the "lower" level of constitutional choice—including some provision for the critical regional issues of slavery and commercial regulation, for executive selection, and for control of the western lands—stood unresolved. Initially, it seemed that the dominant coalition of peripheral states would resolve each of these issues in its own favor against the increasingly desultory opposition of the Middle Atlantic states. As the Middle Atlantic coalition tottered toward collapse, the more cohesive peripheral coalition seemed to gather new strength as its northern and southern wings quickly and smoothly came to an accommodation on the dangerous and divisive regional issues of the slave trade and commercial regulation. Table 7.5 demonstrates that effective opposition to these regional trade-offs was restricted to the nationalist core of the Middle Atlantic coalition. The more moderate Middle Atlantic states either give outright support to the demands of the periphery or they leaned in that direction.

As we noted earlier, even as the original motion by Gerry to appoint a Committee of Detail was being made, General Pinckney of South Carolina was reminding "the Convention that if the Committee should fail to insert some security to the Southern States agst. an emancipation of slaves, and taxes on exports, he shd. be bound by duty to his State to vote agst. their Report" (*Records*, vol. 2, p. 95). As Pinckney's statement indicates, the southerners were particularly concerned that new powers might be ceded to the national government in the areas of commerce and slavery. As representatives of the staple-raising states, the southern delegates wanted to insure that northern majorities in the new Congress could not pass damaging navigation acts that would tax southern bulk exports or force them to use northern shipping at higher than compet-

TABLE 7.5. Expanded Periphery versus Nationalist Core: On Commerce and Slavery; Two-Factor Solution to Votes 330–402, August 21–August 29, Varimax Rotation (Ortho)

	1 Expanded Periphery	2 Nationalist Core	h^2
New Hampshire	(.52)	.44	.46
Massachusetts	(.57)	.30	.42
Connecticut	.47	.06	.23
New York	absent	absent	absent
New Jersey	.05	(.60)	.37
Pennsylvania	.18	(.84)	.74
Delaware	−.03	(.87)	.75
Maryland	.47	−.06	.23
Virginia	(.52)	.23	.32
North Carolina	(.81)	.05	.66
South Carolina	(.77)	.15	.62
Georgia	(.84)	.00	.70
Sum of squares	3.02	2.47	5.49
% Total variance	27.45	22.45	49.90

itive rates. On this they were united. But the southern mind was deeply divided on the slavery question. South Carolina and Georgia demanded the right to continue the unrestricted importation of slaves. Their rice swamps devoured slaves so rapidly that continuous replacement was necessary. On the other hand, North Carolina was nearly self-sufficient, while Maryland and Virginia had an overabundance of slaves, which they could more readily market to their southern neighbors if further importation were halted. In this atmosphere, the Committee of Detail did its work.

It has been widely argued, both within the Convention and among later commentators, that the two southern members of the Committee of Detail, John Rutledge and Edmund Randolph, overwhelmed the three northern men, James Wilson, Nathaniel Gorham, and Oliver Ellsworth, on those issues of commerce and slavery where the regions seemed to clash most directly. Donald L. Robinson contends that the Committee of Detail report "provided virtually everything that Southerners, especially deep Southerners, wanted from the Convention: substantial (three-fifths) representation for their slaves, complete immunity for the slave trade and for slavery in general, prohibition of export taxes, and special majorities for navigation acts and treaties" (Robinson, 1971, p. 218). Nonetheless, it was almost immediately evident that the South would be forced to defend this report on the floor of the Convention. As early as August 8, the issue of slavery and its treatment by the Committee of Detail was raised as a point of contention. King, the Massachusetts nationalist, was disgusted with what he took to be the southern bias in the Committee's report. He called the attention of his Middle Atlantic state allies to the fact that "in two great points the hands of the Legislature were absolutely tied. The importation of slaves could not be prohibited—exports could not be taxed" (*Records*, vol. 2, p. 220).

The debates did not touch the exposed nerves of sectional balance again until August 16, when "Mason urged the necessity of connecting with the power of levying taxes, duties, &c, . . . that no tax should be laid on exports" (ibid., p. 305). Reaction to Mason's concern divided strictly along the dominant periphery versus center cleavage. The deep South's northeastern coalition partners supported it in its efforts to oppose a national power to tax exports, while the partisans of the Middle Atlantic coalition, following Madison, argued that "the power of taxing exports is proper in itself, and as the States cannot with propriety exercise it separately, it ought to be vested in them collectively" (ibid., p. 306). With the Convention still unprepared to face this divisive issue, it was "agreed that the question concerning exports shd. lie over" (ibid., p. 308). This issue, as well as the related questions that went to make up the debate over the closely linked issues of slavery and commerce, was not reached again until August 21.

From August 21 through August 29, this package of issues dominated the agenda. During this nine-day period, 72 roll-call votes were taken. Table 7.6 shows that the Periphery versus Middle states alignment dominated this set of issues as completely as it had the earlier questions of empowerment and the structure of the executive branch. The split in the Middle Atlantic coalition that the periphery, with its superior cohesion, had traditionally been able to exploit was also again evident. Nonetheless, it is very important to note that New Jersey's extended flirtation with the localism of the periphery ceased as the Convention turned to the critical regional issues of slavery and commerce. New Jersey opposed these regional demands so vehemently that she displayed the only negative loading on factor 1 and rejoined the coalition of Middle Atlantic states as a member not of the moderate center but of the more radical nationalist center on factor 3.

By the time debate reached the issues of commerce and slavery, the respective positions and arguments of the contending forces in the

TABLE 7.6. Localist Periphery versus Divided Nationalist Center: On Commerce and Slavery; Three-Factor Solution to Votes 330–402, August 21–August 29, Varimax Rotation (Ortho)

	1 Localist Periphery	2 Moderate Center	3 Nationalist Core	h^2
New Hampshire	(.70)	−.00	.34	.60
Massachusetts	(.70)	.06	.20	.54
Connecticut	.09	(.68)	.06	.48
New York	absent	absent	absent	absent
New Jersey	−.19	.45	(.65)	.66
Pennsylvania	.28	.08	(.81)	.74
Delaware	.15	−.10	(.85)	.76
Maryland	.08	(.68)	−.06	.47
Virginia	.20	(.65)	.21	.51
North Carolina	(.81)	.27	−.06	.73
South Carolina	(.83)	.20	.04	.72
Georgia	(.57)	(.63)	−.07	.73
Sum of squares	2.85	2.07	2.02	6.94
% Total variance	25.90	18.82	18.28	63.00

Convention on the philosophical question of the practicality and advisability of explicit restrictions in the Constitution were already well known. This general range of questions was approached through debate on a resolution which read, in part, "no tax or duty shall be laid by the Legislature on articles exported from any State." Langdon of New Hampshire raised the point that this left open the possibility that "non-exporting States, will be subject to be taxed by the States exporting its produce" (*Records*, vol. 2, p. 359). This problem had plagued several of the states since independence. Nonetheless, Langdon's colleagues in the peripheral coalition could not be convinced that the power to tax exports could safely be lodged at the national level. Williamson argued that though North Carolina's exports had long been taxed by Virginia, the removal of this power to the National government remained totally unacceptable and "would destroy the last hope of an adoption of the plan." South Carolina's Butler called the proposal "unjust and alarming to the staple States" (ibid., p. 360).

The men of the Middle Atlantic states, clearly outgunned on this issue, sought to retain the posture of disinterested nationalism. G. Morris scolded his opponents, saying, "these local considerations ought not to impede the general interest" (ibid.). Dickinson, arguing the classic concern of the Middle Atlantic state men for unfettered government, claimed that although "the power of taxing exports may be inconvenient at present; . . . it must be of dangerous consequence to prohibit it with respect to all articles and for ever" (*Records*, vol. 2, p. 361). Madison warmly supported this line of argument. Clymer reminded the southern delegates "that every State might reason with regard to its particular productions, in the same manner of the Southern States. The middle States may apprehend an oppression of their wheat flour, provisions, &c. . . . They may apprehend also combinations agst. them between the Eastern & Southern States as much as the latter can apprehend them between the Eastern and middle" (ibid., p. 363). Having issued his note of caution, Clymer then sought to get around the objections of the periphery by moving "as a qualification of the power of taxing Exports that it should be restrained to regulations of trade, . . . 'for the purpose of revenue'" (ibid.). This proposal met with an icy reception in which factors 1 and 2 of Table 7.6, the periphery and the moderate center, united to oppose the unremitting nationalists of factor 3. No state varied in its allegiance.

But this expansion of the peripheral coalition to include the moderate states of the Middle Atlantic was to be short lived. The interests of the five southern states on the question of the continued importation of slaves differed so radically, with Maryland and Virginia seeking discontinuance while the deep South demanded continuance, that conflict between the southern members of the peripheral coalition seemed inevitable. The dispute was brought clearly into the open when Luther Martin of Maryland "proposed to . . . allow a prohibition or tax on the importation of slaves," arguing that continued importation "weakened . . . the Union," and was "inconsistent with the principles of the revolution" (*Records*, vol. 2, p. 364). Stern objections and warnings immediately erupted from the South Carolina delegation. Rutledge cautioned his fellows that "the true question at present is whether the Southn. States shall or shall not be parties to the Union." Pinckney declared that "South Carolina can never receive the plan if it prohibits the slave trade" (ibid.).

When debate on the slave trade opened on the morning of August 22, General Charles Cotesworth Pinckney went directly to the regional economics of the conflict between the states of the upper South (Maryland and Virginia of the Middle Atlantic coalition) and the states of the lower South (the Carolinas and Georgia of the peripheral coalition) on this volatile issue. General Pinckney said, "S. Carolina &

Georgia cannot do without slaves. As to Virginia she will gain by stopping the importations. Her slaves will rise in value, & she has more than she wants" (*Records*, vol. 2, p. 371). For the shipping interests so dear to the northern wing of the Peripheral coalition, Pinckney held out the prospect that "the more slaves, the more produce to employ the carrying trade; The more consumption also, and the more of this, the more of revenue for the common treasury" (ibid.). Baldwin, on the other hand, simply denied the Convention's right to deal with matters of merely local or regional interest. Baldwin observed that he "had conceived national objects alone to be before the Convention, not such as like the present were of a local nature. Georgia . . . has always hitherto supposed a Genl Governmt to be the pursuit of the central States who wished to have a vortex for every thing—that her distance would preclude her from equal advantage" (*Records*, vol. 2, p. 372).

With these sentiments in the air, the Convention adjourned for the day, only to face the same issue upon reconvening the next morning in an atmosphere so tense that a dissolution of the Convention was again threatened. The compromise minded delegates from Connecticut quickly sought to disarm the growing conflict by providing reassurances to the ruffled and defensive southern members. Characteristically, the moderate Middle Atlantic states were prepared to be conciliatory toward the South rather than see the current tensions grow to crisis proportions. The moderates were willing to trim and bargain, and in the final analysis, to give in on this issue. Sherman advised that "it was expedient to have as few objections as possible to the proposed scheme of Government." To further this goal, he suggested that the Committee of Detail report be accepted as presented. Sherman sought to legitimize this approach by observing "that the abolition of slavery seemed to be going on in the U. S. & that the good sense of the several States would probably by degrees compleat it" (*Records*, vol. 2, pp. 369–370). Judge Ellsworth also held out the hope that slavery was a dying institution in America, saying, "let us not intermeddle. . . . Slavery in time will not be a speck in our Country" (ibid., p. 371). Baldwin sought to foster this view among the northern men by assuring that Georgia, "if left to herself . . . may probably put a stop to the evil" (ibid., p. 372).

The nationalist center would not condescend to argue economics or to engage in hopeful moralizing. It was determined to stick to the high plane of abstract morality, a position made much easier to assume by the knowledge that it was hopelessly in the minority. Dickinson represented the views of his nationalist colleagues in arguing that he "considered it as inadmissible on every principle of honor & safety that the importation of slaves should be authorized to the States by the Constitution" (ibid.). But Rufus King's practical approach struck a much more responsive note with the states of the moderate center. King argued that this was strictly a political question upon which compromise and conciliation would prove more effective than moralizing. With this in mind, "he remarked on the exemption of slaves from duty whilst every other import was subjected to it, as an inequality that could not fail to strike the commercial sagacity of the Northn. & middle States." General Pinckney, also in the conciliatory mood that strength allows, agreed with his northern colleague that a moderate tax would not be improper. Therefore, "he moved to commit the clause that slaves might be made liable to an equal tax with other imports" (*Records*, vol. 2, p. 373).

G. Morris, noting Pinckney's willingness to compromise on this aspect of the matter, acted to broaden the ground for compromise to include the entire area of slavery, commerce, and export taxes, saying, "these things may form a bargain among the Northern & Southern States." Randolph agreed to the commitment, "in order that some middle ground might, if possible, be found. He could never agree to the clause as it stands. He wd. sooner risk the constitution" (*Records*, vol. 2, p. 374).

The commitment of these three questions to a compromise committee as a package left little doubt as to the expected outcome. The resolution of the issue was rapidly established along the lines of the King-Pinckney exchange of the previous day. Luther Martin, a member of the committee, described the atmosphere within which the committee had to work and the nature of the compromise. Upon entering conference, Martin "found the *eastern* States, notwithstanding their *aversion to slavery*, were very willing to indulge the southern States, at least with a temporary liberty to prosecute the *slave-trade*, provided the southern States would, in their turn, gratify them, by laying *no restriction on navigation acts*; and after a very little time the committee, by a great majority, agreed on a report" (*Records*, vol. 3, pp. 210–211).

This rapid action allowed the committee to report its compromise proposals to the full Convention on the morning of August 24. In place of the provision that allowed unlimited importation of slaves with no tax, the following language was proposed: "the migration or importation of such persons as the several States now existing shall think proper to admit shall not be prohibited by the Legislature prior to the year 1800, . . . but a tax or duty may be imposed on such migration or importation at a rate not exceeding the average of the duties laid on imports" (*Records*, vol. 2, p. 409). Further, the provision concerning the capitation tax was to remain unchanged, while the requirement of a two-thirds majority to pass navigation acts was to be removed entirely. This would leave the northern commercial interests free to regulate national commerce by simple congressional majority.

The Commerce and Slave Trade Compromise was reported to the floor on August 24 but was not debated until August 25. In the interim, the Convention returned to the complex issue of executive selection. Again, the Middle Atlantic states were powerless against a united coalition of the periphery because differences in state size again proved to be their undoing. The precise question before the Convention was whether the periphery's preference for legislative selection would be exercised by separate ballots in the House and Senate or, as Rutledge now suggested, in the hope of driving a wedge between Pennsylvania and Virginia and their small state allies, by "joint ballot" of both houses voting together. Sherman immediately objected that the "joint ballot" would deprive the smaller "*States* represented in the *Senate* of the negative intended them in that house" (*Records*, vol. 2, p. 401). When the vote was taken, New Hampshire, Massachusetts, and the Carolinas were supported by the largest of the Middle Atlantic states, Pennsylvania, Maryland, and Virginia, in approving the measure 7-4. Delegates from the smaller states quickly sought to reestablish their influence in the presidential selection process by proposing that each state delegation should have one vote even if the polling was done by "joint ballot." The motion was lost by a single vote, 5-6, when Pennsylvania and Virginia again joined the peripheral states to turn back their former allies. The remnants of the Middle Atlantic state coalition successfully avoided final defeat by postponing the issue.

With the Commerce and Slave Trade Compromise report before the Convention, a day was given for its consideration. When it came to the floor for debate and decision on August 25, the cohesion of the peripheral coalition and defections from the Middle Atlantic coalition were again decisive. As soon as the report was taken up, General Pinckney moved "to strike out the words 'the year eighteen hundred' (as the year limiting the importation of slaves) and to insert the words 'the year eighteen hundred and eight.'" The northern members of the peripheral coalition were more than willing to allow this additional eight-year increment to their southern colleagues, even over Madison's strenuous objection that "twenty years will produce all the mischief that can be apprehended from the liberty to import slaves" (*Records*, vol. 2, p. 415). The division within the Middle Atlantic coalition on this issue was clearly registered in the vote on Pinckney's motion. Factors 1 and 2, the periphery and the moderate center, again combined to defeat the nationalist center on factor 3. The three states of the Northeast, New Hampshire, Massachusetts, and Connecticut, joined by Maryland and the three states of the deep South against the central states of New Jersey, Pennsylvania, Delaware, and Virginia. A vote was then taken on this clause as amended to read "1808." It passed by an identical vote.

This took care of the southern half of the compromise, but the provisions dealing with the northern interest in commercial policy were postponed. This section did not reappear for four days, until August 29, during which time many of the southern delegates began to reevaluate the potential dangers represented by northern control of commercial regulation. During the interim, the South Carolina delegates were not averse to fishing in troubled waters. An additional piece of the puzzle was supplied on August 28 when, in conjunction with the debate on the provisions concerning the reciprocal dealings between the states, General Pinckney "seemed to wish some provision should be included in favor of property in slaves." Butler and Charles Pinckney formulated as a motion the General's "wish" that "'fugitive slaves and servants . . . be delivered up like criminals'" (Records, vol. 2, p. 443). Though this proposition was withdrawn for the moment, the idea of achieving this extra modicum of security for South Carolina's slaveholders did not leave the minds of that state's delegates. Its attainment would prove to be the further price for their support of the northern position on commerce.

When the commerce section was finally debated, Charles Pinckney immediately moved to renege on the southern half of the compromise committee bargain. He moved to strike out the section of the report calling for simple majority decision on commercial questions, thereby retaining the provision of the Committee of Detail draft requiring a two-thirds vote to pass navigation acts. Fearing that the whole compromise might come unhinged, the older Pinckney chastised his young cousin for mistrusting their northern colleagues. Although the General agreed that "it was the true interest of the S. States to have no regulation of commerce," the "liberal conduct toward the views of South Carolina" demonstrated by the northern states had convinced him that "no fetters should be imposed on the power of making commercial regulations" (Records, vol. 2, pp. 449–450).

Williamson declared on the younger Pinckney's side "in favor of making two thirds instead of a majority requisite, as more satisfactory to the Southern people." Butler also leaned toward this view, because he saw the fundamental interests of the North and the South "as different as the interests of Russia and Turkey" (Records, vol. 2, pp. 450–451). Outside the South Carolina delegation, however, feelings ran strongly to the view of the younger Pinckney and of Williamson that commercial regulation by simple majority was an open invitation to southern destruction. Randolph, who had introduced the Virginia Plan in the first week of the Convention, now declared "that there were features so odious in the Constitution . . . that he doubted whether he should be able to agree to it. A rejection of the motion (Pinckney's for two-thirds majorities) would compleat the deformity of the system" (ibid., p. 452). Despite this warning, the northern delegates pressed their demands. Gorham asked Randolph and his southern colleagues, "If the Government is to be so fettered as to be unable to relieve the Eastern States what motive can they have to join it . . . ?" Gorham then proceeded to reassure the southern delegates, urging "the improbability of a combination against the interest of the Southern States, the different situations of the Northern & Middle States being the security against it" (ibid, p. 453). Nonetheless, despite Gorham's generous assurances, the vote on Pinckney's motion was 4-7 in the negative. A solid bloc of northern and Middle Atlantic states, from New Hampshire to Delaware, joined only by South Carolina, defeated the remaining four southern states of Maryland, Virginia, North Carolina, and Georgia. The payoff to South Carolina was immediately forthcoming when the Convention passed the following resolution without debate: "'If any person bound to service or labor in any of the U-States shall escape into another State, he or she shall not be discharged from such service or labor, . . . but shall be delivered up to the person justly claiming their service or labor'" (ibid., pp. 453–454). With this, the second great compromise of the Convention, and the groundwork for another major realignment of the voting blocs in the Convention, was complete (see Figure 2.3).

Although regional demands for special benefits, assurances, and protections had again threatened to destroy the Convention, compromise had once more forestalled disaster. But at what cost? In fact, the costs were immense. This compromise, and particularly South Carolina's role in it, began a dramatic coalition realignment. The very cohesive and successful coalition of northeastern and southern states did not survive the deal by which South Carolina secured her right to unrestricted importation of slaves until 1808 by giving up the southern veto over navigation acts. An atmosphere of betrayal permeated the southern delegations, destroying the power that that region had previously wielded when acting as a solid bloc of votes. The South was not seen again as a steady and decisive force in the Convention.

With the peripheral coalition broken by the shattering of its southern wing and the coalition of Middle Atlantic states disrupted by a renewed tension between its large and small members, the tone of the Convention's final days was unmistakably set by the debates that began on August 30 over control of the unsettled western lands. One might expect the coalition of Middle Atlantic states to reinstate the provisions constituting a broad empowerment of the national government. But this proved to be impossible. During the same week that saw South Carolina's deft maneuvering, another set of issues proved to be as destructive of the Middle Atlantic coalition as the issues of commerce and slavery were of the peripheral group. To an analysis of these new issues—centering on the rights of the states in this new system, the new cleavage that was activated, and the realignment that followed—we now turn.

CHAPTER 8

Small State Fears and the States' Rights Caucus

In Chapter 7, the progress and passage of the commerce and slave trade proposals were explained in some detail. An important aspect of that explanation involved the gap in time between the approval on August 25 of free importation of slaves until 1808 and the approval on August 29 of commercial regulation by a simple majority vote of the legislature. During this four-day interim, South Carolina's conduct convinced her neighbors that she had very selfishly and dangerously sold out broad regional interests in the control of commercial legislation in favor of her own limited interest in the return of slaves fleeing into other states to escape servitude in South Carolina.

The impact of South Carolina's machinations on the peripheral coalition, in which a solid southern bloc had been a dominant factor, was profound. The peripheral coalition had been effective during the recent debates over the power and flexibility of the proposed national government precisely because it presented a more cohesive front than the opposing coalition of Middle Atlantic states had been able to maintain. This unity was badly disrupted by the profound differences among the southern states on the critical questions surrounding the continuing role of slavery in the region. These debates raged through late August and finally culminated in South Carolina's abandonment of her southern colleagues on the fundamental issue of commercial legislation. Many in the South were convinced that the northern majority would oppress southern commerce if this opportunity was open to them. Commercial legislation by simple majority would provide just such an opportunity, so the South had been unanimous in demanding a special majority of two-thirds. But the right to continue importing slaves under favorable conditions and the guarantee that fugitive slaves would be returned to their owners were thought to be so overwhelmingly important to South Carolina that to secure these benefits, her delegates traded away southern control over commercial legislation by supporting the northern position of passing navigation acts by simple majority.

South Carolina's decision broke the South as a solid voting bloc. (See Table 8.1 below, but more importantly, see Table 9.2 in the following chapter.) With the peripheral coalition lying in disarray, one would expect the Middle Atlantic states to move the Convention decisively back toward a strongly nationalist program. But when this opportunity arose, the Middle Atlantic states were in no position to take advantage of it. The success of the Middle Atlantic coalition depended entirely upon the extent to which the small states of the Middle Atlantic—Connecticut, New Jersey, Delaware, and Maryland—felt comfortable and safe working in close conjunction with the large central states of Pennsylvania and Virginia. The Middle Atlantic coalition was particularly vulnerable to a reemergence of the cleavage that had divided the larger expanding states from the smaller and naturally bounded states. No one believed that the division among the states that had wreaked such havoc on the apportionment debates as they applied both to the legislative and the executive branches had simply disappeared. The small states continuously eyed the larger states for signs that they were attempting to construct a system that benefited them inordinately, while the larger states were under a constant temptation to do precisely that. The consequent lack of harmony between the larger and smaller members slowly but surely drained the strength and morale of the nationalist coalition.

Small State Isolation and the States' Rights Caucus

With the southern half of the Commerce and Slave Trade Compromise approved on August 25 and the troublesome commercial questions postponed until August 29, issues came before the Convention that fundamentally challenged the already strained bonds holding the Middle Atlantic coalition together. In the face of regular defections by the small Middle Atlantic states to the coalition of the periphery, Pennsylvania and Virginia, fearing the impotence of isolation, sought to minimize their vulnerability by forsaking the small states on the long contested and still undecided question of executive selection. Just as the small states had abandoned them in their joint pursuit of electoral selection when the larger states refused during the closing days of July to support their proposed allocation scheme, the large states now sought to preempt the small by making a separate peace with the peripheral coalition and its preferred mode of legislative selection.

Since the early days of the Convention, the peripheral group had supported the traditional Whig mechanism of executive selection by the legislature. The Middle Atlantic states, on the other hand, had just as consistently backed a plan that called for executive selection by specially designated electors. This device was meant to prevent the possibility of legislative dominance of the executive. The more cohesive peripheral group had been able to enforce legislative selection both in early June and again in late July. The question that arose on the morning of August 24 was whether legislative selection would be conducted by separate ballots in the House and the Senate or, as suggested by Rutledge in the hope of driving a wedge between Pennsylvania and Virginia and their small state allies, by "joint ballot" of both houses voting together. Just as Rutledge had hoped they would, Pennsylvania and Virginia jumped at the chance to support legislative selection, after opposing it for months, if it were skewed to maximize their influence at the expense of their small state allies. The small states were depending heavily upon a separate ballot in the Senate to give them some meaningful control over the executive branch. A firm foothold in the executive selection process, together with their equal vote in the Senate, would, they were convinced, supply the institutional means to defend themselves against the large states. But if balloting occurred jointly, the influence of the smaller states would be wiped out by the much more numerous House of Representatives delegations assigned to Virginia (10), Pennsylvania (8), and Massachusetts (8). It would require the votes of every member from Connecticut (5), New Jersey (4), and Delaware (1) just to offset the votes of Virginia, let alone the others.

The states opposing Rutledge's "joint ballot" proposal were the four small states appearing on factor 2 of Table 8.1. The anomalous position of Delaware that we noted earlier is clearly demonstrated by this issue. On the question of a joint ballot selection, Delaware voted with the large state nationalists. But on the very next vote, designed to amend joint ballot selection by adding the clause "each State having One vote," Delaware seemed to recall that selection by joint ballot would give it only one vote compared to Virginia's ten, considering only the House, and that adding Senators would give Delaware only three to Virginia's twelve. The rather sobering mathematics of the situation led Delaware to join the other small Middle Atlantic states on this question. But Pennsylvania and Virginia, still voting with the peripheral states on factor 1 of Table 8.1, helped to defeat the proposal 6-5.

The fearsome implications of the Pennsylvania and Virginia votes in favor of a joint ballot selection were not lost on the small states. Luther Martin reported that at about this point in the Convention, a small state caucus, including members from all of the states loading either negatively on factor 1 or positively on factor 2 of Table 8.1, began to meet regularly. It consisted of "a number of members who considered the

TABLE 8.1.   Three-Factor Solution to Roll-Call Votes 403–441 Taken between August 30 and September 3, Varimax Rotation (Ortho)

	1 Large-State Periphery	2 Small-State Middle	3 Nationalist Middle	h^2
New Hampshire	(.63)	.24	(.52)	.73
Massachusetts	(.69)	.20	.41	.68
Connecticut	.23	(.61)	.38	.58
New York	absent	absent	absent	absent
New Jersey	−.14	(.80)	−.12	.68
Pennsylvania	(.55)	.16	(.64)	.75
Delaware	−.11	−.03	(.77)	.61
Maryland	))−.82((	.02	−.03	.67
Virginia	(.67)	.07	.15	.47
North Carolina	(.75)	.19	−.32	.70
South Carolina	(.61)	(.58)	−.02	.70
Georgia	.28	(.81)	.11	.75
Sum of squares	3.42	2.18	1.72	7.32
% Total variance	31.03	19.82	15.64	66.50

system, as then under consideration and likely to be adopted, extremely exceptionable. . . . Mr. Gerry and Mr. Mason did hold meetings, but with them also met the Delegates from New Jersey and Connecticut, a part of the Delegation from Delaware, an honorable member from South Carolina, one other from Georgia, and myself. . . . the sole object was not to aggrandize the great at the expense of the small, but to protect and preserve, if possible, the existence and essential rights of all the states, and the liberty and freedom of their citizens" (*Records*, vol. 3, p. 282).

Martin's reading of the division between the states is quite clear. Once again the Convention was dealing with a distributive issue at the "lower" level of constitutional choice, and once again, it was the large states against the small. Not only did Martin name virtually all of the states loading negatively on factor 1 or positively on factor 2 of Table 8.1 as members of the states' rights caucus, but the "rationale" for the new division between the states is also clearly stated. Martin said very emphatically that the hope of the caucus was "to protect and preserve . . . the existence and essential rights of *all of the States*." The small states would be hard pressed to fulfill this mission against formidable opposition.

During the interim between August 27 and August 29, the real question seemed to be not whether some faction, but which faction, of the Middle Atlantic alliance would break away and adhere consistently to the periphery. The large states had shown a willingness to defect on the question of joint ballot selection of the chief executive. This inclination was only enhanced when the actions of the small states continued to demonstrate the general futility and impotence of the coalition of Middle Atlantic states. An almost comedic case in point involved the three votes surrounding a motion by Gouverneur Morris to move back to selection by electors. Morris' motion lost 6-5 when Maryland broke the solid ranks of the Middle Atlantic states to vote with the five member peripheral coalition. Broome of Delaware then suggested that the executive question be bound over to a committee of one member from each state in the hope that a compromise might be reached. Maryland's return to the Middle Atlantic group was negated when Connecticut's vote was divided, resulting in a 5-5-1 tie that served to defeat the proposal. Even more frustratingly, on the "abstract question . . . shall be chosen by electors," with Massachusetts absent from the floor and the periphery reduced to four members, the Middle Atlantic states were still unable to prevail as the votes of both Connecticut and Maryland were divided, producing another tie at 4-4-2-1. The Middle Atlantic coalition was obviously and embarrassingly tottering toward impotence.

A New Alignment among the States

The new coalitions that rose in the wake of the decisions made concerning the divisive regional issues of slavery and commerce bore startling similarities to earlier alignments. Initially, the most striking aspect of this new alignment among the states was its resemblance to the patterns that had characterized the earlier debates on legislative representation. The three largest states, Massachusetts, Pennsylvania, and Virginia, load prominently on factor 1, along with two of the three states of the deep South. A new element, the presence on factor 1 of New Hampshire, a small, underpopulated state on the northeastern frontier, is no surprise, given the close historical connection of New Hampshire with its parent state of Massachusetts. Even more interesting, because it anticipated future developments, was Georgia's uncertainty. For the first time in the Convention, Georgia was not solidly aligned with Massachusetts and her southern neighbors. This reflects the dissolution of the southern bloc that resulted from the Commerce and Slave Trade Compromise.

Factor 2 is made up of those states, small and vulnerable or southern

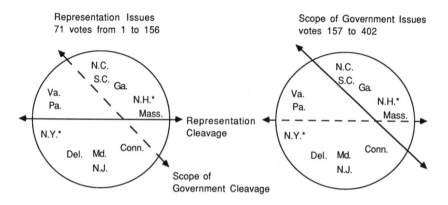

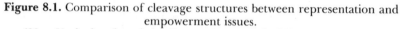

Figure 8.1. Comparison of cleavage structures between representation and empowerment issues.
*New York abandoned the Convention on July 11 at vote #132. New Hampshire did not arrive until July 23 at vote #203.

and conservative, that had been on their guard since the Convention's opening lest they be overwhelmed and rendered powerless in the new government. The obvious response was to retain a prominent place in the new system for the states as independent political entities. Equal representation in the Senate had been a step in the right direction, but the small state men were not satisfied to rest there. They were constantly alert to the possibility that the nationalism in which they had joined as full participants during the Convention's opening days and again from mid-July to the third week in August might again be bent to the service of large state pretensions as it seemed to be whenever distributive questions came to the fore. The temptation was always there, and the small states, knowing it, watched the larger states closely. The third factor allowed the strong nationalism of Delaware's Dickinson and Read to join the nationalist stalwarts Wilson and Morris of Pennsylvania (see Figure 8.1).

The issues that highlight the division between the states during this period clarify the nature of that division. Some questions directly and blatantly divided the states on the basis of present or expected size (such as the questions surrounding the mechanism for executive selection). These issues were similar to those that had dominated the Convention's debates over legislative representation and over the distribution of presidential electors, and they activated a similar cleavage structure. Other questions, such as those dealing with ratification procedures and occasions for the entry of national troops into the states, served to reinforce this division when it became evident to certain of the small state members that the large states were again seeking to dominate the new system and that small state safety could be secured only by firmly establishing the states as legitimate entities in the structure of the national government (see Table 8.2).

By the time these new issues were reached for consideration, the coalition of the periphery, aided by the regular defections of Connecticut, New Jersey, and Maryland, had successfully blunted and then turned back the Middle Atlantic nationalists' attempt to create a broadly empowered and virtually unrestrained national government. Most of the states composing the coalition of the periphery, particularly Massachusetts and the states of the deep South, were satisfied that they had both restrained the central government through a judicious employment of the separation of powers maxim and secured their paramount regional interests in slavery and commerce. Their principal concern was to complete the business at hand and go home rather than to spend time constructing additional barriers between the states and national power. Therefore, neither the periphery nor the large states of the Middle Atlantic were either disposed to or in a position to strengthen the position of the states as independent political entities within the new system. This left the states quite exposed, with only a few of the small Middle Atlantic members as their conscious defenders. These defenders would be hard pressed indeed.

The Small State Opposition on the Defensive

With both of the coalitions that had dominated the Convention's business since mid-July thus weakened, how did the realignment that isolated New Jersey, Delaware, and Maryland against the remaining eight states actually take place? Figure 2.3, the summary graph on coalition realignment, indicates that the coalitions that replaced the periphery versus Middle Atlantic states alignment took shape during the week immediately following the August 24 report of the compromise committee on slavery and commerce. First Virginia, then Pennsylvania, and finally Connecticut abandoned the defunct coalition of Middle Atlantic states to join an expanded and transformed coalition of the periphery. Virginia moved first. It had been dealt a severe blow when free importation of slaves until 1808 was approved on August 25. With its surplus of slaves, Virginia would have had a near monopoly on filling the deep South's continuous need for slave labor if additional importation had been halted. Nonetheless, the more crucial issue of commercial regulation remained. Virginia wanted special congressional majorities of at least two-thirds to pass navigation acts. Therefore, Virginia aban-

TABLE 8.2. Twenty-Four Critical Votes between 352 and 441 as Identified by Factor Scores of 1.25 on Either Factor or 1.0 on Both Factors of the Two-Factor Varimax Solution in Table 8.1

Vote No.	Factor Score	Factor No.	Voting Split	Issue	Date Aug.	*Records,* v.2, p.
353	1.36	2	3-7	To postpone reconsideration of procedure for settling disputes and land questions between states.	24	399
355	1.55	2	2-9	Strike out *legislature,* insert *people,* for direct election of the President.	24	399
356	−1.29 1.82	1, 2	7-4	To insert *joint* before *ballot* in legislative selection of the President.	24	399
357	1.61 −1.55	1, 2	5-6	Add after *legislature,* "each state having one vote," in legislative selection of the President.	24	399
363	−1.47	2	6-4	Attempt to dilute the presidential appointing power.	24	399
369	1.28	1	3-6-1	Dickinson motion to allow the legislature to refer appointments to state executives. Motion was an attempt to limit appointing power.	25	410
382	1.49	2	3-5	Scope of Supreme Court's original jurisdiction.	27	426
392	1.61	2	3-8	Among limitations on the states, "nor lay embargoes."	28	436
394	1.35	2	6-5	Add "or exports" to limitations on state power to tax imports.	28	436
398	−1.60	2	9-2	To commit the full faith and credit article.	29	447
403	1.75	1	3-8	Carroll moved to strike out need for state's consent to be divided.	30	460

TABLE 8.2. *(Continued)*

Vote No.	Factor Score	Factor No.	Voting Split	Issue	Date Aug.	*Records,* v.2, p.
407	1.75	1	3-8	Martin moved that the legislature be entitled to erect and admit new states from both inside and outside claimed territory.	30	460
408	−1.28	1	8-3	Morris moves that state legislatures must approve divisions.	30	460
409	1.61	1	2-8	Martin moves to add "all such claims to western lands to be examined by the Supreme Court."	30	460
417	1.75	1	3-8	Postpone ratification article to take up August 28 report on commercial fairness among the states.	30	460
423	1.76 −1.47	1, 2	4-7	Ten states ratifying will be sufficient to institute the new government.	31	474
427	1.93	2	4-7	To encourage speed in appointment of ratifying conventions.	31	474
428	1.45	1	3-8	Gerry and Mason move to postpone the ratification article.	31	474
430	1.75	2	4-7	Postpone the section of the ratification article that calls for legislative selection of the President.	31	474
432	−1.34	2	8-3	To add "or oblige vessels bound for one state to enter another."	31	474
436	1.45	1	2-8	To adjourn.	Sept. 3	488
437	1.82	2	2-8	Legislators to be ineligible for offices created by the Legislature.	3	488
439	1.98	2	5-5	To add *created* before *during*.	3	488
440	1.62	2	5-4-1	To add "created or emoluments increased."	3	488

doned the Middle Atlantic coalition and rejoined its southern neighbors in the peripheral coalition to stop South Carolina from trading away the economic security of the region for the right to continue the importation of slave labor.

Pennsylvania, on the other hand, was wholly out of sympathy with this exchange of regional advantages between the northern and southern interests. Therefore, it did not follow Virginia in rejoining their former southern allies until that seamy business had been concluded on August 29. With the decks thus cleared of the divisive commerce and slavery questions, a new set of issues quickly arose that were infinitely more in line with the fundamental interests of Pennsylvania as a large state with western land reserves. As soon as the northern states secured approval of their right to set commercial policy by simple majority vote in the national Congress, Morris guided debate to the provision in the Committee of Detail report that dealt with conditions for the admission of new states into the union. This question, and a series of others like it that followed in quick succession, touched directly upon the very sensitive question of the role of the claiming states in the admission of new states into the union. Debate centered on the section that read, "'If the admission be consented to, the new States shall be admitted on the same terms with the original States'" (*Records*, vol. 2, p. 454). Morris moved to strike out that section, arguing that the legislature should not be bound to admit new states on an equal basis under all conditions. Nine states agreed with him. Having thus reduced the western territory to colonial status, a condition in which Morris had long contended that it should be held, he moved the following substitute for Article 17: "'New States may be admitted by the Legislature into this Union: but no new State shall be erected within the limits of any of the present States, without the consent of the Legislature of such State, as well as the Genl. Legislature'" (ibid., p. 455). No issue was more obviously capable of detaching Pennsylvania from the small states of the Middle Atlantic than this question of control over the unsettled lands in the West. Pennsylvania claimed vast stretches of this territory, while the small Middle Atlantic states held claim to almost none. Daniel Carroll of Maryland opened this confrontation by moving to strike out a provision requiring "'the consent of the State to its being divided'" (ibid., p. 461). Carroll argued that this was an absolutely fundamental point with those states that did not hold claims to extensive tracts of the western territory (Rakove, 1979, p. 352; Onuf, 1983, pp. 186–209).

Pennsylvania's James Wilson opposed Carroll's motion, arguing that "he knew of nothing that would give greater or juster alarm than the doctrine, that a political society is to be torn asunder without its own consent" (*Records*, vol. 2, p. 462). This argument struck the delegates from the smaller states as yet another brazen rejection of principle in favor of interest. Luther Martin said that "he wished Mr Wilson had thought a little sooner of the value of *political* bodies. In the beginning, when the rights of the small States were in question, they were phantoms, ideal beings. Now when the Great States were to be affected, political Societies were of a sacred nature" (ibid., p. 464). When the votes were counted, New Jersey, Delaware, and Maryland stood alone.

The small states, all of which had been fighting since the Revolution for national control of the western lands, immediately sensed the danger. Martin said nothing "would so alarm the limited States as to make the consent of the large States claiming the western lands, necessary to the establishment of new States within their limits" (*Records*, vol. 2, p. 455). A particularly troubling case, as Martin mentioned, was that of Vermont, whose territory had long been claimed by New York. Congress had already promised Vermont's early admission into the union. Would New York's consent now be necessary? When the vote was taken, the familiar alignment based on state size reappeared. The three large states of Massachusetts, Pennsylvania, and Virginia joined the Carolinas and Georgia to pass Morris' substitute proposal over the objections of the five smaller states of New Hampshire, Connecticut, New Jersey, Delaware, and Maryland. But the small states were viewing this matter from different perspectives. New Hampshire and Connect-icut tended to fasten their objections on the concrete case of Vermont. Johnson of Connecticut worried that "Vermont would be subjected to N-York," and Langdon said that "his objections were connected with the case of Vermont" (ibid., p. 456).

The small states of the middle Atlantic—New Jersey, Delaware, and Maryland—were not so wedded to Vermont in their thinking that it served as more than an example for them. With Dickinson, they argued the general point that had been stressed in similar situations since the Revolution. This argument stemmed from the clear "impropriety of requiring the small States to secure the large ones in their extensive claims of territory" (ibid.).

This difference in perspective was not one of mere detail and did not go unnoticed by Gouverneur Morris and his colleagues. Morris moved to solve the apparent problem of Vermont and thus to detach New Hampshire and Connecticut from the other small states by substituting in his proposal the word "jurisdiction" in place of the word "limits." Vermont was no longer under New York's jurisdiction since it had already been formed into a state. Only Delaware and Maryland opposed this solution. On seven of the fifteen votes taken on August 30, New

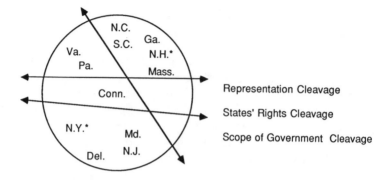

Figure 8.2. Comparison of cleavage structures between representation, empowerment, and the newly dominant states' rights issues.
*New York abandoned the Convention on July 11 at vote #132. New Hampshire did not arrive until July 23 at vote #203.

Jersey, Delaware, and Maryland were in the minority, either 8-3 or 9-2, when one of them wavered. Maryland also had the distinction of being beaten on an additional vote by 10-1, and on the next day, August 31, Maryland was beaten on four of the fifteen votes by either 9-1 or 10-1. Obviously, New Jersey and Delaware, along with Maryland in a particularly fundamental way, were isolated on the states' rights issues (see Figure 8.2). These issues dominated the Convention's debates until September 4.

Factor 1 of Table 8.1 displays the fundamental cleavage that dominated debate in late August and early September. The small central states of New Jersey, Delaware, and Maryland load negatively on the first factor, while the other eight states load positively. Maryland's −.81 shows her to have been in almost complete opposition to the direction in which the Convention's present majority wished to move. The fundamental cleavage that divided the states during this period dealt directly with the position of the states as independent political entities within the new nation.

The disposition of the western lands, now tied to the admission of new states by the Morris proposal, had been a stumbling block for the small Middle Atlantic states since the Revolution. Precisely New Jersey, Delaware, and Maryland had been the last three states to ratify the Articles of Confederation, largely because they were worried about the reluctance of the larger states to relinquish their claims to exclusive control of the vast western territories. Now, in the view of the small central states, the large states were again trying to monopolize the benefits to be derived from this tremendous resource. Carroll of

Maryland made this very point on August 30 when he sought to alter Morris' substitute proposal so that it would no longer require a state's consent for lands over which it claimed "jurisdiction" to be divided into new states. Madison recorded Carroll as warning his colleagues, given "our situation with regard to the Crown lands, and the sentiments of Maryland on that subject, that he perceived we should again be at sea, if no guard was provided for the right of the U. States to the back lands." Carroll closed by calling for a commitment of this issue to a committee of a member from each state, assuring the House that this was "a point of a most serious nature," which if it "be disregarded, he believed that all risks would be run by a considerable minority, sooner than give their concurrance" (*Records*, vol. 2, pp. 461–462). Carroll's colleagues were unimpressed by his warning. When the vote was taken, New Jersey, Delaware, and Maryland stood against the remaining eight states.

Martin then sought to postpone Morris' substitute article in order to take up an alternative reflecting the small state position. His motion proposed that "'the Legislature of the U-S- shall have power to erect New States within as well as without the territory claimed by the several States or either of them, and admit the same into the Union'" (*Records*, vol. 2, p. 464). This motion to postpone was defeated 3-8, with New Jersey, Delaware, and Maryland in the minority. Morris' substitute motion requiring the affected state to consent to any division of its territory was then approved by the same 8-3 margin. This action meant that the small states had been defeated on both the status of the new states that might be created out of the western lands (they would be unequal) and the position of the claiming states in that process (their approval would be necessary). These two decisions, viewed from the perspective of the small Middle Atlantic states, and of the northern states more generally, meant that the future course of national development would be decided by individual states, principally Virginia, or, even more ominously, by the South as a region. Next, the small states had to face a series of issues that went to the heart of the status and importance not of the western territories but of the very states for which they sat as representatives.

Article 18 of the Committee of Detail draft read, "'The United States shall guarantee to each State a Republican form of Government; and shall protect each State against foreign invasions, and, on the application of its Legislature, against domestic violence'" (*Records*, vol. 2, p. 466). This article explicitly outlined certain duties and responsibilities of the central government to the states. But some nationalist delegates were disturbed by the fact that the final clause left it up to the states to declare when they required national assistance to maintain the peace. Dickinson immediately sought to remove this state prerogative by striking out the phrase "'on the application of the Legislature,'" arguing that "he thought it of essential importance to the tranquility of the U-S. that they (the central government) should in all cases suppress domestic violence" (ibid., vol. 2, pp. 466–467). The small Middle Atlantic states split. New Jersey and Delaware were willing to see national troops suppress domestic violence wherever and whenever it might occur, while Maryland remained adamant about controlling the pretext under which national troops could enter the state. When the vote was taken, the nationalist delegations of New Jersey, Delaware, and Pennsylvania supported Dickinson's motion, while the localist majority from the other eight states opposed.

Although Maryland felt the security of a solid majority in this instance, it was to be short-lived. The nationalists then sought marginally to strengthen the federal hand by Dickinson's motion to add the phrase "'or Executive'" after "'application of its Legislature,'" citing the possibility that disturbances might make it impossible for the legislature to meet. The Convention's moderate majority agreed that such an instance might arise, and so they moved to deal with it. When Dickinson's motion passed 8-2-1, with Maryland's vote divided, Luther Martin, the strongest advocate of states' rights present in the Convention, sought to restrain the executive in his right to summon federal troops to cases "'in the recess of the Legislature.'" The vote was 1-9, with Maryland alone in favor, and when the final vote on the article as amended was taken, only Delaware and Maryland opposed (*Records*, vol. 2, p. 467).

After Articles 19 and 20 of the Committee of Detail draft had been agreed to with little opposition, Article 21 generated a sharp clash. Article 21 read, "'The ratifications of the Conventions of____States shall be sufficient for organizing this Constitution.'" The ominous question was: If not unanimity, if not the approval of every state, how many would it take to launch this new government? This clash demonstrated both the reasoning of those who were already tending toward opposition to the new Constitution and the growing impatience of the majority.

Wilson proposed that the ratification of seven states, a simple majority, be sufficient to put the new government under way. But the small states were hesitant to discuss ratification until they had been assured of equal treatment on a number of matters that still remained undecided. Recent developments had done little to convince the smaller states that their larger neighbors were particularly mindful of their interests. Therefore, Carroll of Maryland moved to postpone further consideration of the ratification article in order to take up a committee report of

August 28 that had been designed to alleviate small state fears that preferential treatment would be given to the ports of the larger commercial states. New Jersey, Delaware, and Maryland, again isolated 3-8, were unwilling to discuss ratification until they had been assured of evenhanded commercial treatment. The Convention's moderate majority would have no part of this delay in the main business. The majority could finally see themselves nearing the end of the Committee of Detail report after nearly a month. McHenry noted the impatience of his colleagues, observing that the mood of the delegates was "averse to taking anything up till this system is got through" (*Records*, vol. 2, p. 470).

With the small states pushed to one side, the majority returned to the main business of passing the ratification article. Sherman proposed ten, Randolph favored nine as "a respectable majority of the whole," Wilson mentioned eight as his earlier proposal of seven had generated little support, and Madison thought that either seven, eight, or nine was acceptable. Most of the delegates seemed to agree with Wilson that "we must . . . in this case go to the original powers of Society, The House on fire must be extinguished, without a scrupulous regard to ordinary rights." Virtually no one felt that his long labors should be subject to rejection by a single state. Rhode Island had refused even to participate, and Maryland was far out of step with the rest of the Convention, declaring unanimity to be "necessary to dissolve the existing confederacy which had been unanimously established" (*Records*, vol. 2, p. 469). Nonetheless, accepting a number less than thirteen left uncertain whether the new government would operate over all of the states once the requisite number had ratified or only over those that had actually confirmed the proposed document. King moved to add the words "'between the said States' so as to confine the operation of the Govt. to the States ratifying it" (ibid., p. 475). Only Maryland voted against this proposal. In the end, the number 9 was used to fill up the blank. The final vote found all in favor except Maryland.

Once the decision was made that nine states would be sufficient to institute the new government, the delicate question of how the proposed Constitution should pass through the lame duck Confederation Congress on the way to the states for ratification was taken up. Article 22 read, "'This Constitution shall be laid before the U-S. in Congs. assembled for their approbation; and it is the opinion of this Convention that it should be afterwards submitted to a Convention chosen (in each State) under the recommendation of its Legislature, in order to receive the ratification of such Convention'" (*Records*, vol. 2, p. 478).

G. Morris and Charles Pinckney immediately set to work revising the ratification article to facilitate the proposed Constitution's rapid passage through both the Confederation Congress and the state conventions. First, they moved to strike out "'for their approbation,'" so that the only responsibility of the Congress would be to pass the proposed Constitution on to the states. By this means, the Convention's majority sought to prevent the possibility that a jealous Congress would vacillate or even withhold approval. They were successful by a vote of 8-3, with only Massachusetts, Maryland, and Georgia opposed.

Next, Morris and Pinckney sought further to reduce the role of the state legislatures in the ratification process. But they did so in such a heavy handed way that they drew major opposition down upon themselves and convinced several of those leaning toward opposition that the work of the Convention was out of hand. Morris sought to encourage the state legislatures to call "'Conventions within the respective States as speedily as circumstances will permit.'" He argued quite explicitly that this change was necessary to insure passage of the new Constitution before the opposition had a chance to mobilize, reasoning that "when it first appears, with the sanction of this Convention, the people will be favorable to it. By degrees the State officers, & those interested in the State Govts will intrigue & turn the popular current against it" (ibid.).

Those delegates who had been concerned throughout the Convention's deliberations with fashioning a document that would be acceptable to the majority of the states and their citizens were clearly incensed by this approach. A large majority of the delegates felt that the Constitution could not only withstand but would thrive in the light of day, and that Morris' proposal was a mean spirited intrigue against a rational appraisal of the Convention's work. Another group, those who would ultimately refuse to sign the document, also took this opportunity to state their objections. Maryland's Luther Martin facetiously agreed with Morris "that the people would be agst. it," but not because of the schemes of local politicians; rather, because it was unworthy of them: "They would not ratify it unless hurried into it by surprise." Elbridge Gerry of Massachusetts spoke in support of Martin, representing the "system as full of vices." Virginia's George Mason declared himself fundamentally opposed to the Constitution, saying "that he would sooner chop off his right hand" than sign the document as it then stood. Mason said "he wished to see some points not yet decided brought to a decision. . . . Should these points be improperly settled, his wish would then be to bring the whole subject before another general Convention." Edmund Randolph, also of Virginia, looked with Mason to another convention, whose responsibility it would be to correct the shortcomings of this one. Randolph worried that "in case the final form of the Constitution should not permit him to accede to it, that the State Conventions should be at liberty to propose amendments to be submitted to another General Convention" (*Records*, vol. 2, pp. 478–479).

Though the delegates were unwilling to join Morris in pushing the state legislatures into unseemly haste, rejecting his proposal 7-4, they were equally unwilling to join Mason and Randolph in risking the exigencies of another convention. The matter was resolved when it was decided that the document would go to the Congress as a courtesy to the body that had called the Convention, rather than for its express approbation. The Congress would then forward the document to the state legislatures, which would call state ratifying conventions where the full and considered judgment of the people's representatives would be rendered on the Convention's work.

A very short debate then ensued on Article 23, the final section of the Committee of Detail report and the last needing action. Article 23 specified how the states were to communicate their ratifications to the Congress and how the waiting governmental machinery would be set in motion when the requisite nine ratifications had been achieved. The article concluded with the statement that "'the members of the Legislature should meet at the time and place assigned by Congress, and should, as soon as may be, after their meeting, choose the President of the United States, and proceed to execute this Constitution'" (*Records*, vol. 2, p. 480).

Article 23 was quickly approved up to the words "'by Congress,'" but the phrase "'choose the President of the United States and'" was struck out because the mode of executive selection remained undecided. With this vote, consideration of the Committee of Detail draft, under scrutiny since August 6, was virtually complete. All that remained was the perfunctory approval of the committee report of August 28, which barred preferential treatment of the ports of some states over those of other states. This point, which Maryland had sought to make a test of the motives of the larger states several days earlier, was now approved overwhelmingly.

With the Committee of Detail draft completed, Sherman proposed that one member from each state be appointed to a committee to consider "such parts of the Constitution as have been postponed, and such parts of Reports as have not been acted on" (*Records*, vol. 2, p. 481). What remained were the tough ones, the points upon which the Convention had so far been unable to achieve a satisfactory resolution. Once again, the Convention hoped that a carefully chosen committee would be able to reach a compromise around which support could be rallied on the floor. As every delegate understood, the central element in the solution to these remaining questions would revolve around the executive, that is his mode of selection, tenure, reeligibility, and powers.

It was eminently clear to the delegates from the smaller states that the Convention was once again slipping out of control and that dangerous consequences could result. If the large states effectively dominated the executive selection process and the vast resources represented by the unsettled lands in the west, their stature in the new system could only be enhanced, while that of the smaller states would just as certainly decline. With these concerns foremost in the minds of the delegates from the smaller states, a committee of one member from each state was appointed on August 31 to resolve the matters that still remained undecided. The Brearley Committee on postponed and undecided parts reported briefly on September 1, but it was not until September 4 and 5 that this committee delivered the main components of its complex and controversial compromise report to the full Convention. The compromise solutions arrived at by the Brearley committee and the coalitions that had formed within the committee and that emerged to enforce its proposals on the floor of the Convention are perhaps the least well understood and the most dramatic of the entire Convention. To their origins, operation, and impact we now turn.

CHAPTER 9

The Brearley Committee Report
and a New Northern Majority

The coalition pattern that pitted the five states of the periphery against the six states from the Middle Atlantic region organized the business of the Convention for the six weeks from mid-July to the end of August. During that time, it became obvious that both coalitions possessed an exploitable and ultimately debilitating weakness when confronting issues at the "lower level" of constitutional choice. The peripheral coalition was subject to disruption by explicitly regional concerns, while the coalition of Middle Atlantic states could be destroyed by questions that might once again separate the large states from the small. When the questions confronting the Convention derived from considerations at the "higher level" of constitutional choice (for example, How powerful and unrestrained should this new government be?), the localists of the periphery opposed the more cosmopolitan delegates from the Middle Atlantic states. Generally, the advantage went to the periphery because it was the more cohesive of the two coalitions. Nonetheless, it was quite clear that if questions arose that appealed not to philosophical dispositions but to interests based in region or state size, one or both coalitions might rapidly disintegrate. As we have seen, cleavages based on both region and state size were consciously and directly stimulated during the final week of August, and the results were predictably destructive.

Direct clashes during the final week of August over control of the western lands and influence over the process of executive selection, following so closely on the heels of the Commerce and Slave Trade Compromise, irrevocably split both coalitions, leaving the executive questions and several other matters to be turned over to the Brearley Committee on postponed parts, to which one delegate from each state was appointed on August 31. The Convention was "again at sea," as Maryland's Daniel Carroll described it. But, as had happened after the Connecticut Compromise five weeks earlier, new bargains were struck, and new working majorities were formed—this time within the Brearley Committee itself—that were to dominate the Convention's crucial last ten working days.

During the first week of September, while Connecticut, New Jersey, and Maryland struggled to maintain the integrity of the states in the new system, the Brearley Committee on postponed and undecided parts did its work, reporting its major proposals on September 4 and 5. Attention was immediately drawn to the provisions dealing with the executive, as these had proven to be among the most perplexing aspects of the new system. Precedents seemed to be totally lacking for the establishment of a Chief Magistrate who was both powerful enough to be effective and constrained enough to be responsible. Much of this perplexity arose not simply from thinking about the structure of the presidency itself, but about how the executive branch should relate to other parts of an integrated constitutional system. The solution proposed by the Brearley Committee report of September 4, particularly as it envisioned sharing several critical powers between the President and the Senate, provoked consternation in many delegates.

The Riddle of a Republican Executive Is Solved

The executive question once again became the Convention's full-time concern on September 4, when the Brearley Committee reported their newly formulated compromise solution. But the climate within the Convention was now very different from what it had been immediately following the Connecticut Compromise, when two evenly balanced coalitions (periphery vs. middle), aligned behind coherent solution packages (legislative selection vs. electoral selection), had confronted one another. Now a single coalition centering on the smaller northern states was clearly dominant on the executive question, and all that the scattered opposition could hope to accomplish was amendment of the new system's most objectionable aspects. Most of the members of the new majority of small and northern states had long preferred executive selection by specially chosen electors to legislative selection. The Brearley Committee report envisioned a return to electoral selection, but perhaps more importantly, the failure of any one candidate to achieve a majority of the electoral votes would result in the referral of the five leading candidates to the Senate (where the small states had an equal vote with the large states) for final selection. Further, treaties, as well as ambassadorial, Supreme Court, and other major administrative appointments, were to be made by the President only "with the advice and Consent of the Senate" (*Records*, vol. 2, p. 498). And finally, although the House would charge the President in impeachable offenses, the final disposition of these charges would occur in the Senate. These provisions gave the smaller states what many of the delegates feared would be too much direct control over the appointment, conduct in office, and removal of the President. Both the larger states and the deep South opposed these dramatic enhancements of senatorial authority. Madison explained that the compromise was between the small state men, who wanted to concentrate power in the Senate, where they held equal votes, and certain large state men (Madison had King and Morris in mind) who "wished a high mounted Govt," with a strong, aristocratic Senate, and who hoped to win support from other large state men (he mentioned Gerry and Mason) who "set great value" on control of money bills in the lower house (*Records*, vol. 2, p. 514).

As a member of the Brearley committee, Madison was in a good position to understand the elements that had gone into the compromise, but sharing his delegation's dissatisfaction with the report, he tended to exaggerate some aspects of the compromise and to ignore the most important, namely, the balance between the roles of the electors and of the Senate in the selection of the President. In this aspect of the compromise, the small states had gained such an advantage (as both they and their opponents thought) that they were willing not only to concede money bills to the House but also to transfer the initiative regarding appointments and treaties from the Senate to the President.

When the report concerning the executive was taken up, Charles Pinckney opposed the process for executive selection because "as the President's reappointment will thus depend on the Senate he will be the mere creature of that body" (*Records*, vol. 2, p. 511). Such a decisive influence over the process of executive selection posed the danger of a Senate-based aristocracy, a possibility that many were coming to apprehend as more ominous than the potential for monarchy that lurked in the presidency. Mason agreed with Pinckney that "considering the powers of the President & those of the Senate, if a coalition should be established between these two branches, they will be able to subvert the Constitution." These and other delegates shared Williamson's concern that the powers given to the Senate by the committee report "lays a certain foundation for corruption & aristocracy" (ibid., p. 512). Therefore, the remainder of the Convention's substantive debates centered on attempts by interests remaining outside the consensus of the dominant northern majority to reduce and control the influence of the Senate in the new system. Yet, as the Convention entered its final days, neither the large states nor the southern states were in a position to effectively oppose the Brearley Committee report and the determined phalanx of small Middle Atlantic and northeastern states that stood behind it.

Not since the small states had stood as one against the large state bid for proportional representation in both houses of the proposed Congress

TABLE 9.1.   Two-Factor Solution to 58^a Executive Votes among
Votes 442–569 Taken between September 4 and September 17,
Varimax Rotation (Ortho)

	1 Northern Majority	2 Large State Opposition	h^2
New Hampshire	(.76)	.47	.80
Massachusetts	(.77)	.27	.66
Connecticut	(.86)	.10	.74
New York	absent	absent	absent
New Jersey	(.80)	.15	.67
Pennsylvania	.24	(.77)	.65
Delaware	(.84)	.02	.70
Maryland	(.63)	.31	.50
Virginia	.13	(.84)	.72
North Carolina	−.19	.20	.08
South Carolina	.37	.40	.29
Georgia	(.76)	.09	.58
Sum of squares	4.50	1.89	6.39
% Total variance	40.91	17.18	58.09

^{a}Executive votes after September 4 were Nos. 445–495, 497–500, and 548.

had they been more united or more adamant than they were on the question of who would control the process for electing the Chief Executive. On this issue, the small states came out of the Brearley Committee no longer a defensively minded four-state minority of Connecticut, New Jersey, Delaware, and Maryland in uneasy collaboration with powerful Pennsylvania and Virginia, or as a group of small states isolated on states' rights issues, but as the core members of a solid seven-state majority, joined by their neighbors to the north, New Hampshire and Massachusetts, and by Georgia, which was the only southern state consistently to join the new northern majority. The smaller states had been radicalized by the large state attempt to control presidential selection by balloting jointly in the legislature, by their blatant attempt to maintain control of the western lands, and by their attempts to minimize the role of the states in the proposed system. Therefore, in direct response to these large state initiatives, the small states within the Brearley Committee determined irrevocably to maintain final control of the most important new office in this new government—the presidency. What is more, as Table 9.1 indicates, they had the power to do so.

Table 9.1 highlights the magnitude of the changes that occurred in the

TABLE 9.2.   Four-Factor Solution to 58 Executive Votes among
Votes 442–569 Taken between September 4 and September 17,
Varimax Rotation (Ortho)

	1 Northern Majority	2 Large-State Opposition	3 Southern Opposition	4	h^2
New Hampshire	(.72)	.40	.37	.12	.82
Massachusetts	(.82)	.31	.04	.05	.77
Connecticut	(.94)	.16	−.03	.02	.90
New York	absent	absent	absent	absent	absent
New Jersey	(.74)	.10	.35	−.04	.68
Pennsylvania	.15	(.80)	.27	−.19	.77
Delaware	(.78)	.02	.26	−.17	.70
Maryland	.46	.19	(.60)	−.11	.62
Virginia	.17	(.87)	.03	.11	.80
North Carolina	−.05	−.03	.03	(.98)	.96
South Carolina	.12	.14	(.85)	.10	.77
Georgia	(.64)	.02	.43	−.13	.61
Sum of squares	3.91	1.76	1.66	1.07	8.40
% Total variance	35.55	16.00	15.09	9.73	76.37

voting coalitions active in the Convention as a result of the decisions and compromises taken by the Brearley Committee. Factor 1, which now describes a new northern majority on the executive question, accounts for nearly 41% of the variance in this set of fifty-eight executive votes. Factor 2 provides an additional 17% variance explained by describing the vehement opposition of the large states of Pennsylvania and Virginia. Of almost equal interest is the voting behavior that this two-factor solution does not capture, that of the two Carolinas, neither of which load significantly on either factor. South Carolina splits its very modest loadings almost equally (.37 and .40) between the two factors. The loadings of North Carolina on both factors are even lower, and that state actually has the only negative loading on factor 1.

The four-factor solution in Table 9.2 not only clarifies the position of the Carolinas, but more generally, it highlights the dissolution of the South as a cohesive voting bloc on the executive issues. The three states of the deep South traditionally had been the hub of the old peripheral coalition, especially before New Hampshire's late arrival, while the isolated Massachusetts delegation wavered; now these states were dissociated, and no two participate on the same factor.

Factor 1 still describes nearly 36% of the total variance in the voting on this set of issues. Only Maryland and Georgia, which shared some of their southern neighbors' apprehension over a powerful Senate, had partially abandoned the first factor to participate with South Carolina on the third. Neither abandonment is total. Factor 2 is virtually unchanged. It is still made up of the large states of Pennsylvania and Virginia. The delegates from both states were adamant in their demand that final selection of the executive be moved from the Senate, where equality weakened the large states, to the House, where Pennsylvania and Virginia alone expected to hold nearly one-third of the seats. Factor 3 describes the behavior of South Carolina, which in the two-factor analysis was committed to neither group, but now loads at .85 on this factor with the partial support of Maryland and Georgia. Maryland still maintains a loading of .46 on factor 1, only slightly below the .50 loading that we have defined as the lower bound of coalition membership, while loading at .60 on factor 3. Georgia's strongest loading is still .64 on the first factor, but Georgia does join South Carolina and Maryland on the third factor with a loading of .43. The fourth factor describes the unremitting opposition of North Carolina to the likelihood of the Senate's ultimate selection of the Chief Executive. North Carolina loads on the fourth factor at .98, with no other state loading at more than .12.

The extent to which the South as a regional bloc of votes was broken as a force in the Convention—not only on the executive issue, but more generally on all issues during the final two weeks—is demonstrated by Table 9.3. Only Virginia, of the five states south of Delaware, maintained a consistent opposition to the small states of the new northern majority. In fact, Maryland and Georgia actually joined the small states to the north in writing federalism into the structure of the executive branch. Further, the South displayed no identifiable, coordinated set of positions on the remaining issues discussed during the Convention's final ten days. While the small northern states labored, over the vehement opposition of Pennsylvania and Virginia, to give the Constitution its final polish of moderate federalism, the states of the South seemed resigned to depart for home unsure whether their cup was half full or half empty, as indicated by the almost precisely balanced loadings of Maryland, South Carolina, and Georgia on the two factors of Table 9.3.

Even in the face of this new northern majority, a broadly acceptable solution to the complex package of executive issues was not immediately forthcoming. As the factor score list in Table 9.4 indicates, the executive issues were the nearly exclusive focus of discussion through the first week of September.

TABLE 9.3. Two-Factor Solution to Roll-Call Votes 442–569
Taken Between September 4 and September 17, Varimax Rotation (Ortho)

	1 Northern Majority	2 Large-State Opposition	h^2
New Hampshire	(.75)	.45	.76
Massachusetts	(.65)	.34	.54
Connecticut	(.79)	.14	.64
New York	absent	absent	absent
New Jersey	(.82)	.06	.67
Pennsylvania	.22	(.68)	.51
Delaware	(.75)	.07	.56
Maryland	.49	.47	.46
Virginia	−.00	(.85)	.72
North Carolina	.08	.46	.22
South Carolina	.42	.49	.42
Georgia	.49	.51	.50
Sum of squares	3.55	2.45	6.00
% Total variance	32.27	22.27	54.54

Resolving Problems Associated with Electoral Selection

Before the compromise engineered by the Brearley Committee, two major objections had been raised against the use of electors: that the most qualified persons would be unwilling to serve because it would entail a long journey to the seat of the national government for the sole purpose of balloting for President, and that, when thus assembled, the electors would be the objects of undesirable intrigues. Both of these objections were eliminated by the new idea of having the electors ballot in their home states.

This idea, however, gave additional weight to a third concern, that the electors would tend to vote for citizens of their own state and thus scatter their votes. This objection was overcome, in part, by the idea that they should vote for two candidates, one of whom could not be from the elector's home state. Thus was born the vice-presidency. With these three objections removed, an electoral system became more available as an alternative to legislative election.

The Brearley Committee did not stop with merely proposing a

TABLE 9.4.   Twenty-Nine Critical Votes Taken during the Convention's Closing Days, between Roll-Call Votes 442 and 569, September 4–17, as Identified by Factor Scores of 1.25 on Either Factor or 1.0 on Both Factors of the Two-Factor Solution in Table 9.3

Vote No.	Factor Score	Factor No.	Voting Split	Issue	Date, Sept.	*Records,* v.2, p.
447	1.33	1	3-7-1	To strike out 'Senate' and put in 'Legislature' for final selection of the executive.	5	508
451	1.63	1	4-7	Madison moves to insert after 'delegates,' the phrase 'who shall have balloted.'	5	508
461	−1.90 1.32	1, 2	8-3	Candidate with highest electoral vote to win 'provided that number be a majority.'	6	520
462	1.36 −1.09	1, 2	5-6	Majority of the electors appointed 'and who shall have given their votes.'	6	520
468	−1.54	2	8-3	Election to be on the same day throughout the U.S.	6	520
469	−1.30	2	8-3	House of Representatives to elect (rather than the Senate) in the absence of an electoral vote majority.	6	520
484	−1.30	2	8-3	To strike 'except treaties of peace' from the clause requiring a two-thirds vote.	8	546
487	−1.35	2	5-6	To require a majority of all of the members of the Senate to make a treaty.	8	546
488	1.24 −1.01	1, 2	5-6	Two-thirds of the Senate must be present to pass a treaty.	8	546
499	1.38	2	3-8	The legislature shall have the sole right to establish offices not herein provided for.	8	546

TABLE 9.4.   (*Continued*)

Vote No.	Factor Score	Factor No.	Voting Split	Issue	Date, Sept.	*Records,* v.2, p.
500	−1.29 −1.21	1, 2	7-4	President may convene both houses or either house for extra sessions.	8	546
513	−1.45	2	7-3	To amend restriction on states' taxing exports to allow duties to defray inspection costs.	12	583
518	1.92	2	3-8	To strike out 'and direct taxes' from Art. 1, Sec. 2.	13	606
519	1.44	1	3-8	President to return bills to Congress within ten days	13	606
528	1.32	1	4-7	Issue unrecorded.	14	611
531	−1.37	1	8-3	To strike out Congress may by 'joint ballot' appoint a treasurer.	14	611
533	−1.09 1.49	1, 2	6-5	To strike 'punish' before 'offenses against the law of nations' to allow the U.S. both to 'define and punish' such offenses.	14	611
534	1.47	1	3-8	To grant letters for the incorporation of canals.	14	611
535	1.40	1	4-6-1	To establish a university.	14	611
536	1.28	1	2-9	To denounce though not disallow standing armies in peacetime.	14	611
546	1.56	1	3-7-1	To strike out 'all such laws shall be subject to the revision and control of the Congress' from the state prohibition on taxing imports and exports.	15	622
547	−1.52 1.55	1, 2	6-4-1	'That no state shall lay any duty on tonnage without the consent of Congress.'	15	622

TABLE 9.4.   (*Continued*)

Vote No.	Factor Score	Factor No.	Voting Split	Issue	Date, Sept.	*Records,* v.2, p.
548	−1.33	2	7-4	The President 'shall not receive any other emolument from the U.S. or any of them.'	15	622
555	1.80	2	2-9	Issue unrecorded.	15	622
556	2.04	2	3-7-1	To strike 'three-quarters' from the clause on the ratification of amendments.	15	622
558	2.42	2	3-8	'No state shall without its consent be effected in its internal police or deprived of its equal suffrage in the Senate.'	15	622
559	2.31	2	2-8-1	To strike out the amending article altogether.	15	622
562	1.53	2	6-3-1	Issue unrecorded.	15	622
563	1.25	1	3-7	That no navigation acts be passed before 1808 unless by two-thirds vote of both houses.	15	622

method for selecting the President; its plan included a well-understood distribution among the states of control over the two phases of executive selection: nomination and final election. The small state men on the Brearley Committee believed that, even with the new plan of electors voting for two candidates, the votes would still be scattered and would rarely result in majority support for anyone. But even if no one was expected to attract a majority, candidates from the large states could be expected to get more votes, giving those states an advantage in the first round of the process. This indicated the need for a second round, in the interest of majority election, and in this round, the advantage of the large states needed to be balanced. How better to achieve this balance than to entrust final election to the Senate, where all states exercised an equal vote? Many of the large state men agreed with their small state colleagues that the first round of the process would seldom be determinative. And as several of the more obvious objections to the use of an electoral system had already been corrected, the delegates increasingly focused their attention on improving the position of their own states and those similarly circumstanced, rather than on further analyzing the implications of a state oriented electoral system. Substantive consideration of the merit and purpose of a selection system characterized by electors gave way to unabashed competition at the "lower level" of constitutional choice for control of the process itself (Thach, 1923, p. viii).

It is clear from the debates of September 4 and 5 that this distinction between the nomination and the election of the President, as well as its implications for control, was well understood. Madison feared that "the attention of the electors would be turned too much to making candidates." In that case, "the election would in fact be consigned to the Senate altogether," and "the nomination of the candidates to the largest States" (*Records*, vol. 2, p. 500). Gouverneur Morris "concurred in, and enforced" Madison's remarks, and similar statements were made by Pinckney, Sherman, King, and Hamilton, while Mason estimated that "nineteen times in twenty," the choice would fall to the Senate (ibid., pp. 500, 501, 512, 514, 525).

Others were not so sure of this. Baldwin thought that "important characters" would, in time, be "less & less unknown; and the Senate would consequently be less & less likely to have the eventual appointment thrown into their hands" (*Records*, vol. 2, p. 501). Morris and Wilson professed similar expectations, while Madison, Mason, and Williamson adopted the practical defensive tactic of putting forward a series of amendments designed to reduce the probability that the electors would fail to elect (ibid., pp. 501, 512, 514–515). Yet the fact that they could rally only four or fewer votes for any of these amendments points clearly to the determination of the northern majority, with its small state core, that the election would normally take place in the Senate.

Sherman, very early in the discussion, sought explicitly to keep the small state demand for control of the process before the Convention by reminding "the opponents of the new mode proposed that if the Small States had the advantage in the Senate's deciding among the five highest candidates, the Large States would have in fact the nomination of these candidates" (*Records*, vol. 2, pp. 512–513). The problem for those in opposition was obviously one of convincing the northern majority, with its overwhelming voting advantage and its patent stake in maintaining Senate authority, that there was real danger in failing to prevent an undue concentration of power in a branch of government so naturally disposed to aristocracy. But as long as the small states saw the Senate as the only mechanism by which they could retain control of the presidential selection process, to tamper with that mechanism was out of the question. Even in the face of an increasingly general reaction against the Senate as an invitation to aristocracy, it was not possible to reach an agreement until a solution was found that preserved small state control without involving the Senate.

The great fear of many delegates was that the powers added to the Senate in order to enhance the influence of the small states in the new government had, at least potentially, set the stage for aristocracy. Much of September 5 was taken up by the expression of such fears and by the search for ways to alleviate them without reducing the influence of the smaller states over the process of executive selection. Mason feared that "considering the powers of the President & . . . the Senate, if a coalition should be established between these two branches, they will be able to subvert the Constitution" (*Records*, vol. 2, p. 512). Randolph's comments "dwelt on the tendency of such an influence in the Senate over the election of the President in addition to its other powers, to convert that body into a real & dangerous Aristocracy" (ibid., p. 513).

Several attempts to remove final selection from the Senate were made without success until Gerry suggested on September 6 that, at least in the case of an incumbent President's failing to receive a majority of the electoral votes, the "eventual election should be made by the Legislature—This he said would relieve the President from his particular dependence on the Senate for his continuance in office." Many delegates, from both North and South, favored this partial move away from the Senate as a judicious attempt to prevent the possibility that a domineering aristocracy would develop in that body. However, even though King declared himself in favor of "the idea, as calculated to satisfy particular members & promote unanimity," Williamson "espoused it as a reasonable precaution against the undue influence of the Senate," and Gouverneur Morris thought "it would free the President from being tempted . . . to Conform to the will of the Senate," the question was never brought to a vote. It was understood that the northern majority would not give up its trump card without compensation (*Records*, vol. 2, p. 522). Alexander Hamilton, who "had been restrained from entering into the discussions by his dislike of the Scheme of Govt in General," also spoke in favor of change in the executive selection mechanism. He agreed with those delegates who thought that no candidate would achieve a majority and that the Senate would, therefore, select the President on most occasions. Hamilton argued that "Considering the different views of different States, & the different districts Northern Middle & Southern, he concurred with those who thought that the votes would not be concentered, and that the appointment would consequently in the present mode devolve on the Senate" (ibid., pp. 524–525). Even though a growing number of northern and Middle Atlantic state delegates were coming to share the southern concern over an aristocratic Senate, no electoral mode was apparent in which they could maintain final control of the process and, at the same time, obviate the increasingly general perception that the Senate was threatening to overbalance the system.

Three things were obvious to every member of the Convention: first, that the voting advantage of the Northern majority, as shown on factor 1 of Table 9.1 could not be overcome; second, that they were demanding final control of the process; and third, that the opposition—southern even more than large states—was adamant that this power not be housed in the Senate. All major groups were immediately relieved of their principal concerns when Williamson suggested that instead of the Senate, "this choice should be made by the Legislature, voting *by states* and not *per capita*." To simplify matters, Sherman suggested that the Senate be dropped, leaving final selection to the House of Representatives voting by states, a proposal that passed over the opposition of only Delaware (*Records*, vol. 2, p. 527). The small states of the new northern majority believed that they had gained what they most wanted, final control over the process of executive selection, while the opposition believed that they had avoided what they most feared, a major addition to the power of an already potentially aristocratic Senate. With adjournment now in sight, everyone was, if not wholly satisfied, at least resigned.

Other Major Issues in the Brearley Committee Report

The Brearley Committee resolved a number of questions beyond the process of executive selection. Charles Warren noted that "the Report of the Special Committee of September 4 . . . disposed of four of the great questions which had divided the Convention—the election of the President, the power of appointment, the treaty-making power, and the power of trial of impeachment—and had settled each by compromises which in their final result were favorable to Senatorial authority" (Warren, 1928, p. 664). Over each element of this formidable list of powers, the coalitions that confronted one another during the Convention's final days did battle.

On September 6, the day that the responsibility for the final selection of the President in the event that no candidate achieved a majority in the

Electoral College was moved from the Senate to the House of Representatives voting by states, James Wilson raised serious questions concerning the other powers that the Brearley Committee had assigned to the Senate. He indicated that "he thought the new mode of appointing the President, with some amendments, a valuable improvement; but he could never agree to purchase it at the price of the ensuing parts of the Report" (*Records*, vol. 2, p. 523). The remaining battles of the Convention were fought over precisely these "ensuing parts of the Report." Both the large state and the southern factions, on factors 2, 3, and 4 of Table 9.2, consistently attempted to modify provisions of the Brearley Committee report by removing powers from the Senate where possible, while the northern majority, on factor 1 of Table 9.2, sought to defend and maintain the advantages that they had written into the Committee report.

The provisions of the nine-part report that most concerned the large state and southern recalcitrants were the following. *Sections 3 and 9 on impeachment:* "The Senate of the U-S-shall have power to try all impeachments." Particularly disturbing was that the President himself, the chief executive officer of the federal government, "shall be removed from his office on impeachment by the House of Representatives, and conviction by the Senate." *Section 6 on the role of the Vice President:* "The vice-president shall be ex officio President of the Senate." *Section 7 on treaties and appointments:* "The President by and with the advice and Consent of the Senate, shall have power to make Treaties; and he shall nominate and by and with the advice and consent of the Senate shall appoint ambassadors, and other public Ministers, Judges of the Supreme Court, and all other officers of the U-S-, whose appointments are not otherwise herein provided for" (*Records*, vol. 2, pp. 497–499). Factor score Table 9.4 above indicates how thoroughly these "ensuing parts of the Report" dominated the Convention's attention once the issue of executive selection was resolved.

Many of these questions were decided amid much clamorous debate but with little real change as the northern majority held its ground against opposition from both the large states and the South. In a very real sense, the tables had been completely turned on the original proponents of the Virginia Plan. Initially, the Convention had feared the House of Representatives as the "vortex" into which all power might inevitably slip unless great care was taken. But events had taken such a turn that the large states, particularly Pennsylvania, Virginia, and the Carolinas, now feared that the Senate as constituted in the report before the Convention might soon incorporate all of the authority and functions of the new government. Their goal was to weaken the Senate in favor of institutions, most obviously the House, in which they were more favorably situated. The source and extent of their frustration in this endeavor is graphically reflected in Figure 2.3, the summary description of coalition alignment and realignment in the Convention, as these four states were isolated, Pennsylvania and Virginia fundamentally so, against the dominant northern majority and its small state core.

The Appointing Power

The first clash between these coalitions over the "ensuing parts of the Report" came on September 7 over the Senate's role in the appointment process. The President was to nominate and appoint ambassadors and other high government officials with the advice and consent of the Senate. Wilson immediately "objected to the mode of appointing, as blending a branch of the Legislature with the Executive" (*Records*, vol. 2, p. 538). Gouverneur Morris and King, both of whom had been members of the Brearley committee and had worked with the small state members to increase the authority of the Senate and of the national government generally, moved to the defense of this aspect of the report. Morris argued that the new plan would provide both responsibility and security, whereas "Congress now make(s) appointments there is no responsibility." On the entire clause—"'He shall nominate & by & with the advice and consent of the Senate, shall appoint ambassadors, and other public ministers (and Consuls) Judges of the supreme Court'"—the concerns and reservations of Wilson and Pinckney were overridden without formal vote. On the clause immediately following—"'And all other officers of U. S-'"— the Convention took the time formally to defeat Pennsylvania and South Carolina by a recorded vote of 9-2 (*Records*, vol. 2, p. 539).

The Treaty Power

The question of appointments by the President with the "advice and consent" of the Senate concerned and irritated the large states, especially Pennsylvania, but they did not interpret the issue as being vital to their interests. However, as debate began on September 8, a question that involved southern security was directly confronted. On the question of the treaty making power, the shattered bloc of southern votes, which Table 9.2 shows to be distributed across three factors, temporarily reunited. The South was extremely sensitive to the treaty power because violent battles in the Confederation Congress had recently centered on John Jay's 1786 negotiations with the Spanish in which closure of the

Mississippi River, a move that the South saw as purposely and devastatingly detrimental to its interests, played a prominent part (Davis, 1977, p. 109; Rakove, 1979, pp. 349–350). In eleven roll-call votes, each showing a straight North–South division, the northern majority in the Confederation Congress had shown its disposition to ignore and override strong southern views on this issue.

Now, in the Convention, a solid South rallied to defend its common regional interests in an ability to block objectionable treaties. Rutledge moved on behalf of an apprehensive South that "'no Treaty be made without the consent of two thirds of all the members of the Senate.'" The last clause of section seven of the committee report had read, "'consent of two-thirds of the members present.'" The South hoped by passage of this amendment to make approval more difficult, but the Carolinas and Georgia were defeated, 3-8. In light of the fact that only two-thirds of the members present were to be required to approve a treaty, Madison sought to insure against the possibility that a treaty would be hastily approved in the absence, planned or coincidental, of objecting senators. Madison moved "that a Quorum of the Senate," to conduct any business, "consist of two-thirds of all the members" (*Records*, vol. 2, p. 549). He was apparently hoping that in an extreme event a boycott by southern senators could deprive that body of a legal quorum, thereby stopping action on a treaty to which they strongly objected. The vote was very close, as the five southern states from Maryland to Georgia stood against the six northern states from New Hampshire to Delaware. If a treaty could pass by a vote of two-thirds of the members present, and if consideration of a treaty could not be stopped by depriving the Senate of a two-thirds quorum, the South asked that at the very least, "no Treaty shd. be made witht. previous notice to the members, & a reasonable time for their attending" (ibid., pp. 549–550). The northern majority again denied the Carolinas and Georgia, 8-3. After all of the noise created by the South's attempt to decrease the Senate's control over the treaty approval process, the committee report of September 4 was approved 8-3.

The Impeachment Power

With the questions of Senate participation in appointments and in the treaty making power settled in favor of the Brearley Committee report and the northern majority that had written it, a related question, that of the Senate's position as trial court in the impeachment process, came up for discussion. Three quick votes again demonstrate the stance being taken toward the ascendancy of the Senate by contending groups in the Convention. On the impeachment questions, as on those discussed above, Pennsylvania and Virginia sought to modify the Senate's new powers, while the northern majority, particularly its small state core, sought to maintain and even to build upon them.

Madison "objected to a trial of the President by the Senate" as rendering "The President . . . improperly dependent." G. Morris defended the committee report by arguing that he "thought no other tribunal than the Senate could be trusted," while "Pinckney disapproved of making the Senate the Court of Impeachments, as rendering the President too dependent on the Legislature" (*Records*, vol. 2, p. 551). On Madison's motion that "by the Senate" be struck out of the impeachment clause, the vote was 9-2 against. Only Pennsylvania and Virginia, the very large states on factor 2 of Table 9.2, were prepared to remove this authority from the Senate. On the clause as amended to read "'conviction by the Senate, for Treason, bribery, or other high crimes & misdemeanors against the United States,'" the vote was 10-1, with Pennsylvania remaining unalterably opposed (ibid., p. 552).

The decisions taken on these "ensuing parts of the Report" are important because they show the new northern majority to be active not just on the highly visible executive selection issue but on a whole series of secondary issues as well. Each incremental contribution to an increased senatorial authority also increased the sense on the part of the smaller states that they were well placed to defend themselves in the new system. They would not only have an equal vote in the Senate as a result of the Connecticut Compromise, but that vote would now be exercised across a broad range of issues of content and consequence: appointment of the President in the event that the electoral process was not definitive; advice and consent responsibility on the appointment of all major officials, ambassadors, and judges; trial of all impeachments; and the amendment of money bills. In defense of these powers, the northerners successfully resisted demands for change on the part of both the large state and the southern minorities, while restraining their own more zealous members when these members sought to extend these authorities beyond the carefully negotiated Brearley Committee report.

These issues decided, the Convention appointed a committee of five—Johnson, Hamilton, G. Morris, Madison, and King—"to revise the stile of and arrange the articles which had been agreed to by the House" (*Records*, vol. 2, p. 553). Only a few minor points remained to be decided before the Convention could turn the results of four months of intense deliberations over to these five men so that the draft document could receive its final organization and polish. September 10 saw the treatment of most of these remaining issues, particularly those dealing with the amendment and ratification procedures. This accomplished, all of the provisions adopted thus far were consigned to the Committee on Style, along with an instruction that they "'prepare an address to the people, to accompany the present Constitution, and to be laid with the same before the U—States in Congress'" (ibid., p. 564). The Committee on Style took only two days to do its work, reporting back to the Convention on September 12. The Committee report was ordered reproduced for distribution to the delegates, and the remainder of the day was given to its close examination and analysis.

The Northern Majority Stands Its Ground

Madison reported that on September 13, "The Report of the Committee of stile and arrangement, was taken up, in order to be compared with the articles of the plan as agreed to by the House & referred to the Committee and to receive the final corrections and sanction of the Convention," but little of note was accomplished on this day. September 14 and 15 saw the continuation and completion of the Convention's consideration and amendment of the Committee of Style report. With the Convention nearing the end of its task, the votes were taken rapidly and often with very limited debate. Complicating the analysis of these last few days is the fact that the subject of many of the votes was not even listed by Madison or by the *Journal*. In an editorial footnote to the votes of September 12, Farrand notes that "from this point on the records of the Journal are more unsatisfactory than ever, and it is impossible to reach any satisfactory conclusion with regard to the various questions and votes" (*Records*, vol. 2, p. 582).

This problem is most acute for September 14 and 15, when the votes were coming quickly and, in many cases, on very minor points. On only two of the first eight roll-calls taken on September 14 can the issue be identified. Nonetheless, on the major issues on which controversy and conflict still centered, the *Journal* seems to be substantially complete. The issue content is identified for eight of the next nine votes, and five of these are highlighted in factor score table 9.4 above. In each case, the large states, often with southern support, sought to add particular powers to the Congress or to defend powers that the smaller states wanted to remove. In no instance did the northern majority allow the desired change or fail to remove a power to which it objected.

In the first case, a motion was made to strike out the clause stating that the Congress "'may by joint ballot appointed a Treasurer.'" Rutledge wanted the treasurer to "be appointed in the same manner with other officers." This of course meant nomination by the President with the advice and consent of the Senate. The large state men reacted immediately. Retention of appointment by "joint ballot" would favor them just as it would have in the earlier cases of legislative representation and presidential selection. Gorham and King, both of Massachusetts, argued that this "would have a mischievous tendency. The people are accustomed & attached to that mode of appointing Treasurers, and the innovation will multiply objections to the System" (*Records*, vol. 2, p. 614). Morris supported these arguments, but when the vote was recorded, the three largest states—Massachusetts, Pennsylvania, and Virginia—whose authority would be most enhanced by a "joint ballot" selection, stood alone against the remaining eight.

That the large states on factor 2 of Table 9.2, even at this late date, still hoped to add new powers to the central government is clearly demonstrated by the debate over Franklin's motion to add after "post roads" in Section 8 of Article 1 the rather limited additional authority "to provide for cutting canals where deemed necessary." Wilson seconded the motion, but Sherman spoke against it, and it probably would have been rejected on its merits even if Madison had not "suggested an enlargement of the motion into a power 'to grant charters of incorporation where the interest of the U. S. might require & the legislative provisions of individual States may be incompetent'" (*Records*, vol. 2, p. 615). Madison claimed that "his primary object" in proposing this expansion was merely "to secure an easy communication between the States," but other delegates, King in particular, saw a legislative Pandora's box in this motion (ibid.). King was concerned that "the States will be prejudiced and divided into parties by it—In Philada. & New York, It will be referred to the establishment of a Bank. . . . In other places it will be referred to mercantile monopolies" (ibid., p. 616). Wilson sought to minimize the importance of King's concerns, but Mason expressed the sentiments of a majority when he said that "he was afraid of monopolies of every sort" and wished to see the vote taken, not on Madison's expanded motion, but on the single case of canals (ibid.). Even this single case was rejected 3-8, with only Pennsylvania, Virginia, and Georgia in favor.

A similar fate awaited the large state and southern minorities when they joined to support Madison's and Pinckney's motion to add "in the list of powers vested in Congress a power—'to establish an University, in which no preferences or distinctions should be allowed on account of religion.'" Morris merely observed that the power was "not necessary. The exclusive power at the Seat of Government, will reach the object," and when the vote was taken, the large states of Pennsylvania and Virginia shared the 7-4 defeat with the southern states of North and South Carolina (*Records*, vol. 2, p. 616).

September 15 was the last day of significant debate in the Convention. Fully 26 roll calls occurred on that day, more than on any other single day in the Convention, and nine of them are identified by high factor scores as being central to the conflicts still unresolved in these final days. On two of these nine votes, the issue goes unidentified, while three of them center on the South's continuing anxiety over northern control of commercial regulation, and two others deal with the small states' demand that their equal suffrage in the Senate not be subject to amendment. These were obviously issues that had been critical to these groups since the Convention's opening day, and they were, on this last day of substantive debate, still unwilling to let them go without one last effort at a satisfactory resolution. Predictably, given the balance of forces existing in the Convention during its final days, the small states succeeded in getting their changes into the document, while the South failed to get its.

Early on September 15, the South moved to reduce national control over the regulation of commerce. Article 1, section 10, paragraph 2, read "'No State shall, without the consent of Congress, lay any imposts or duties on imports or exports, except what may be absolutely necessary for executing its Inspection laws; and the nett produce of all duties and imposts, laid by any State on imports or exports, shall be for the use of the Treasury of the U-S-; and all such laws shall be subject to the revision and controul of the Congress'" (*Records*, vol. 2, p. 624). The South no longer even tried to object to the requirement that Congress must consent to imposts and duties laid by the states, or even to the further requirement that all monies generated above those needed "for executing its Inspection laws" should go into the national coffers. They simply sought to strike out as unduly meddlesome the last clause, that "all such laws shall be subject to the revision and controul of the Congress." Without debate, the motion was rejected 3-7-1. The southern states of Virginia, North Carolina, and Georgia voted for the motion, the Pennsylvania vote was divided, and South Carolina again joined the six northern states to insure their control of all commercial regulation.

McHenry, Mason, and Carroll then sought to address a related question that had particular relevance to their Chesapeake Bay region. The Maryland delegates moved that "no State shall be restrained from laying duties on tonnage for the purpose of clearing harbours and erecting light houses." Morris sought to assure them that "the States are not restrained from laying tonnage as the Constitution now Stands," but Madison was not so sure, arguing that "whether the states are now restrained . . . depends on the extent of the power 'to regulate commerce.' These terms are vague but seem to exclude this power of the

States." As far as New Hampshire's Langdon was concerned, there was no doubt "that the regulation of tonnage was an essential part of the regulation of trade, and that the States ought to have nothing to do with it." To clarify this point in the mind of anyone who still harbored doubts, Langdon proposed a countermotion to that of McHenry and Carroll that bluntly stated "'that no State shall lay any duty on tonnage without the Consent of Congress'" (*Records*, vol. 2, p. 625). The large states and the South joined to oppose this restriction, Pennsylvania, Virginia, North Carolina, and Georgia voting no, but South Carolina again joined five northern states to defeat her southern neighbors on still another question concerning the South's control of its own commercial destiny.

That the South could make no headway against the northern majority on an issue as critical to them as commercial regulation is striking, but matters were quite different when the small states wanted an additional increment of security to be written into the document for their benefit. Sherman "moved . . . to annex to the end of the (Amending) article a further proviso 'that no State shall without its consent be affected in its internal police, or deprived of its equal suffrage in the Senate.'" Madison warned his colleagues that if they "begin with these special provisos, . . . every State will insist on them" (*Records*, vol. 2, p. 630). Many were apparently convinced because when the vote was taken the three small states of Connecticut, New Jersey, and Delaware were in the uncommon position of being isolated 3-8. Instead of accepting this judgment of the Convention, the small states moved boldly to strike out the entire amending clause. The message was clear: If it is to be possible to amend away our equal vote in the Senate, we will have no amendments whatever to this new Constitution. The small states were not successful in this measure; only Connecticut and New Jersey actually voted to strike out Article 5, with Delaware's vote divided, but their opponents got the message. G. Morris quickly proposed that the small states be given the added security of knowing that "'no State, without its consent shall be deprived of its equal suffrage in the Senate'" (ibid., p. 631).

Mason was emboldened by the small state success to again express his "discontent at the power given to Congress by a bare majority to pass navigation acts." Mason moved "a further proviso (to the amending article) 'that no law in nature of a navigation act be passed before the year 1808, without the consent of two-thirds of each branch of the Legislature'" (ibid.). The South was again denied, 3-8. With North Carolina absent from the floor, South Carolina joined the six northern states from New Hampshire to Delaware in turning back Maryland, Virginia, and Georgia.

Immediately following this vote, Randolph, Mason, and Gerry, the only delegates who remained to adjournment yet refused to sign the document, presented their objections for a final time. Randolph expressed "the pain he felt at differing from the body of the Convention, on the close of the great & awful subject of their labors, and anxiously wishing for some accommodating expedient which would relieve him from his embarrassments." To relieve himself of these embarrassments, Randolph proposed "'that amendments to the plan might be offered by the State Conventions, which should be submitted to and finally decided on by another general Convention'" (ibid.). Failing this, he would be unable to sign the proposed Constitution, although he indicated that this did not finally determine him to oppose it in Virginia. He simply wanted all options left open to "his final judgement."

Mason followed Randolph in these final declarations of opposition, presenting his belief that the Constitution "would end either in monarchy, or a tyrannical aristocracy; which, he was in doubt, but one or other, he was sure." Gerry agreed with them both, and after enumerating several specific objections, he joined them in calling "for a second general Convention" (*Records*, vol. 2, pp. 623–633).

Madison's record of the Convention's response to these declarations of irreconcilable opposition on the part of distinguished members is as eloquent as it is sparse:

> On the question on the proposition of Mr Randolph.
> All the States answered—no
> On the question to agree to the Constitution. as amended.
> All the States ay.
> The Constitution was then ordered to be engrossed. (*Records*, vol. 2, p. 633)

The Signing

The delegates came together one final time, on Monday, September 17, not to debate, discuss, and contend any further, but to urge their few wavering colleagues of the benefits of unanimity and to put their signatures to the final document. Franklin, the oldest and most venerable member of the Convention, undertook the task of urging unanimity in a prepared speech read for him by Wilson. Franklin urged that "there are several parts of this Constitution which I do not at present approve, but I am not sure I shall never approve them. . . . Thus I consent, Sir, to this Constitution because I expect no better, and because I am not sure, that it is not the best. The opinions I have had of its errors, I sacrifice to the public good. . . . I cannot help expressing a wish that every member of the Convention who may still have objections to it, would with me, on this occasion doubt a little of his own infallibility—

and to make manifest our unanimity, put his name on this instrument" (*Records*, vol. 2, pp. 641–643).

To facilitate the signing of some undecided members, Franklin suggested a form provided by Gouverneur Morris and "put into the hands of Docr. Franklin that it might have a better chance of success." It read, "'Done in Convention, by the unanimous consent of *the States* present the 17th. of Sepr. &c—In Witness whereof we have hereunto subscribed our names'" (*Records*, vol. 2, p. 643). The suggestion was that members who still had serious reservations could sign by way of witnessing the fact that the states, and not necessarily they as individuals, had unanimously approved the Constitution. This minor subterfuge made little difference to most of the delegates. Randolph, Gerry, and Mason still refused to sign. Only Blount of North Carolina claimed that "he was relieved by the form proposed and would without committing himself attest to the fact that the plan was the unanimous act of the States in Convention" (ibid., p. 646).

But even at this late date, with the mode of signing already approved, one substantive issue still bothered several of the delegates, including many who were well disposed toward the plan and fully prepared to sign: "Gorham said if it was not too late he could wish, for the purpose of lessening objections to the Constitution, that the clause declaring 'the number of Representatives shall not exceed one for every forty thousand-' which had produced so much discussion, might be yet reconsidered, in order to strike out 40,000 & insert 'thirty thousand'" (*Records*, vol. 2, pp. 643–644). King and Carroll immediately seconded Gorham's motion, but this same general proposal had been made twice in recent days and had been defeated both times by identical 6-5 votes.

On both September 8 and 14, Williamson had moved to reconsider "the clause relating to the number of the House of Representatives . . . for the purpose of increasing the number." The intention behind increasing the size of the House was to give it a more broadly popular and representative quality. On both the eighth and the fourteenth, remnants of the conservative peripheral alignment reappeared to strike it down. On both occasions, New Hampshire, Massachusetts, Connecticut, and New Jersey, in the North, joined with South Carolina and Georgia to defeat a contiguous block of Middle Atlantic states ranging from Pennsylvania to North Carolina. A similar outcome might have been expected on this third occasion, but the unprecedented and magisterial intervention of Washington decided the matter otherwise in a surprising demonstration of the awe in which the delegates still held this man after some four months of close daily association.

When Washington "rose, for the purpose of putting the question, he

said that although his situation (presiding officer) had hitherto restrained him from offering his sentiments . . . he could not forbear
expressing his wish that the alteration proposed might take place. . . . he
thought this of so much consequence that it would give much satisfaction
to see it adopted." Madison records that after Washington's expression
of his sentiments on this point, the delegates unanimously gave him this
satisfaction: "No opposition was made to the proposition of Mr. Gorham
and it was agreed to unanimously" (*Records*, vol. 2, p. 644).

With this last substantive decision taken, "the members then proceeded to sign the instrument" (the United States Constitution is
reproduced in Appendix E). The Convention then "dissolved itself by an
Adjournment sine die" (*Records*, vol. 2, p. 649), and as Washington
describes it in his diary, "The business thus being closed, the Members
adjourned to the City Tavern, dined together and took a cordial leave of
each other." Washington then returned to his lodgings "and retired to
meditate on the momentous wk. which had been executed" (ibid., vol. 3,
p. 81).

CHAPTER 10

Summary and Conclusion

The American Constitutional Convention met in Philadelphia between May 25 and September 17, 1787. For nearly all of that time, the delegates struggled over control of the proposed government, over the proper relationship between the state and national governments, and over the nature of an effective and safe relationship between the several departments of a government in the republican form. Proposals of every description were offered and considered. Previous analysts have concluded that, beyond the early polarization between large states and small over the representation question, the debates lacked objective structure. Therefore, the debates have consistently been treated as political spectacle—the battle of the demigods—wherein great men clashed over great principles and the political world was wrought anew.

This book began with an argument about the interaction of alternative visions of a community's general interest with the partial and exclusive interests of the individuals, groups, classes, states, and regions that comprise the community. I have demonstrated that the debates and decisions of the Federal Convention bear the distinctive marks of that grudging accommodation between principles and interests that is characteristic of democratic politics. General principles, such as republicanism, federalism, separation of powers, checks and balances, and bicameralism, define the structure of government only in vague outlines. Therefore, a discussion of general principles serves merely to identify the broad paths along which the general interests and common good of the community can be pursued. Other considerations, primarily deriving from diverse political, economic, and geographic interests, suggest and often virtually determine the modifications, adjustments, and allowances that principled consistency must make to political expediency.

James Madison made precisely this point in a letter that accompanied a copy of the new Constitution sent to Jefferson in Paris in late October 1787. Madison explained that "the nature of the subject, the diversity of human opinion, . . . the collision of local interests, and the pretentions of the large & small States will . . . account . . . for the irregularities which will be discovered in (the new government's) structure and form" (*Records*, vol. 3, p. 136). Similarly, Alexander Hamilton felt constrained to warn his readers in the first number of *The Federalist* that though "our choice should be directed by a judicious estimate of our true interests, unperplexed and unbiased by considerations not connected with the public good, . . . the plan . . . affects too many particular interests, not to involve in its discussion a variety of objects foreign to its merits" (Modern Library ed., 1937, p.3). Nor was this reading of the dynamic interplay between principles and interests in the Convention merely the temporary view of the Founders. After nearly half a century's reflection, Madison remained convinced that "the abstract leanings of opinions" and "the question of power" were the separate though intimately related tracks along which the Convention's debates had moved. Madison wrote to Theodore Sedgwick in a letter of February 12, 1831, that "the two subjects, the structure of the Govt and the question of power entrusted to it were more or less inseparable in the minds of all, as depending a good deal, the one on the other, (though) after the compromise wch gave the small States an equality in one branch of the Legislature, and the large States an inequality in the other branch, the abstract leaning of opinions would better appear" (*Records*, vol. 3, p. 496). Nor was this reading of the Convention's dynamics restricted to participants such as Hamilton and Madison. Alexis de Tocqueville, in his classic *Democracy In America* (1835), presented a reading of the interplay of principles and interests in the Convention that is very similar to that of Hamilton and Madison and to the analysis presented in this book. Tocqueville argued that "two interests were opposed to each other in the establishment of the Federal Constitution. These two interests had given rise to two opinions. It was the wish of one party to convert the Union into a league of independent states. . . . The other party desired to unite the inhabitants of the American colonies . . . to establish a government that should act as the sole representative of the nation. . . . Under these circumstances the result was that the rules of logic were broken, as is usually the case when interests are opposed to arguments . . . these principles and interests are so many natural obstacles to the rigorous application of any political system" (Vintage Books ed., 1954, vol. 1, pp. 122–123).

The interaction between principles and interests in the Federal Convention has been illustrated and examined through a theoretical distinction between a "higher" level of constitutional choice, where the influence of principle guided action, and a "lower" level of constitutional choice, where the influence of political and economic interests were decisive. The argument and the evidence presented in this study make clear that the Federal Convention of 1787, from its opening day on May 25 until its final adjournment on September 17, confronted two distinct, but intimately related, aspects of constitutional design. The first was general. What kind of republican government should be constructed? As the delegates considered and discussed alternative visions of the relationship between human nature, the institutions of government, and the quality of the resulting social order, the temper and tone of their deliberations were quiet and philosophical. Some measure of detachment was possible at the "higher" level of constitutional choice because the debates over general principles provided little indication of precisely how the choice of one set of principles over another would affect the specific interests of particular individuals, states, and regions. On these issues, the nationalists of the Middle Atlantic states regularly lined up against the localists of New England and the lower South.

While the delegates considered questions of basic constitutional design, they seemed almost oblivious to the conflicts of interest that inevitably arose as they moved to the "lower" level of constitutional choice, where their theories and principles would be shaped and molded into practical arrangements for governing. When distributional questions came to the fore, debate intensified, tempers flared, and conflict predominated. Questions touching upon the allocation of representatives and presidential electors, the status of slavery, and regulation of the nation's commerce and its western lands directly affected the political, economic, and social interests of distinct persons, classes, states, and regions. Indeed, it was only at this "lower" level of constitutional construction, where interests clashed so loudly, that the Convention was threatened with dissolution. On these issues, the large states lined up against the small states, the North opposed the South, the commercial states opposed the staple states, and the states with extensive claims to western lands sought to maintain them against the objections of the states which had no such claims to press.

This study has demonstrated that the activities of the Convention were by no means as fluid and unstructured as past interpretations have indicated. The positions and arguments of individual delegates, when aggregated by state delegation as the operative voting unit, show such a remarkable degree of stability that the contours of the opposing arguments can be intricately traced. But that stability was decisively and irrevocably breached on four occasions during the course of the deliberations. In each case, as the Convention resolved one set of critical issues, other issues, still unresolved and subject to intense dispute, rose to the fore and the voting coalitions realigned to contest and do battle over them.

Perhaps the most important claim that can be made for this study is that it has opened an explicit dialogue between the data left by the Convention (in the form of both debates and roll-call votes) and the many conflicting interpretations of those data that have been advanced both by Convention participants and by later analysts. Figure 2.3 and the tables and figures presented throughout the text of this book constitute an empirically verifiable description of the voting coalitions that dominated each phase of the Convention's work. Therefore, explanations of the Convention's debates, deliberations, and eventual decisions which postulate active opposition patterns that are not consonant with those displayed here should be viewed with skepticism. For example, an interpretation of the Convention's work that stresses state size (large versus small) or region (North versus South) as characteristic of the entire Convention must be confounded by the actual alignments that appeared during the Convention's opening days and again during the five-week period from mid-July to late-August, when the largest and the smallest states joined hands in a coalition of Middle Atlantic states to oppose the northern and southern periphery.

The Realignment Model Revisited

In discussing various dimensions of the Convention's activities, I have sought to demonstrate that the "critical realignment model," developed by Key, Burnham, Sundquist, and others to explain step-level changes in the structure of the American political party system, also enlightens and informs the performance of voting coalitions in the Convention. In fact, my hope is that the detailed records of the theoretical and practical arguments offered by the delegates to explain and justify the votes cast by their state delegation, in conjunction with the limited number of actors (12 state delegations) and the very manageable time frame (4 months), have enriched and expanded our understanding of the "critical realignment model" (Burnham, 1970, pp. 13–15).

Previous studies involving the realignment phenomenon have been forced to deal almost exclusively with fluctuations in the percentage of the total vote garnered by the candidates of the major parties in national, state, and local elections. These studies have identified the realignment phenomenon with a more or less inherently ambiguous change in the distribution of the two-party vote that has seemed to persist over time. A realignment of the relevant decision-makers in the present study was marked by the explicit movement of one or more of the state voting delegations from one voting coalition to another. In addition, the actor who changed his allegiance here is a state voting delegation, made up of several of the first citizens of each of the states, many of whom went to great lengths to explain exactly what they were doing, why, and what they hoped to achieve. So we not only know which states chose regularly to vote together at each stage in the Convention's business, we have over one thousand pages of recorded debate in which the delegates sought to justify, explain, and promote the position being taken by their state. We not only know what they did (the roll-call votes), we know why they said they did it (the debates).

Consequently, by analyzing both the votes and the debates, I have been able to demonstrate quite clearly that there were only four coalition realignments over the course of the Convention's proceedings. Between the realignments occurred five well-defined periods of stability in the voting coalitions. The result is a dynamic picture of voting behavior in the Convention that is directly analogous to Burnham's description of the "normal structure of American national politics at the mass base" as a "dynamic . . . polarization between long-term inertia and concentrated bursts of change in . . . [an] open system of action" (Burnham, 1970, pp. 17, 27).

I have sought to expand the relevance of Burnham's argument by demonstrating that similar dynamics operate at all levels of the American political system, from the aggregate level of mass politics, where it was initially discovered and described, to the level of small groups such as the American Constitutional Convention. In each case, a number of individual actors must deal serially with a diverse set of issues, all of which require some firm disposition. To reach effective decisions on these questions, actors are inevitably forced to form voting coalitions with others who may be somewhat differently motivated. E. E. Schattschneider has expressed this broad insight with characteristic directness by arguing that "political conflicts are waged by coalitions of inferior interests held together by a dominant interest. The effort in all political struggles is to exploit cracks in the opposition while attempting to consolidate one's own side" (Schattschneider, 1960, pp. 69–70). There is virtually no clearer case of this strategy in operation than that described in Chapters 6 and 7 of this book, where the five-member peripheral coalition consistently and effectively acted to separate the four smaller members of the coalition of Middle Atlantic states from the larger states of Pennsylvania and Virginia.

Furthermore, I believe that this study has helped to elaborate Schattschneider's contention that the key to understanding the coalitions that actually form in any political conflict is to first "discover the hierarchies of unequal interests, of dominant and subordinate interests" (op. cit., p. 71). It should come as no surprise that the coalitions

characterizing any period of political conflict in the Convention tended
to form around the issue that the combatants saw as most crucial. Why,
after all, should coalitions form around secondary or subordinate issues?
Chapters 3, 4, and 5 show just how assiduously James Madison worked
to establish an agenda for the Convention that would lead to the early
consideration of his two dominant concerns—representation and the
further question of the scope of the powers that the new government
would wield.

Schattschneider's insight warns the analyst of an ongoing decision
system facing an agenda full of important issues to be alert to the
changing salience of the issues confronting the system. This is particularly the case if the resonance of the issues gaining in importance is
different from that of the issues previously thought to be fundamental.
The new issues may very well redetermine the pattern of conflict and
the possibilities for coalition alignment in the system. What people want
most, what they see as the central question demanding resolution, will
largely determine whom they must work with to achieve their major
policy goals. Coalitions do not form and then go in search of issues.
Issues arise or are pushed to the forefront by circumstances or by
political entrepreneurs, and then coalitions form to do battle over them
(Sundquist, 1973, pp. 11–25). Once again, E. E. Schattschneider has
stated this principle of politics most succinctly: "In politics as in everything else it makes a great difference whose game we play." When an
important issue sweeps to the fore, initial positions are adopted, sides are
formed, and a dynamic is put into operation in which "unification and
division are part of the same process . . . conflicts divide people and
unite them at the same time. . . . The more fully the conflict is
developed, the more intense it becomes, the more complete is the
consolidation of the opposing camps" (Schattschneider, 1960, pp. 48,
64).

In the American Constitutional Convention, the "consolidation of
opposing camps" involved the confrontation between more or less
cohesive coalitions of state voting delegations. These coalitions confronted one another over a critical issue or set of related critical issues
until every argument had been plumbed to its depths. Conflict continued until it became obvious that the balance of forces was too even to
allow victory to either side and that the question was too important to go
unresolved. The Convention's consistent response was to go to a
compromise committee where passions might be more restrained and
delegates of moderate opinion might be assigned the task of arriving at
an acceptable solution.

Each time that a compromise solution to an issue that had dominated debate and had provided the "rationale" for the division of states into opposing coalitions was finally reached, the old voting alignments disappeared very suddenly. Each compromise solution to a fundamental issue unleashed a powerful dynamic in the Convention as new issues fought for predominance and new coalitions rapidly formed to contest them. The most striking example of this process occurred on July 16 and 17, when the Convention's attention shifted from the question of legislative representation to the structure of the executive branch, almost without missing a beat. It was widely understood that once the representation question was settled, control would have to be established over the Chief Magistrate and his executive branch. Around this new struggle; this new critical issue, new coalitions formed.

Schattschneider's very general analysis of the realignment phenomenon observes that "a radical shift of alignment becomes possible only at the cost of a change in relations and priorities of all of the contestants" (op. cit., p. 65). The demise of one critical issue and the rise of another to replace it "involves a total reorganization of political alignments. . . . Every shift of the cleavage line . . . will determine the place of each individual in the political system, what side he is on, who else is on his side, who is opposed to him, how large the opposing sides are, what the conflicts are about, and who wins" (ibid., pp. 62–63). Therefore, with Schattschneider's characterization of the structure of political conflict as a guide, one of the central aims of this study has been to define very precisely the cleavages that separated the participants and to identify the issues that energized the active cleavages at the expense of other cleavages that might have divided the states differently. I have also sought to identify the active membership of the coalitions during each stable period and to be quite explicit about the extent or depth of the commitment of each participant (state) to its coalition. Further, I have sought to chart the movement of every participant during a realignment crisis and to explain the considerations that motivated the decision either to realign and break old alliances or to ride out the storm holding fast to familiar colleagues.

As the circular model with multiple cleavages suggested, and as Figure 10.1 demonstrates, Sundquist was quite correct to argue that "successive realignments can best be understood as new patterns drawn on transparent overlays" (Sundquist, 1973, p. 7). The five stable voting alignments that occurred during the course of the Convention can be represented using the circular model by visualizing the states as stationary within the voting universe and observing the way in which changes in the location of the cleavage lines generate each of the opposition patterns.

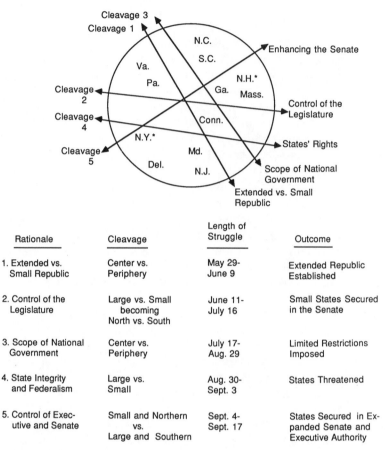

Figure 10.1. Cleavage lines active during the Convention.
*New York abandoned the Convention on July 11 at vote #132. New Hampshire did not arrive until July 23 at vote #203.

Rationale	Cleavage	Length of Struggle	Outcome
1. Extended vs. Small Republic	Center vs. Periphery	May 29–June 9	Extended Republic Established
2. Control of the Legislature	Large vs. Small becoming North vs. South	June 11–July 16	Small States Secured in the Senate
3. Scope of National Government	Center vs. Periphery	July 17–Aug. 29	Limited Restrictions Imposed
4. State Integrity and Federalism	Large vs. Small	Aug. 30–Sept. 3	States Threatened
5. Control of Executive and Senate	Small and Northern vs. Large and Southern	Sept. 4–Sept. 17	States Secured in Expanded Senate and Executive Authority

On the Issues:
A Summary of Who Won, What and When

The Convention's opening days, May 29 through June 9, were dominated by a brilliant clash at the "higher" level of constitutional choice between the advocates of an "extended republic," with the locus of power at the national level, and a disparate opposition generally favoring "small republics" and local control. Though each delegate arrived in Philadelphia knowing that the central purpose of the Convention was to strengthen government at the national level, this first active cleavage in the Convention reflected the fact that the delegates differed fundamentally about the theoretical and institutional basis of national power in a republic constituted along federal lines and, perhaps even more fundamentally, about the degree to which government should be strengthened.

The initial debates centered on alternatives that were most clearly articulated by, on the one hand, James Madison and, on the other, first by John Dickinson and later by William Paterson. Madison, supported most consistently and forcefully by Hamilton, Wilson, and G. Morris, argued in favor of a government national and supreme, based on citizens in their individual capacities, and possessing the authority to displace state power completely where the states were judged to be incompetent and to monitor it closely in other areas through the use of a national negative on state legislation. John Dickinson, speaking for a group of delegates led by Gerry, Sherman, Paterson, Mason, and the South Carolinians C. C. Pinckney, Rutledge, and Butler, argued in favor of enhancements of national power conceived of as amendments to the Articles of Confederation. These delegates, speaking for New England and the South, wanted the new national government to remain collateral to and supportive of the state governments and to be based firmly on the state governments, rather than directly upon the citizens of the states. Modest regulatory powers at the national level, principally in commerce and taxation, would, in this view, stabilize the state governments, simultaneously making them both the basis for and the bulwark of the new system, and rendering a national negative on state laws completely unnecessary.

The ground of battle changed dramatically from principles to interests on June 9, when Madison, Wilson, and the advocates of an extended republic—having already won agreement to the construction of a government national and supreme, with seats in both the House and the Senate distributed among the states on the basis of population—demanded an absolute veto over laws passed by the state legislatures. This move provoked a very strong and determined reaction among the delegates from the small states, and eventually among some others, particularly the delegates from Massachusetts and South Carolina, who, though favoring proportional representation, wished to defend the integrity of the states as political actors within the new system. This second active cleavage to divide the Convention posed the raw question of power: Who will dominate this new government? Madison's Virginia Plan, serving as the Convention's agenda through the first nine weeks, clearly envisioned the dominance of the most populous and wealthy states. A group favoring proportional representation centered on the three most populous states (Massachusetts, Pennsylvania and Virginia) and the three rapidly growing states of the deep South (North Carolina, South Carolina and Georgia). Consistent opposition to proportional representation in both houses of the national legislature was supplied by a federalist coalition of New York, New Jersey, and Delaware, with Maryland uncertain and Connecticut generally cooperative but undependable.

The confrontation over the distribution among the states of legislative representation occurred in phases. The first phase was the storied confrontation between the large states and the small, which, though it ushered the Convention to the brink of dissolution, culminated in the compromise committee report of July 5 that included equal representation for the small states with the large in the Senate. Nonetheless, this grudging acknowledgement of the demands of the small states for equality in the Senate only served to focus attention more directly upon the still unresolved issue of the distribution of seats in the House of Representatives, where the nation's opposing regions, the North and the South, would still be distinctly, and perhaps dangerously, unequal. This second battle was contested primarily between the large populous states of the North and South, with the southern states convinced that their initial minority status would render them vulnerable to northern domination, particularly on the very sensitive issues of slavery and commerce.

Thus, during the seven-week representation debate, two interrelated but variously motivated battles were fought, culminating in pitched battles over the several committee reports of early July. In the first stage, the small states achieved the equal representation in the Senate that allowed them to feel secure in the new governmental structure. Later, during mid-July, the southern states, over the direct opposition of their former large state colleagues, achieved a mandatory adjustment of representation in the House on the basis of population. It was widely assumed that this would give them majority control of that branch within a few short years if demographic trends continued in their favor. This staged unfolding of the conflict also explains why Pennsylvania abandoned the powerful large-state–deep-South coalition before Virginia did. When proportional representation in the Senate was lost in early July and the southern members of large-state–deep-South coalition turned to consolidating the position of their region in the House of Representatives, Pennsylvania abandoned them without hesitation to side with its northern neighbors, while Virginia remained to assure the regional gains in which it would share.

Immediately, and for the next five weeks, from July 17 to August 24, debate moved decisively back to the "higher" level of constitutional choice. Consequently, this third active cleavage in the Convention saw the original coalitions, pitting the "extended republic" nationalists of the Middle Atlantic states against the more locally oriented "small republic" federalists of the periphery, reappear almost intact. The two theories of republican government that had surfaced during the Convention's opening days seemed to call for entirely different relationships between the executive and legislative branches and between the government and its citizenry.

The Convention gave the nature, structure, and powers of the executive in a republican government its full attention from July 17 to July 26. Those advocating a powerful "extended republic" wanted an independent executive strong enough to check a volatile legislature, while the more traditional "small republic" view called for an executive dependent upon, even selected by, the legislature. This principled clash at the "higher" level of constitutional choice was tentatively resolved in favor of executive selection by an independent college of electors. It was thought by this mechanism that the potential for cabal and corruption inherent in legislative selection would be avoided, particularly in the case of of an incumbent President seeking a second term. But how would the presidential electors be distributed among the states? This question, quite predictably, plunged the Convention briefly, but decisively, back into the "lower" level of constitutional choice as the delegates sought feverishly to secure the power and position of their individual states within this new executive selection mechanism. The large states demanded a distribution of the electors based on population, while the smaller states called, once again, for an equal distribution. When neither side would relent, legislative selection was temporarily readopted, and the Convention adjourned to allow the Committee of Detail time to prepare a draft constitution.

When the Convention reconvened on August 6, debate continued to focus on issues at the "higher" level of constitutional choice. The central questions facing the Convention as it began to work its way through the Committee of Detail draft concerned the stance that the new nation would take toward its current citizens, its future immigrants, and its component parts, particularly the new states then rising in the West. The choices seemed to be relatively restricted. On the one hand, the nationalists from the Middle Atlantic states held a cautious but optimistically positive view of the ordinary citizens' ability to participate in a properly balanced and structured government broadly empowered to govern freely as changing times and an indeterminate future might dictate. On the other hand, the localist orientation of the delegates from New England and the South promoted a much less optimistic view of the quality of citizen input and of the feasibility of constructing adequate Checks and Balances in any government awarded great discretion. Therefore, in the later view, it was thought both wise and expedient to depart as little as possible from a pure theory of Separation of Powers. Failure to heed this ancient dictum, they believed, lay at the root of England's constitutional degeneration. Additionally, they believed that one might fight tyranny and corruption by anticipating its varied forms and by building in defensive restrictions and qualifications wherever experience had exposed weaknesses in the once noble English model. Behind this more constricted view of a desirable national government were also aligned the major regional interests fearing the vague and uncertain impact of national policies on their foremost concerns: commerce in the North and slavery in the South. Basically, the dispute was one of the degree to which the delegates were prepared to put confidence in men, properly selected, and in government, properly structured. The delegates from the periphery sought long residency requirements for both suffrage and officeholding; some even wanted to restrict these privileges to the native-born. Delegates from the Middle Atlantic states commonly sought to keep the pathways to government open to a full, even if mediated, citizen involvement. These issues held the Convention's attention into late August.

The fourth stable opposition pattern to appear in the Convention shows Connecticut, New Jersey, and Maryland to have been isolated against the remaining eight states. These three are obviously the states, both small and vulnerable, that had been on their guard since the Convention's opening day lest they be overwhelmed and rendered powerless in the new government. Some measure of security had been achieved with equal representation in the Senate, but the small state men continued to be wary. They feared, with good reason, that the nationalism in which they had joined as members of the Middle Atlantic coalition might once again be bent to the political interests of the large states. The temptation to grab for political control of the new government was always there for the large states, and the small states, knowing it, watched them closely.

On the morning of August 24, the coalitions that had dominated the Convention's business since mid-July began to unravel as the worst fears of the small states concerning their putative large state allies were confirmed on the critical and still-unresolved issue of executive selection. The specific question was: If selection of the Chief Executive is to be a legislative responsibility, should this selection be conducted by separate ballots in the House and Senate, or by "joint ballot" of both houses voting together? The small states had been depending heavily upon a separate ballot in the Senate to give them some meaningful control over the executive branch. Obviously, the reemergence of a cleavage based on size promised to severely disrupt the nationalist coalition of Middle Atlantic states, as that coalition was an amalgam of the very large (Pennsylvania and Virginia) and the very small (Connecticut, New Jersey, Delaware and Maryland). Over the waning days of August, the small state delegates became ever more firmly convinced that the large states were again seeking dominance and that small state safety could be secured only if the states themselves remained as legitimate power centers within the new system.

The vulnerability of the smaller states was further demonstrated by an unbroken series of stunning defeats during the final week of August, leaving no doubt, even in the minds of some confirmed nationalists from the smaller Middle Atlantic states, that additional defenses had to be secured. They were profoundly radicalized by adverse decisions regarding control of western land reserves, the method for admitting new states into the Union, conditions under which federal troops might enter individual states, and ratification procedures. With these questions decided in favor of a broad nationalism that seemed favorable to the larger states, several remaining issues, foremost among them the still unresolved executive questions, were turned over to the Brearley Committee on Postponed Parts, to which one delegate from each state was appointed on August 31.

New bargains were struck and new working majorities were formed within this compromise committee, just as they had been following the Connecticut Compromise five weeks earlier and after the Commerce and Slave Trade Compromise only the week before. Out of the Brearley Committee came a new coalition structure, dominated by a powerful northern bloc of five small states from the Northeast and the Middle Atlantic: New Hampshire, Connecticut, New Jersey, Delaware, and Maryland. They were joined by the only large northern state, Massachusetts, and by the weakest and most vulnerable of the Southern states, Georgia, to form a controlling seven-state majority. Steady opposition to this new northern majority was supplied by the two Carolinas, fearing that southern interests were in jeopardy, and by Pennsylvania and Virginia, fearing that the small states were close to consolidating a too powerful position in the new government. This fifth and final stable coalition pattern dominated the Convention's last ten working days.

For most of the states making up the new seven-state majority, especially its small state core, the Convention had proven to be a rough passage. Through the first seven weeks, it had taken repeated threats of a determination physically to withdraw from the Convention merely to establish the right to equality in one branch of the legislature. Through most of the debates since, the small states had been wary allies in support of the centralizing programs of the large state nationalists, powerful, persuasive men like Madison, Wilson, Morris, and King. The willingness of these large state delegates, late in the Convention, to sacrifice once again the interests of their putative small state partners by supporting "joint ballot" selection of the President and by attempting to retain exclusive control of the western lands deeply impressed the small states with their continued vulnerability.

The small states emerged from the Brearley Committee as a tightly cohesive and highly determined majority demanding final control of the process by which the President was to be chosen. Many delegates, from both large states and small, were convinced that electors isolated in their respective states could not coordinate their votes to elect a President on the first round and that, as a result, "nineteen times in twenty," this task would fall to the Senate, and so, effectively, to the small central and northern states. To make this selection system palatable to Pennsylvania, Virginia, and the Carolinas, states that were opposed to such a prominent role for the Senate in presidential selection, the Convention searched for a means by which small state control could be maintained while fulfilling the opposition demands that an ominously powerful Senate be somehow separated from the process. This was achieved by transferring responsibility for final selection from the Senate to the House of Representatives voting by states. Both the northern majority and the large state and Southern minorities were satisfied with this solution. The majority thought that they had achieved effective control of presidential selection and, hence, a power base in addition to the Senate from which to defend their interests, while the opposition minorities, resigned to the small state victory, sought only to remove the Senate from the process, thus reducing their great fear that it would become an oppressive aristocracy.

In addition, the Brearley Committee resolved a number of questions beyond the process of executive selection, including sensitive issues touching upon the conduct of foreign affairs, the power of appointment, and the impeachment trials of federal officials, including the President. In each case, the power and significance of the Senate were maximized. The remaining battles of the Convention were fought over precisely these additions to senatorial authority and, indirectly, over the additions to the power and influence of the small states in the new system that these Senate powers represented. Pennsylvania, Virginia, and the Carolinas consistently attempted to remove these powers from the Senate, or to require that they be shared with the House, just as they had on the executive issues, while the new northern majority sought to defend and maintain the advantages that they had written into the Brearley Committee report. The northern majority firmly rejected each attempt to remove or even to moderate the powers to be wielded by the Senate.

In a very real and fundamentally important sense, as the Convention finished its work, the tables had been turned on the original proponents and beneficiaries of the Virginia Plan. Although the Virginia Plan set the early tone of the Convention in favor of a powerful and truly national government, the small Middle Atlantic states clearly controlled the Convention's latter days. During the Convention's closing days, the Constitution was given its final gloss of moderate federalism. The small states had merely been the last major group in the Convention to attain the security that all required before they could endorse the new Constitution. So on September 17, 1787, the Convention sent the proposed Constitution on to the Congress, the states, and an uncertain future.

The ultimate impact of shifting cleavages generating new patterns of allegiance among the participants was that no major group was fundamentally dissatisfied with the product of the Convention's long deliberations. In Charles Warren's words:

> One of the most fortunate features of the Constitution was that it was the result of compromises and adjustments and accommodations. . . . It did not represent the complete supremacy of the views of any particular man or set of men, or any State or group of States. The claims and interests of neither the North nor the South prevailed. . . . Moreover, it represented neither an extreme Nationalist point of view nor an extreme States' Rights doctrine. The adherents of each theory had been obliged to yield. (Warren, 1928, p. 733)

But the other and equally important side of this coin is that although "the adherents of each theory" and of each regional interest were "obliged to yield" on their full program, at some point most of the delegates, states, and regions participated in the core of a winning coalition which secured for them their dearest aims, if not all of their aims. Thus, the delegates, almost to a man, departed the Convention convinced that their constitutional glass was at least half full as opposed to half empty.

Notes

Chapter 2

1. For unstated reasons Ulmer used a source—E. H. Carr, Editor, *Journal of the Federal Convention kept by James Madison* (Chicago: Scotts-Foresman Company, 1898)—that includes only 421 of the 569 roll-call votes taken in the Convention. '

2. All factor analyses (SPSS) in this study proceed from a matrix of correlation coefficients. Since voting in the Convention was by state delegation, rather than by individual delegate, treating each state as a dichotomous variable, after the pairwise deletion of absences and divided votes, allows each cell of the matrix to show the degree of association between pairs of states in yes and no voting. Votes were coded for analysis as follows: 1-yes; 2-no; 3-divided; 4-absent. There were only 146 occasions upon which delegations are recorded as having divided their votes evenly, our code 3. The greatest concentration of absences, our code 4, occurred during the first few days and weeks of the Convention, when some of the states were late in achieving a legal quorum in their delegations. Still, missing data, prior to the Connecticut Compromise, accounted for an average of only 7.7% per state and a much lower average in later periods.

    Twelve states attended the Convention, although never more than eleven were present at any one time. Those states—New Hampshire, Massachusetts, Connecticut, New York, New Jersey, Pennsylvania, Delaware, Maryland, Virginia, North Carolina, South Carolina, and Georgia—will comprise the variables in this study. The range of cases is also very clearly limited. They are the 569 roll-call votes taken over the course of the Convention. (See Farrand, 1911, *Records of the Federal Convention of 1787*; cited in the text as *Records*.)

3. One much quoted description of factor analysis and its intent is that of Harry H. Harman. Harman says that "the principal concern of factor analysis is the resolution of a set of variables linearly in terms of (usually) a small number of categories or 'factors.' . . . A satisfactory solution will yield factors which convey all of the essential information of the original set of data. Thus, the chief aim is to attain scientific parsimony or economy of description" (Harman, 1976, p. 4).

4. Equally enlightening, and perhaps even more directly to the point of this study, is Rudolph J. Rummel's comment: "If the investigator has a matrix of intricately related variables, say UN votes (or say Constitutional Convention votes), . . . factor analysis will bare the separate patterns of interrelationships involved. Moreover, the relationship of each variable to the separate patterns . . . can be determined" (Rummel, 1970, p. 29).

5. The present study is a Q-factor analysis throughout, as we are concerned with grouping states, or entities in the matrix columns, on the basis of voting-response pattern, or characteristics (votes), found in the matrix rows. The tables reported in the text are orthogonal varimax solutions, although in almost every instance, both orthogonal (varimax) and oblique

(direct oblimin) rotations have been performed with only minor variations in the patterns described.

Chapter 4

1. Single quotes within double quotes in passages from *Records* refer to resolutions, motions, or proposed wording of the Constitution.
2. Occasional words in parentheses are as found in the original of *Records*. They are Madison's interpolations. The author's occasional interpolations are given in brackets, [. . .], according to the usual style.

Bibliography

Adair, Douglass (1957). That politics may be reduced to a science. *Huntington Library Quarterly* 20: 343–360.

Adams, Henry (1889). *History of the United States during the First Administration of Thomas Jefferson.* New York: Scribner's.

Alker, Hayward (1964). Dimensions of conflict in the general assembly. *American Political Science Review* 58: 642–657.

Alker, Hayward, and Russett, Bruce (1965). *World Politics in the General Assembly.* New Haven, CT: Yale University Press.

Anderson, Lee F., Watts, Meredith W., Jr., and Wilcox, Allen R. (1966). *Legislative Roll-Call Analysis.* Evanston, IL: Northwestern University Press.

Appleby, Joyce (1976). Liberalism and the American Revolution. *The New England Quarterly* 49: 3–26.

Appleby, Joyce (1978). The social origins of American revolutionary ideology. *Journal of American History* March, pp. 935–958.

Appleby, Joyce (1984). *Capitalism and a New Social Order: the Republican Vision of the 1790's.* New York: New York University Press.

Bailyn, Bernard (1967). *The Ideological Origins of the American Revolution.* Cambridge, MA: Harvard University Press.

Bailyn, Bernard (1973). The central themes of the American Revolution: an interpretation. In Stephen G. Kurtz and James H. Hutson (eds.), *Essays on the American Revolution.* New York: W. W. Norton.

Bancroft, George (1882). *History of the United States: Vol. 6. The Formation of the American Constitution.* New York: Little, Brown.

Banning, Lance (1974). Republican ideology and the triumph of the Constitution. *William And Mary Quarterly* 31: 167–188.

Beard, Charles A. (1913). *An Economic Interpretation of the Constitution of the United States.* New York: Macmillan.

Bellah, Robert N., Madsen, Richard, Sullivan, William M., Swidler, Ann, and Tipton, Stephen M. (1985). *Habits of the Heart: Individualism and Commitment in American Life.* New York: Harper & Row.

Benson, Lee (1960). *Turner and Beard: American Historical Writing Reconsidered.* Glencoe, IL: Free Press of Glencoe.

Birkby, Robert H. (1966). Politics of accommodation: the origins of the Supremacy Clause. *Western Political Quarterly* 19: 123–135.

Bonomi, Patricia U. (1973). The middle colonies: Embryo of the new political order. In Alden T. Vaughn and George Athan Billias (eds.), *Perspectives on American History*, pp. 63–92. New York: Harper & Row.

Breen, Timothy H. (1975). Persistent localism: English social change and the shaping of New England institutions. *William and Mary Quarterly* 32: 3–28.

Brown, Robert E. (1956). *Charles Beard and the Constitution*. Princeton, NJ: Princeton University Press.

Buchanan, James M., and Tullock, Gordon (1962). *Calculus of Consent: Logical Foundations of Constitutional Democracy*. Ann Arbor, MI: University of Michigan Press.

Burnham, Walter Dean (1970). *Critical Elections and the Mainsprings of American Politics*. New York: W. W. Norton.

Carey, George W. (1978). Separation of powers and the Madisonian model: a reply to the critics. *American Political Science Review* 72: 151–164.

Cash, W. J. (1941). *The Mind of the South*. New York: Knopf.

Collier, Christopher, and Collier, James Lincoln (1986). *Decision in Philadelphia: The Constitutional Convention of 1787*. New York: Random House.

Crowl, Philip A. (1947). Anti-federalism In Maryland, 1787–1788. *William and Mary Quarterly* 4: 446–469.

Dahl, Robert A. (1967). *Pluralist Democracy in the United States: Conflict and Consent*. Chicago: Rand McNally.

Davis, Joseph L. (1977). *Sectionalism in American Politics*. Madison: University of Wisconsin Press.

Devine, Donald J. (1972). *The Political Culture of the United States*. Boston: Little, Brown.

Diamond, Martin (1972). The Federalist. In Leo Strauss and Joseph Cropsey (eds.), *History of Political Philosophy*, 2nd ed., pp. 631–651. Chicago: Rand McNally.

Diamond, Martin (1976). The American idea of man: the view from the founding. In Irving Kristol and Paul Weaver (eds.), *The Americans: 1976*. Lexington, MA: Lexington Books, pp. 1–23.

Diamond, Martin (1981). *The Founding of the Democratic Republic*. Itasca, IL.: F. E. Peacock.

Diggins, John (1984). *The Lost Soul of American Politics: Virtue, Self-Interest and the Foundations of Liberalism*. New York: Basic Books.

Eidelberg, Paul (1968). *The Philosophy Of The American Constitution*. New York: Free Press.

Elazar, Daniel J. (1972). *American Federalism: A View from the States*, 3rd ed. New York: Harper & Row.

Elazar, Daniel J., and Zikmund, Joseph (1975). *The Ecology of American Political Cultures: Readings*. New York: Thomas Y. Crowell.

Farrand, Max (1904). Compromises of the Constitution. *American Historical Review*. 9: 479–489.

Farrand, Max, ed. (1911). *Records of the Federal Convention of 1787*. 4 vols. New Haven, CT: Yale University Press.

Farrand, Max (1913). *The Framing of the Constitution of the United States*. New Haven, CT: Yale University Press.

The Federalist, Edward M. Earle (ed.). New York: Modern Library, 1937.

Ferguson, E. James (1983). Political economy, public liberty, and the formation of the Constitution. *William and Mary Quarterly* 40: 389–412.

Fiske, John (1888). *The Critical Period in American History*. Boston: Houghton, Mifflin.

Greenberg, Douglas (1979). The middle colonies in recent American historiography. *William and Mary Quarterly* 36: 396–427.

Greene, Jack P. (1967). *The reappraisal of the American Revolution in the recent historical literature*. Washington, DC: American Historical Association Publication No. 68.

Greene, Jack P. (1978). "Virtus et libertas:" political culture, social change, and the origins of the American Revolution in Virginia, 1763–1776. In Jeffrey J. Crow and Larry E. Tise (eds.), *The Southern Experience in the American Revolution*. Chapel Hill: The University of North Carolina Press.

Greene, Jack P. (1982). The background of the Articles of Confederation. *Publius* 12: 15–44.

Grumm, John R. (1963). A factor analysis of legislative behavior. *Midwest Journal of Political Science* 7: 336–356.

Hall, David D. (1978). Understanding the Puritans. In John M. Mulder and John W. Wilson (eds.), *Religion in American History: Interpretive Essays*, pp. 1–16. Englewood Cliffs, NJ: Prentice-Hall.

Harman, Harry H. (1976). *Modern Factor Analysis*, 3rd ed. Chicago: University of Chicago Press.

Harris, C. W. (1948). A factor analysis of selected Senate roll-calls, 80th Congress. *Educational and Psychological Measurement* 8: 583–591.

Hartz, Louis (1955). *The Liberal Tradition In America: An Interpretation of American Political Thought Since The Revolution*. New York: Harcourt, Brace.

Henderson, H. James (1974). *Party Politics in the Continental Congress*. New York: McGraw-Hill.

Hofstadter, Richard (1954). *The American Political Tradition*. New York: Vintage Books.

Hunt, Gaillard (1901). *The Life of James Madison*. New York: Doubleday, Page.

Huntington, Samuel P. (1982). American ideals and American institutions. *Political Science Quarterly* 97: 1–37.

Isaac, Rhys (1982). *The Transformation of Virginia, 1740-1790*. Chapel Hill: University of North Carolina Press.

Jensen, Merrill (1940). *The Articles of Confederation: An Interpretation of the Social-Constitutional History of the American Revolution 1774–1781*. Madison: University of Wisconsin Press.

Jensen, Merrill (1950). *The New Nation: A History of the United States during the Confederation 1781–1789*. New York: Vintage Books.

Jensen, Merrill (1964). *The Making of the Constitution*. New York: Van Nostrand Reinhold.

Jillson, Calvin (1978). Voting bloc analysis in the Constitutional Convention: implications for an interpretation of the Connecticut Compromise. *Western Political Quarterly* 31: 535–547.

Jillson, Calvin (1979). The executive in republican government: the case of the American founding. *Presidential Studies Quarterly* 9: 386–402.

Jillson, Calvin (1981a). Constitution-making: alignment and realignment in the Federal Convention of 1787. *American Political Science Review* 75: 598–612.

Jillson, Calvin (1981b). The representation question in the Federal Convention of 1787: Madison's Virginia Plan and its opponents. *Congressional Studies* 8: 21–41.

Jillson, Calvin, and Eubanks, Cecil (1984). The political structure of constitution-making: the Federal Constitution of 1787. *American Journal of Political Science* 28: 435–458.

Kelley, Robert (1979). *The Cultural Pattern in American Politics: The First Century.* New York: Knopf.

Kenyon, Cecilia M. (1955). Men of little faith: the anti-federalists on the nature of representative government. *William and Mary Quarterly* 12: 3–43.

Ketcham, Ralph (1984). *Presidents above Party: The First American Presidency, 1789–1829.* Chapel Hill: University of North Carolina Press.

Key, V. O. (1955). A theory of critical elections. *Journal of Politics.* 17: 3–18.

Key, V. O. (1959). Secular realignment and the party system. *Journal of Politics* 21: 198–210.

Kincaid, John (1982). *Political Culture, Public Policy, and the American States.* Philadelphia: Ishi Press.

Klein, Milton M. (1978). Shaping the American tradition: the microcosm of colonial New York. *New York History*, April, pp. 173–197.

Kramnick, Isaac (1982). Republican revisionism revisited. *American Historical Review* 87: 629–664.

Lippmann, Walter (1955). *The Public Philosophy.* New York: Mentor.

Lipset, Seymour M. (1963). *The First New Nation.* New York: Anchor Books.

Lynd, Staughton (1967). *Class Conflict, Slavery, and the United States Constitution.* New York: Bobbs-Merrill.

Main, Jackson Turner (1973). *The Sovereign States, 1775–1783.* New York: Franklin Watts, Inc.

McDonald, Forrest (1958). *We the People.* Chicago: University of Chicago Press.

McDonald, Forrest (1965). *E Pluribus Unum: The Formation of the American Republic.* Boston: Houghton Mifflin.

McDonald, Forrest (1985). *Novus Ordo Seclorum: The Intellectual Origins of the Constitution.* Lawrence: University Press of Kansas.

McLaughlin, Andrew C. (1905). *The Confederation and the Constitution.* New York: Harper & Brothers.

Meyers, Marvin (1973). *The Mind of the Founder: Sources of the Political Thought of James Madison.* New York: Bobbs-Merrill.

Morgan, Edmund S. (1967). The Puritan Ethic and the American Revolution. *William and Mary Quarterly* 24: 3–43.

Onuf, Peter (1983). *The Origins of the Federal Republic: Jurisdictional Controversies in the United States, 1775–1787*. Philadelphia: University of Pennsylvania Press.

Ostrom, Vincent (1979). Constitutional level of analysis: problems and prospects. Convention paper delivered at the meetings of the Western Political Science Association in Portland, OR, March 22–24, 1979.

Pomper, Gerald (1967). Classification of presidential elections. *Journal of Politics* 29:535–566.

Pomper, Gerald (1970). Conflicts and coalitions at the American Constitutional Convention. In E.W. Kelley, S.O. Groennings, M. Leiserson (eds.), *The Study of Coalition Behavior: Theoretical Perspectives and Cases from Four Continents*, pp. 209–225. New York: Holt, Rinehart & Winston.

Pool, William (1950). An economic interpretation of the Federal Constitution in North Carolina. *North Carolina Historical Review* 27: 119–141, 284–313, 437–461.

Rakove, Jack N. (1979). *The Beginnings of National Politics: An Interpretive History of the Continental Congress*. New York: Knopf.

Riker, William H. (1984). The heresthetics of constitution-making: the presidency in 1787, with comments on determinism and rational choice. *American Political Science Review* 78: 1–16.

Robinson, Donald L. (1971). *Slavery in the Structure of American Politics, 1765–1820*. New York: Harcourt, Brace, Jovanovich.

Roche, John P. (1961). The Founding Fathers: a reform caucus in action. *American Political Science Review* 55: 799–816.

Rossiter, Clinton (1966). *1787: The Grand Convention*. New York: New American Library.

Rummel, Rudolph J. (1967). Understanding factor analysis. *Journal of Conflict Resolution* 11: 444–478.

Rummel, Rudolph J. (1970). *Applied Factor Analysis*. Evanston, IL: Northwestern University Press.

Russett, Bruce M. (1966). Discovering voting groups in the United Nations. *American Political Science Review* LX: 327–329.

Schattschneider, E. E. (1960). *The Semi-Sovereign People: A Realist's View of Democracy In America*. New York: Holt, Rinehart & Winston.

Schubert, Glendon (1962). The 1960 term of the Supreme Court: a psychological analysis. *American Political Science Review* 56: 90–107.

Shalhope, Robert E. (1972). Toward a republican synthesis: the emergence of an understanding of republicanism in American historiography. *William and Mary Quarterly* 29: 49–80.

Shalhope, Robert E. (1982). Republicanism and early American historiography. *William and Mary Quarterly* 39: 334–356.

Smith, David G. (1965). *The Convention and the Constitution*. New York: St. Martin's Press.

Smith, J. Allen (1907). *The Spirit of American Government*. Cambridge, MA: Harvard University Press.

Smith, Page (1980). *The Shaping of America: A People's History of the Young Republic.* Vol. 3. New York: McGraw-Hill.

Stoudinger, Susan (1968). An analysis of voting behavior in the Constitutional Convention of 1787. Unpublished master's thesis: University of Maryland.

Sundquist, James L. (1973). *Dynamics of the Party System: Alignment and Realignment of Political Parties in the United States.* Washington, DC: The Brookings Institution.

Sydnor, Charles (1952). *American Revolutionaries in the Making.* Chapel Hill: University of North Carolina Press.

Szatmary, David P. (1980). *Shay's Rebellion: The Making of an Agrarian Insurrection.* Amherst: The University of Massachusetts Press.

Thach, Charles C. (1923). *The Creation of the Presidency: 1775–1789.* Baltimore: Johns Hopkins Press.

Thomas, Robert E. (1953). The Virginia Convention of 1788: a criticism of Beard's An Economic Interpretation of the Constitution. *Journal of Southern History* 19: 63–72.

Tocqueville, Alexis de (1835). *Democracy In America.* Phillips Bradley (ed.), 2 vols. New York: Vintage Books, 1954.

Tolles, Frederick B. (1966). The historians of the middle colonies. In Ray Allen Billington, *The Reinterpretation of Early American History*, pp. 65–79. San Marino,CA: The Huntington Library.

Ulmer, S. Sidney (1968). Sub-group formation in the Constitutional Convention. *Midwest Journal of Political Science* 10: 288–303.

Vile, M. J. C. (1967). *Constitutionalism and the Separation of Powers.* Oxford: Clarendon Press.

Warren, Charles (1928). *The Making of the Constitution.* New York: Barnes & Noble, reprint, 1967.

Wolfe, Christopher (1977). On understanding the Constitutional Convention of 1787. *Journal of Politics* 39: 97–118.

Wood, Gordon S. (1966). Rhetoric and reality in the American Revolution. *William and Mary Quarterly* 23: 3–32.

Wood, Gordon S. (1969). *The Creation of the American Republic 1776-1787.* New York: W. W. Norton.

Appendix A
THE DATA
569 Roll-Call Votes Taken in the Constitutional Convention

Data were coded as follows:
1 = Yes, 2 = No, 3 = Divided, 4 = Absent
The number of each roll-call vote is listed, followed by the vote of each of the twelve states that were represented during some or all of the Convention's work. Rhode Island failed to send a delegation and so is not listed. The first column is for New Hampshire, the last column is for Georgia, with states listed roughly North to South as follows: New Hampshire, Massachusetts, Connecticut, New York, New Jersey, Pennsylvania, Delaware, Maryland, Virginia, North Carolina, South Carolina, and Georgia.

001	411242142214		040	421112112222
002	412341141114		041	412221221111
003	411141441114		042	412121221111
004	411142141114		043	411221221111
005	413121341121		044	421212112222
006	422222342222		045	412221221111
007	412222241212		046	412224331111
008	413111141111		047	422111111221
009	432111141222		048	411111121111
010	422141212222		049	422111111121
011	422341212222		050	412211111121
012	411142121111		051	412211111121
013	421242222211		052	431122232112
014	422242122222		053	412111111111
015	412143111112		054	422222212222
016	411142222111		055	411211131112
017	411241221111		056	421211222323
018	412141222111		057	412121211112
019	422242222222		058	432311111111
020	422242222222		059	431222122212
021	412141121111		060	412111111111
022	412141111121		061	422122121222
023	412141211111		062	411111111111
024	411141112122		063	411441111111
025	431212211211		064	411113111111
026	421121111222		065	421112132222
027	431312222111		066	411221111111
028	412321111121		067	411221231111
029	421212222212		068	421112132222
030	421122221222		069	422112112222
031	422221222222		070	411221231111
032	411111111111		071	421212132212
033	411111111111		072	411121131111
034	412221321222		073	411231221111
035	412111111211		074	422311222223
036	422222322222		075	411322222113
037	411221231111		076	411111111111
038	411111211111		077	431212112112
039	411121211111	215	078	421312111112

079	412313322121	131	411111111211
080	412211211223	132	422422122211
081	421112211111	133	412421122211
082	431212222222	134	411411221122
083	431112111112	135	422421222222
084	422123112212	136	421422221121
085	422122221211	137	412411121112
086	422222211111	138	411411111111
087	411112112111	139	412422221111
088	421111122211	140	411411111111
089	411112232111	141	422422222222
090	421221131122	142	421411312212
091	421211131222	143	421411222222
092	421221131122	144	412421111111
093	411221111122	145	422422222211
094	422221121222	146	422412322222
095	411221111122	147	431421211131
096	411221212212	148	421412112222
097	411111111121	149	412421222111
098	421112222211	150	412423221111
099	412221111222	151	411411311111
100	421221111122	152	411411111111
101	421122111112	153	411422112112
102	411111111111	154	411423112222
103	412221221222	155	422421211212
104	411111111111	156	431412112122
105	421112132222	157	421422211211
106	412221231111	158	422411211122
107	421111211111	159	412411211113
108	422114432224	160	421422212222
109	411111111111	161	412411112122
110	421112112223	162	411411111122
111	411121211111	163	412422221122
112	411112111111	164	411411111111
113	422142222212	165	422421222222
114	422242222214	166	422422112222
115	411221231111	167	411411111111
116	422111111211	168	411411212221
117	431312111221	169	422411121222
118	431312112123	170	412421122122
119	411211112111	171	411441111114
120	431112112123	172	411442112114
121	411211112222	173	411441111114
122	411221111111	174	411442112324
123	411211111121	175	412441222224
124	422222222211	176	412441211224
125	422222222111	177	411441112214
126	422222122111	178	411441111111
127	422222221111	179	422442221122
128	422222121222	180	411441111111
129	411111111122	181	411411111211
130	422222222212	182	431411111222

183	411411112121		235	111441111111
184	422422222112		236	111441222122
185	432412222311		237	112441121211
186	411411211111		238	212441111111
187	412421221111		239	222442222211
188	422412112222		240	222442122222
189	421411221211		241	222442132224
190	421422222211		242	222441111224
191	411421221112		243	111442222234
192	412422222212		244	221441111114
193	421411111121		245	112411111111
194	411411111111		246	222412211212
195	141421111111		247	222422222211
196	411411111111		248	222422222211
197	412411111211		249	222412232111
198	421443211223		250	111411111111
199	411441111111		251	222422122111
200	412441221222		252	111421211111
201	421442112111		253	222412222222
202	422441222222		254	222411111211
203	221442112222		255	222421432222
204	111441211111		256	222422412111
205	222441222222		257	121411111231
206	111441111111		258	322422221122
207	111441121111		259	122412222211
208	111442122111		260	122412222211
209	112442111111		261	122412222211
210	222442222222		262	122412121311
211	111441111111		263	222412222222
212	222442122222		264	221411422221
213	111442212212		265	112422422221
214	111441111111		266	221421111122
215	112412122111		267	121411111112
216	221421311222		268	212422122222
217	112411111222		269	111413111111
218	121421212222		270	111413111111
219	221411211222		271	222422211212
220	112422222111		272	312422111111
221	111411111121		273	222422221222
222	221412121122		274	211422222222
223	212411111111		275	111411111111
224	142412211111		276	311412221121
225	141412223111		277	111411111111
226	111411121111		278	212411221222
227	112412211111		279	111411112111
228	212422212321		280	111421121131
229	111421111112		281	221421211222
230	222422222121		282	122422222211
231	111411111111		283	221422211222
232	222441411224		284	221411211222
233	222441111214		285	221423211222
234	222442111224		286	112412121111

287	311421112222
288	112422221122
289	112422222122
290	212422222222
291	122421111223
292	121411111121
293	221422221222
294	112422221111
295	222422111222
296	222422112222
297	221423111112
298	212422122122
299	444444444444
300	222424111222
301	221411111111
302	111411121111
303	212422111211
304	111421121111
305	222412211122
306	112421421111
307	222441112212
308	212441121111
309	112441112211
310	121443221311
311	121444221221
312	142444422312
313	242441121122
314	241441111111
315	222442222222
316	211423221111
317	111412121111
318	112421131111
319	222422112221
320	212422212222
321	222411211321
322	422412221222
323	411411112211
324	111421112211
325	112421122212
326	221412211121
327	112411211112
328	121411111322
329	111411111122
330	111411211111
331	212422222312
332	121422211122
333	442412232222
334	222411122222
335	112411122222
336	211422211111
337	241412211111
338	112421111111

339	212421112222
340	112422111311
341	212412211121
342	111411111111
343	222412212221
344	221422222222
345	112411121111
346	122422222212
347	111411212122
348	111411111111
349	122421111222
350	422411111222
351	422421222322
352	211414121411
353	122424222121
354	111414111212
355	222421122222
356	112421121112
357	221412112221
358	111421111111
359	221411121222
360	223411111222
361	243411131222
362	221422222422
363	221411211421
364	111411111411
365	111411111111
366	221422222222
367	111422212111
368	111422212111
369	221442231221
370	111441111111
371	111441121111
372	221442222222
373	122442212112
374	141441211421
375	141441211411
376	141441221411
377	141441221411
378	241442222422
379	242442231424
380	242442211424
381	141442211411
382	142441122422
383	242442121422
384	141441111411
385	111441121111
386	111441111222
387	111441132111
388	112421111111
389	121411112111
390	111411111111

391	142411122111	443	112422111411
392	212422122212	444	111411111111
393	122412122122	445	322422222112
394	112411122122	446	222422222122
395	121411121111	447	322421221212
396	121411121111	448	222422221122
397	111411111123	449	222422221122
398	221411111111	450	222422222112
399	222422211121	451	222421211122
400	111411111111	452	111411112211
401	111411122111	453	122422221122
402	212421221111	454	222422222112
403	222412112222	455	111411111211
404	111421222212	456	111411111211
405	111411221111	457	111411111221
406	111421111222	458	222422222122
407	222412112222	459	111411111211
408	111421221111	460	322411111111
409	222412212422	461	111412112211
410	111411121111	462	212421221112
411	222411122222	463	111411111211
412	222412221111	464	142422211111
413	121411142111	465	111411211111
414	222422212222	466	111411111211
415	111411221111	467	111411111111
416	113411131211	468	121421211111
417	222412112222	469	111421221111
418	111411421111	470	111421111211
419	123421112221	471	111411111111
420	221421111222	472	211421221122
421	221421212421	473	322411211211
422	222422212422	474	111421121411
423	221412212221	475	222421222222
424	111411112221	476	222421212112
425	111411121111	477	111411111111
426	121421121112	478	111411111111
427	112421122222	479	111412111121
428	222412212122	480	222422212211
429	111411121111	481	111422111112
430	212422121122	482	222422211221
431	211411131121	483	111411111111
432	241411111121	484	111421221111
433	312444111111	485	223422122222
434	411411422112	486	222422222111
435	112411411111	487	211422122211
436	222422411222	488	222422211111
437	222421422122	489	222422222111
438	222421411122	490	211412222121
439	112421421122	491	111422211121
440	112421421123	492	222421221222
441	112441421123	493	111411111111
442	222422222122	494	111412111111

495	111411111111
496	111411111111
497	111411221111
498	111412112111
499	211422222221
500	121412112121
501	222421111122
502	311421111111
503	122421111222
504	111411111111
505	311411211111
506	321412111121
507	321412111121
508	221422222222
509	111411111111
510	321412212111
511	242422222222
512	141411111111
513	241421211111
514	142411111111
515	111442211121
516	212422222222
517	111411111111
518	222412112222
519	222421211222
520	112422221111
521	222421212132
522	111424112111
523	222421111122
524	222422221222
525	221422222211
526	222412212121
527	111413211111
528	222422211121
529	212421222212
530	221412112111
531	121412112111
532	111421112112

533	121412122112
534	222421221221
535	223421221112
536	222422221221
537	222422222222
538	112422211212
539	142411111121
540	411411111111
541	222421111242
542	121423111111
543	122422112121
544	222422211111
545	111411112111
546	222423221121
547	113412112212
548	112421211211
549	223422221221
550	121411232122
551	321422311121
552	221421111111
553	222422222212
554	222422222222
555	212422122222
556	311412222222
557	221422222222
558	221412122222
559	221412322222
560	322422112122
561	222422122422
562	322412112422
563	222422211421
564	222422222422
565	111411111411
566	111411111411
567	111411111111
568	111411111131
569	111411121111

Appendix B

THE VIRGINIA PLAN
Presented by Edmund Randolph, May 29, 1787

1. Resolved that the articles of Confederation ought to be so corrected & enlarged as to accomplish the objects proposed by their institution; namely. "common defence, security of liberty and general welfare."

2. Resd. therefore that the rights of suffrage in the National Legislature ought to be proportioned to the Quotas of contribution, or to the numbers of free inhabitants, as the one or the other rule may seem best in different cases.

3. Resd. that the National Legislature ought to consist of two branches.

4. Resd. that the members of the first branch of the National Legislature ought to be elected by the people of the several States every _____ for the term of _____ ; to be of the age of _____ years at least, to receive liberal stipends by which they may be compensated for the devotion of their time to public service; to be ineligible to any office established by a particular State, or under the authority of the United States, except those peculiarly belonging to the functions of the first branch, during the term of service, and for the space of _____ after its expiration; to be incapable of re-election for the space of _____ after the expiration of their term of service, and to be subject to recall.

5. Resold. that the members of the second branch of the National Legislature ought to be elected by those of the first, out of a proper number of persons nominated by the individual Legislatures, to be of the age of _____ years at least; to hold their offices for a term sufficient to ensure their independency, to receive liberal stipends, by which they may be compensated for the devotion of their time to public service; and to be ineligible to any office established by a particular State, or under the authority of the United States, except those peculiarly belonging to the functions of the second branch, during the term of service, and for the space of _____ after the expiration thereof.

6. Resolved that each branch ought to possess the right of originating Acts; that the National Legislature ought to be empowered to enjoy the Legislative Rights vested in Congress by the Confederation & moreover to legislate in all cases to which the separate States are incompetent, or in which the harmony of the United States may be interrupted by the exercise of individual Legislation; to negative all laws passed by the several States, contravening in the opinion of the National Legislature the articles of Union; and to call forth the force of the Union agst. any member of the Union failing to fulfil its duty under the articles thereof.

7. Resd. that a National Executive be instituted; to be chosen by the National Legislature for the term of _____ years, to receive punctually at stated times, a fixed compensation for the services rendered, in which no increase or diminution shall be made so as to effect the Magistracy; existing at the time of increase or diminution, and to be ineligible a second time; and that besides a

general authority to execute the National laws, it ought to enjoy the Executive rights vested in Congress by the Confederation.

8. Resd. that the Executive and a convenient number of the National Judiciary, ought to compose a council of revision with authority to examine every act of the National Legislature before it shall operate, & every act of a particular Legislature before a Negative thereon shall be final; and that the dissent of the said Council shall amount to a rejection, unless the Act of the National Legislature be again passed, or that of a particular Legislature be again negatived by _____ of the members of each branch.

9. Resd. that a National Judiciary be established to consist of one or more supreme tribunals, and of inferior tribunals to be chosen by the National Legislature, to hold their offices during good behaviour; and to receive punctually at stated times fixed compensation for their services, in which no increase or dimunition shall be made so as to affect the persons actually in office at the time of such increase or dimunition. that the jurisdiction of the inferior tribunals shall be to hear & determine in the first instance, and of the supreme tribunal to hear and determine in the dernier resort, all piracies & felonies on the high seas, captures from an enemy; cases in which foreigners or citizens of other States applying to such jurisdictions may be interested, or which respect the collection of the National revenue; impeachments of any National officers, and questions which may involve the national peace and harmony.

10. Resolvd. that provision ought to be made for the administration of States lawfully arising within the limits of the United States, whether from a voluntary junction of Government & Territory or otherwise, with the consent of a number of voices in the National legislature less than the whole.

11. Resd. that a Republican Government & the territory of each State, except in the instance of a voluntary junction of Government & territory, ought to be guaranteed by the United States to each State.

12. Resd. that provision ought to be made for the continuance of Congress and their authorities and privileges, until a given day after the reform of the articles of Union shall be adopted, and for the completion of all their engagements.

13. Resd. that provision ought to be made for the amendment of the Articles of Union whensoever it shall seem necessary, and that the assent of the National Legislature ought not to be required thereto.

14. Resd. that the Legislative Executive & Judiciary powers within the several States ought to be bound by oath to support the articles of Union.

15. Resd. that the amendments which shall be offered to the Confederation, by the Convention ought at a proper time, or times, after the approbation of Congress to be submitted to an assembly or assemblies or Representatives, recommended by the several Legislatures to be expressly chosen by the people, to consider & decide thereon.

Appendix C

THE NEW JERSEY PLAN
Presented by William Paterson, June 15, 1787

Mr. Patterson, laid before the Convention the plan which he said several of the deputations wished to be substituted in place of that proposed by Mr. Randolp. After some little discussion of the most proper mode of giving it a fair deliberation it was agreed that it should be referred to a Committee of the Whole, and that in order to place the two plans in due comparison, the other should be recommitted. At the earnest desire of Mr. Lansing & some other gentlemen, it was also agreed that the Convention should not go into Committee of the whole on the subject till tomorrow, by which delay the friends of the plan proposed by Mr. Patterson wd. be better prepared to explain & support it, and all would have an opportuy of taking copies. * —[See note]

The propositions from N. Jersey moved by Mr. Patterson were in the words following.

1. Resd. that the articles of Confederation ought to be so revised, corrected & enlarged, as to render the federal Constitution adequate to the exigences of Government, & the preservation of the Union.

2. Resd. that in addition to the powers vested in the U. States in Congress, by the present existing articles of Confederation, they be authorized to pass acts for raising a revenue, by levying a duty or duties on all goods or merchandizes of foreign growth or manufacture, imported into any part of the U. States, by Stamps on paper, vellum or parchment, and by a postage on all letters or packages passing through the general post-Office, to be applied to such federal purposes as they shall deem proper & expedient; to make rules & regulations for the collection thereof; and the same from time to time, to alter & amend in such manner as they shall think proper: to pass Acts for the regulation of trade & commerce as well with foreign nations as with each other: provided that all punishments, fines, forfeitures & penalties to be incurred for contravening such acts rules and regulations shall be adjudged by the Common law Judiciarys of the State in which any offence Contrary to the true intent & meaning of such Acts rules & regulations shall have been committed or perpetrated, with liberty of commencing in the first instance all suits & prosecutions for that purpose in the superior Common law Judiciary in such State, subject nevertheless, for the correction of all errors, both in law & fact in rendering judgment, to an appeal to the Judiciary of the U. States.

3. Resd. that whenever requisitions shall be necessary, instead of the rule for making requisitions mentioned in the articles of Confederation, the United States in Congs. be authorized to make such requisitions in proportion to the whole number of white & other free citizens & inhabitants of every age sex and condition including those bound to servitude for a term of years & three fifths of all other persons not comprehended in the foregoing description, except

Indians not paying taxes; that if such requisitions be not complied with, in the time specified therein, to direct the collection thereof in the non complying States & for that purpose to devise and pass acts directing & authorizing the same; provided that none of the powers hereby vested in the U. States in Congs. shall be exercised without the consent of at least _____ States, and in that proportion if the number of Confederated States should hereafter be increased or diminished.

4. Resd. that the U. States in Congs. be authorized to elect a federal Executive to consist of _____ persons, to continue in office for the term of _____ years, to receive punctually at stated times a fixed compensation for their services, in which no increase or diminution shall be made so as to affect the persons composing the Executive at the time of such increase or diminution, to be paid out of the federal treasury; to be incapable of holding any other office or appointment during their time of service and for _____ years thereafter; to be ineligible a second time, & removeable by Congs. on application by a majority of the Executives of the several States; that the Executives besides their general authority to execute the federal acts ought to appoint all federal officers not otherwise provided for, & to direct all military operations; provided that none of the persons composing the federal Executive shall on any occasion take command of any troops, so as personally to conduct any enterprise as General, or in other capacity.

5. Resd. that a federal Judiciary be established to consist of a supreme Tribunal the Judges of which to be appointed by the Executive, & to hold their offices during good behaviour, to receive punctually at stated times a fixed compensation for their services in which no increase or diminution shall be made, so as to affect the persons actually in office at the time of such increase or diminution; that the Judiciary so established shall have authority to hear & determine in the first instance on all impeachments of federal officers, & by way of appeal in the dernier resort in all cases touching the rights of Ambassadors, in all cases of captures from an enemy, in all cases of piracies & felonies on the high seas, in all cases in which foreigners may be interested, in the construction of any treaty or treaties, or which may arise on any of the Acts for regulation of trade, or the collection of the federal Revenue: that none of the Judiciary shall during the time they remain in Office be capable of receiving or holding any other office or appointment during their time of service, or for thereafter.

6. Resd. that all Acts of the U. States in Congs. made by virtue & in pursuance of the powers hereby & by the articles of confederation vested in them, and all Treaties made & ratified under the authority of the U. States shall be the supreme law of the respective States so far forth as those Acts or Treaties shall relate to the said States or their Citizens, and that the Judiciary of the several States shall be bound thereby in their decisions, any thing in the respective laws of the Individual States to the contrary notwithstanding; and that if any State, or any body of men in any State shall oppose or prevent ye. carrying into execution such acts or treaties, the federal Executive shall be authorized to call forth ye power of the Confederated States, or so much thereof as may be necessary to

enforce and compel an obedience to such Acts, or an Observance of such Treaties.

7. Resd. that provision be made for the admission of new States into the Union.

8. Resd. the rule for naturalization ought to be the same in every State.

9. Resd. that a Citizen of one State committing an offence in another State of the Union, shall be deemed guilty of the same offence as if it had been committed by a Citizen of the State in which the Offence was committed.

[Note]*This plan had been concerted among the deputations or members thereof, from Cont. N. Y. N. J. Del. and perhaps Mr Martin from Maryd. who made with them a common cause on different principles. Cont. and N. Y. were agst. a departure from the principle of the Confederation, wishing rather to add a few new powers to Congs. than to substitute, a National Govt. because its patrons considered a proportional representation of the States as the basis of it. The eagourness displayed by the Members opposed to a Natl. Govt. from these different [motives] began now to produce serious anxiety for the result of the Convention.- Mr. Dickenson said to Mr. Madison you see the consequence of pushing things too far. Some of the members from the small States wish for two branches in the General Legislature, and are friends to a good National Government; but we would sooner submit to a foreign power, than submit to be deprived of an equality of suffrage, in both branches of the legislature, and thereby be thrown under the domination of the large States.

Appendix D

COMMITTEE OF DETAIL REPORT
PROCEEDINGS OF THE CONVENTION,
JUNE 19—JULY 23

1. Resolved That the Government of the United States ought to consist of a Supreme Legislative, Judiciary and Executive.

2. Resolved That the Legislature of the United States ought to consist of two Branches.

3. Resolved That the Members of the first Branch of the Legislature of the United States ought to be elected by the People of the several States—for the Term of two Years—to be of the Age of twenty five Years at least—to be ineligible to and incapable of holding any Office under the Authority of the United States (except those peculiarly belonging to the Functions of the first Branch) during the Time of Service of the first Branch.

4. Resolved That the Members of the second Branch of the Legislature of the United States ought be chosen by the Individual Legislatures—to be of the Age of thirty Years at least—to hold their Offices for the Term of six Years; one third to go out biennially—to receive a Compensation for the Devotion of their Time to the public Service—to be ineligible to and incapable of holding any Office under the Authority of the United States (except those peculiarly belonging to the Functions of the second Branch) during the Term for which they are elected, and for one Year thereafter.

5. Resolved. That each Branch ought to possess the Right of originating Acts.

6. Resolved That the Right of Suffrage in the first Branch of the Legislature of the United States ought not to be according to the Rules established in the Articles of Confederation but according to some equitable Ratio of Representation.

7. Resolved That in the original Formation of the Legislature of the United States the first Branch thereof shall consist of sixty five Members of which Number New Hampshire shall send *three*—Massachusetts *eight*—Rhode Island *one*—Connecticut *five*—New York *six*—New Jersey *four*—Pennsylvania *eight*—Delaware *one* —Maryland *six*—Virginia *ten*—North Carolina *five*—South Carolina *five*—Georgia *three*..

But as the present Situation of the States may probably alter in the Number of their Inhabitants, the Legislature of the United States shall be authorised from Time to Time to apportion the Number of Representatives; and in Case any of the States shall hereafter be divided, or enlarged by Addition of Territory, or any two or more States united, or any new States created within the Limits of the United States, the Legislature of the United States shall possess Authority to regulate the Number of Representatives in any of the foregoing Cases, upon the Principle of the Number of their Inhabitants, according to the Provisions herein after mentioned namely—Provided always that Representation ought to be proportioned according to direct taxation: And in order to ascertain the Alteration in the direct Taxation, which may be required from Time to Time, by the Changes in the relative Circumstances of the States —

Resolved that a Census be taken, within six years from the first Meeting of the Legislature of the United States, and once within the Term of every ten Years afterwards, of all the Inhabitants of the United States in the Manner and according to the Ratio recommended by Congress in their Resolution of April 18th. 1783—And that the Legislature of the United States shall proportion the direct Taxation accordingly.

Resolved that all Bills for raising or Appropriating Money, and for fixing the Salaries of the Officers of the Government of the United States shall originate in the first Branch of the Legislature of the United States, and shall not be altered or amended by the second Branch; and that no money shall be drawn from the public Treasury but in Pursuance of Appropriations to be originated by the first Branch

Resolved that from the first Meeting of the Legislature of the United States until a Census shall be taken, all Monies for supplying the public Treasury by direct Taxation shall be raised from the several States according to the Number of their Representatives respectively in the first Branch

8. Resolved That in the second Branch of the Legislature of the United States each State shall have an equal Vote.

Resolved That the Legislature of the United States ought to possess the legislative Rights vested in Congress by the Confederation; and moreover to legislate in all Cases for the general Interests of the Union, and also in those Cases to which the States are separately incompetent, or in which the Harmony of the United States may be interrupted by the Exercise of individual Legislation.

Resolved That the legislative Acts of the United States made by Virtue and in Pursuance of the Articles of Union, and all Treaties made and ratified under the Authority of the United States shall be the supreme Law of the respective States so far as those Acts or Treaties shall relate to the said States, or their Citizens and Inhabitants; and that the Judicatures of the several States shall be bound thereby in their Decisions, any thing in the respective Laws of the individual States to the contrary notwithstanding.

Resolved That a national Executive be instituted to consist of a single Person— to be chosen for the Term of six Years—with Power to carry into Execution the national Laws—to appoint to Offices in Cases not otherwise provided for—to be removeable on Impeachment and Conviction of mal Practice or Neglect of Duty—to receive a fixed Compensation for the Devotion of his Time to public Service—to be paid out of the public Treasury.

Resolved That the national Executive shall have a Right to negative any legislative Act, which shall not be afterwards passed, unless by two third Parts of each Branch of the national Legislative.

Resolved That a national Judiciary be established to consist of one Supreme Tribunal—the Judges of which shall be appointed by the second Branch of the national Legislature—to hold their Offices during good Behaviour—to receive punctually at stated Times a fixed Compensation for their Services, in which no Diminution shall be made so as to affect the Persons actually in Office at the Time of such Diminution.

Resolved That the Jurisdiction of the national Judiciary shall extend to Cases arising under the Laws passed by the general Legislature, and to such other Questions as involve the national Peace and Harmony.

Resolved That the national Legislature, be empowered to appoint inferior Tribunals.

Resolved That Provision ought to be made for the Admission of States lawfully arising within the Limits of the United States, whether from a voluntary Junction of Government and Territory, or otherwise, with the Consent of a number of Voices in the national Legislature _____ less than the whole.

Resolved That a Republican Form of Government shall be guarantied to each State; and that each State shall be protected against foreign and domestic Violence.

Resolved That Provision ought to be made for the Amendment of the Articles of Union, whensoever it shall seem necessary.

Resolved That the legislative, executive and judiciary Powers, within the several States, and of the national Government, ought to be bound by Oath to support the Articles of Union.

Resolved That the Amendments which shall be offered to the Confederation by the Convention ought at a proper Time or Times, after the Approbation of Congress, to be submitted to an Assembly or Assemblies of Representatives, recommended by the several Legislatures, to be expressly chosen by the People to consider and decide thereon.

Resolved That the Representation in the second Branch of the Legislature of the United States consist of two Members from each State, who shall vote *per capita*.

Appendix E

THE CONSTITUTION OF THE UNITED STATES

We the people of the United States, in Order to form a more perfect Union, establish Justice, insure domestic Tranquility, provide for the common defence, promote the general Welfare, and secure the Blessings of Liberty to ourselves and our Posterity, do ordain and establish this Constitution for the United States of America.

Article I.

Section 1. All legislative Powers herein granted shall be vested in a Congress of the United States, which shall consist of a Senate and House of Representatives.

Section 2. The House of Representatives shall be composed of Members chosen every second Year by the People of the several States, and the Electors in each State shall have [the] Qualifications requisite for Electors of the most numerous Branch of the State Legislature.

No Person shall be a Representative who shall not have attained to the Age of twenty five Years, and been seven Years a Citizen of the United States, and who shall not, when elected, be an Inhabitant of that State in which he shall be chosen.

Representatives and direct Taxes shall be apportioned among the several States which may be included within this Union, according to their respective Numbers, which shall be determined by adding to the whole Number of free Persons, including those bound to Service for a Term of Years, and excluding Indians not taxed, three fifths of all other Persons. The actual Enumeration shall be made within three Years after the first Meeting of the Congress of the United States, and within every subsequent Term of ten Years, in such Manner as they shall by Law direct. The Number of Representatives shall not exceed one for every thirty Thousand, but each State shall have at Least one Representative; and until such enumeration shall be made, the State of New Hampshire shall be entitled to chuse three, Massachusetts eight, Rhode-Island and Providence Plantations one, Connecticut five, New-York six, New Jersey four, Pennsylvania eight, Delaware one, Maryland six, Virginia ten, North Carolina five, South Carolina five, and Georgia three.

When vacancies happen in the Representation from any State, the Executive Authority thereof shall issue Writs of Election to fill such Vacancies.

The House of Representatives shall chuse their Speaker and other Officers; and shall have the sole Power of Impeachment.

Section 3. The Senate of the United States shall be composed of two Senators from each State, chosen by the Legislature thereof, for six Years; and each Senator shall have one Vote.

Immediately after they shall be assembled in Consequence of the first Election, they shall be divided as equally as may be into three Classes. The Seats of the Senators of the first Class shall be vacated at the Expiration of the second Year, of the second Class at the Expiration of the fourth Year, and of the third Class at the Expiration of the sixth Year, so that one third may be chosen every second Year; and if Vacancies happen by Resignation, or otherwise, during the Recess of the Legislature of any State, the Executive thereof may make temporary Appointments until the next Meeting of the Legislature, which shall then fill such Vacancies.

No Person shall be a Senator who shall not have attained to the Age of thirty Years, and been nine Years a Citizen of the United States, and who shall not, when elected, be an inhabitant of that State for which he shall be chosen.

The Vice President of the United States shall be President of the Senate, but shall have no Vote, unless they be equally divided.

The Senate shall chuse their other Officers, and also a President pro tempore, in the Absence of the Vice President, or when he shall exercise the Office of President of the United States.

The Senate shall have the sole Power to try all Impeachments. When sitting for that Purpose, they shall be on Oath or Affirmation. When the President of the United States [is tried,] the Chief Justice shall preside: And no Person shall be convicted without the Concurrence of two thirds of the Members present.

Judgment in Cases of Impeachment shall not extend further than to removal from Office, and disqualification to hold and enjoy any Office of honor, Trust or Profit under the United States: but the Party convicted shall nevertheless be liable and subject to Indictment, Trial, Judgment and Punishment, according to Law.

Section 4. The Times, Places and Manner of holding Elections for Senators and Representatives, shall be prescribed in each State by the Legislature thereof; but the Congress may at any time by Law make or alter such Regulations, except as to the Places of chusing Senators.

The Congress shall assemble at least once in every Year, and such Meeting shall be on the first Monday in December, unless they shall by Law appoint a different Day.

Section 5. Each House shall be the Judge of the Elections, Returns and Qualifications of its own Members, and a Majority of each shall constitute a Quorum to do Business; but a smaller Number may adjourn from day to day, and may be authorized to compel the Attendance of absent Members, in such Manner, and under such Penalties as each House may provide.

Each House may determine the Rules of its Proceedings, punish its Members for disorderly Behaviour, and, with the Concurrence of two thirds, expel a Member.

Each House shall keep a Journal of its Proceedings, and from time to time publish the same, excepting such Parts as may in their Judgment require Secrecy; and the Yeas and Nays of the Members of either House on any question shall, at the Desire of one fifth of those Present, be entered on the Journal.

Neither House, during the Session of Congress, shall, without the Consent of the other, adjourn for more than three days, nor to any other Place than that in which the two Houses shall be sitting.

Section 6. The Senators and Representatives shall receive a Compensation for their Services, to be ascertained by Law, and paid out of the Treasury of the United States. They shall in all Cases, except Treason, Felony and Breach of the Peace, be privileged from Arrest during their Attendance at the Session of their respective Houses, and in going to and returning from the same; and for any Speech or Debate in either House, they shall not be questioned in any other Place.

No Senator or Representative shall, during the Time for which he was elected, be appointed to any civil Office under the Authority of the United States, which shall have been created, or the Emoluments whereof shall have been encreased during such time; and no Person holding any Office under the United States, shall be a Member of either House during his Continuance in Office.

Section 7. All Bills for raising Revenue shall originate in the House of Representatives; but the Senate may propose or concur with Amendments as on other Bills.

Every Bill which shall have passed the House of Representatives and the Senate, shall, before it become a Law, be presented to the President of the United States; If he approve he shall sign it, but if not he shall return it, with his Objections to that House in which it shall have originated, who shall enter the Objections at large on their Journal, and proceed to reconsider it. If after such Reconsideration two thirds of that House shall agree to pass the Bill, it shall be sent, together with the Objections, to the other House, by which it shall likewise be reconsidered, and if approved by two thirds of that House, it shall become a Law. But in all such Cases the Votes of both Houses shall be determined by yeas and Nays, and the Names of the Persons voting for and against the Bill shall be entered on the Journal of each House respectively. If any Bill shall not be returned by the President within ten Days (Sundays excepted) after it shall have been presented to him, the Same shall be a Law, in like Manner as if he had signed it, unless the Congress by their Adjournment prevent its Return, in which Case it shall not be a Law.

Every Order, Resolution, or Vote to which the Concurrence of the Senate and House of Representatives may be necessary (except on a question of Adjournment) shall be presented to the President of the United States; and before the Same shall take Effect, shall be approved by him, or being disapproved by him, shall be repassed by two thirds of the Senate and House of Representatives, according to the Rules and Limitations prescribed in the Case of a Bill.

Section 8. The Congress shall have Power To lay and collect Taxes, Duties, Imposts and Excises, to pay the Debts and Provide for the common Defence and general Welfare of the United States; but all Duties, Imposts and Excises shall be uniform throughout the United States;

To borrow Money on the credit of the United States;

To regulate Commerce with foreign Nations, and among the several States, and with the Indian Tribes;

To establish an uniform Rule of Naturalization, and uniform Laws on the subject of Bankruptcies throughout the United States;

To coin Money, regulate the Value thereof, and of foreign Coin, and fix the Standard of Weights and Measures;

To provide for the Punishment of counterfeiting the Securities and current Coin of the United States;

To establish Post Offices and post Roads;

To promote the Progress of Science and useful Arts, by securing for limited Time to Authors and Inventors the exclusive Right to their respective Writings and Discoveries;

To constitute Tribunals inferior to the supreme Court;

To define and punish Piracies and Felonies committed on the high Seas, and Offences against the Law of Nations;

To declare War, grant Letters of Marque and Reprisal, and make Rules concerning Captures on Land and Water;

To raise and support Armies, but no Appropriation of Money to that Use shall be for a longer Term than two Years;

To provide and maintain a Navy;

To make Rules for the Government and Regulation of the land and naval Forces;

To provide for calling forth the Militia to execute the Laws of the Union, suppress Insurrections and repel Invasions;

To provide for organizing, arming, and disciplining, the Militia, and for governing such Part of them as may be employed in the Service of the United States, reserving to the States respectively, the Appointment of the Officers, and the Authority of training the Militia according to the discipline prescribed by Congress;

To exercise exclusive Legislation in all Cases whatsoever, over such District (not exceeding ten Miles square) as may, by Cession of Particular States, and the Acceptance of Congress, become the Seat of the Government of the United States, and to exercise like Authority over all Places purchased by the Consent of the Legislature of the State in which the Same shall be, for the Erection of Forts, Magazines, Arsenals, dock-Yards, and other needful Buildings;—And

To make all Laws which shall be necessary and proper for carrying into Execution the foregoing Powers, and all other Powers vested by this Constitution in the Government of the United States, or in any Department or Officer thereof.

Section 9. The Migration or Importation of such Persons as any of the States now existing shall think proper to admit, shall not be prohibited by the Congress prior to the Year one thousand eight hundred and eight, but a Tax or duty may be imposed on such Importation, not exceeding ten dollars for each Person.

The Privilege of the Writ of Habeas Corpus shall not be suspended, unless when in Cases of Rebellion or Invasion the public Safety may require it.

No Bill of Attainder or ex post facto Law shall be passed.

No Capitation, or other direct, Tax shall be laid, unless in Proportion to the Census of Enumeration herein before directed to be taken.

No Tax or Duty shall be laid on Articles exported from any State.

No Preference shall be given by any Regulation of Commerce or Revenue to the Ports of one State over those of another: nor shall Vessels bound to, or from, one State, be obliged to enter, clear, or pay Duties in another.

No Money shall be drawn from the Treasury, but in Consequence of Appropriations made by Law; and a regular Statement and Account of the Receipts and Expenditures of all public Money shall be published from time to time.

No Title of Nobility shall be granted by the United States: And no Person holding any Office of Profit or Trust under them, shall, without the Consent of the Congress, accept of any present, Emolument, Office, or Title, of any kind whatever, from any King, Prince, or foreign State.

Section 10. No State shall enter into any Treaty, Alliance, or Confederation;

grant Letters of Marque and Reprisal; coin Money; emit Bills of Credit; make any Thing but gold and silver Coin a Tender in Payment of Debts; pass any Bill of Attainder, ex post facto Law, or Law impairing the Obligation of Contracts, or grant any Title of Nobility.

No State shall, without the Consent of [the] Congress, lay any Imposts or Duties on Imports or Exports, except what may be absolutely necessary for executing it's inspection Laws: and the net Produce of all Duties and Imposts, laid by any State on Imports or Exports, shall be for the Use of the Treasury of the United States; and all such Laws shall be subject to the Revision and Controul of [the] Congress.

No State shall, without the Consent of Congress, lay any Duty of Tonnage, keep Troops, or Ships of War in time of Peace, enter into any Agreement or Compact with another State, or with a foreign Power, or engage in War, unless actually invaded, or in such imminent Danger as will not admit of delay.

Article II.

Section 1. The executive Power shall be vested in a President of the United States of America. He shall hold his Office during the Term of four Years, and, together with the Vice President, chosen for the same Term, be elected, as follows:

Each state shall appoint, in such Manner as the Legislature thereof may direct, a Number of Electors, equal to the whole Number of Senators and Representatives to which the State may be entitled in the Congress: but no Senator or Representative, or Person holding an Office of Trust or Profit under the United States, shall be appointed an Elector.

The Electors shall meet in their respective States, and vote by Ballot for two Persons, of whom one at least shall not be an Inhabitant of the same State with themselves. And they shall make a List of all the Persons voted for, and of the Number of Votes for each; which List they shall sign and certify, and transmit sealed to the Seat of the Government of the United States, directed to the President of the Senate. The President of the Senate shall, in the Presence of the Senate and House of Representatives, open all the Certificates, and the Votes shall then be counted. The Person having the greatest Number of Votes shall be the President, if such Number be a Majority of the whole Number of Electors appointed; and if there be more than one who have such Majority, and have an equal Number of Votes, then the House of Representatives shall immediately chuse by Ballot one of them for President; and if no Person have a Majority, then from the five highest on the List the said House shall in like Manner chuse the President. But in chusing the President, the Votes shall be taken by States, the Representation from each State having one Vote; A quorum for this Purpose shall consist of a Member or Members from two thirds of the States, and a Majority of all the States shall be necessary to a Choice. In every Case, after the Choice of the President, the Person having the greatest Number of Votes of the Electors shall be the Vice President. But if there should remain two or more who have equal Votes, the Senate shall chuse from them by Ballot the Vice President.

The Congress may determine the Time of chusing the Electors, and the Day on which they shall give their Votes; which Day shall be the same throughout the United States.

No Person except a natural born Citizen, or a Citizen of the United States, at the time of the Adoption of this Constitution, shall be eligible to the Office of President; neither shall any Person be eligible to that Office who shall not have attained to the Age of thirty five Years, and been fourteen Years a Resident within the United States.

In Case of the Removal of the President from Office, or of his Death, Resignation, or Inability to discharge the Powers and Duties of the said Office, the Same shall devolve on the Vice President, and the Congress may by Law provide for the Case of Removal, Death, Resignation or Inability, both of the President and Vice President, declaring what Officer shall then act as President, and such Officer shall act accordingly, until the Disability be removed, or a President shall be elected.

The President shall, at stated Times, receive for his Services, a Compensation, which shall neither be encreased nor diminished during the Period for which he shall have been elected, and he shall not receive within that Period any other Emolument from the United States, or any of them.

Before he enter on the Execution of his Office, he shall take the following Oath or Affirmation:—"I do solemnly swear (or affirm) that I will faithfully execute the Office of President of the United States, and will to the best of my Ability, preserve, protect and defend the Constitution of the United States."

Section 2. The President shall be Commander in Chief of the Army and Navy of the United States, and of the Militia of the several States, when called into the actual Service of the United States; he may require the Opinion, in writing, of the principal Officer in each of the executive Departments, upon any Subject relating to the Duties of their respective Offices, and he shall have Power to grant reprieves and Pardons for Offences against the United States, except in Cases of Impeachment.

He shall have Power, by and with the Advice and Consent of the Senate, to make Treaties, provided two thirds of the Senators present concur; and he shall nominate, and by and with the Advice and Consent of the Senate, shall appoint Ambassadors, other public Ministers and Consuls, Judges of the supreme Court, and all other Officers of the United States, whose Appointments are not herein otherwise provided for, and which shall be established by Law: but the Congress may by Law vest the Appointment of such inferior Officers, as they think proper, in the President alone, in the Courts of Law, or in the Heads of Departments.

The President shall have Power to fill up all Vacancies that may happen during the Recess of the Senate, by granting Commissions which shall expire at the End of their next Session.

Section 3. He shall from time to time give to the Congress Information of the State of the Union, and recommend to their consideration such Measures as he shall judge necessary and expedient; he may, on extraordinary Occasions, convene both Houses, or either of them, and in Case of Disagreement between them, with Respect to the Time of Adjournment, he may adjourn them to such Time as he shall think proper; he shall receive Ambassadors and other public Ministers; he shall take Care that the Laws be faithfully executed, and shall Commission all the Officers of the United States.

Section 4. The President, Vice President and all civil Officers of the United States, shall be removed from Office on Impeachment for, and conviction of, Treason, Bribery, or other high Crimes and Misdemeanors.

Article III.

Section 1. The judicial Power of the United States, shall be vested in one supreme Court, and in such inferior Courts as the Congress may from time to time ordain and establish. The Judges, both of the supreme and inferior Courts, shall hold their Offices during good Behaviour, and shall, at stated Times, receive for their Services, a Compensation, which shall not be diminished during their Continuance in Office.

Section 2. The judicial Power shall extend to all Cases, in Law and Equity, arising under this Constitution, the Laws of the United States, and Treaties made, or which shall be made, under their Authority;—to all Cases affecting Ambassadors, other public Ministers and Consuls;—to all Cases of admiralty and maritime Jurisdiction;—to Controversies to which the United States shall be a Party;—to Controversies between two or more States;—between a State and Citizens of another State;—between Citizens of different States,—between Citizens of the same State claiming Lands under Grants of different States, and between a State, or the Citizens thereof, and foreign States, Citizens or Subjects.

In all Cases affecting Ambassadors, other public Ministers and Consuls, and those in which a State shall be Party, the supreme Court shall have original Jurisdiction. In all the other Cases before mentioned, the supreme Court shall have appellate Jurisdiction, both as to Law and Fact, with such Exceptions, and under such Regulations as the Congress shall make.

The Trial of all Crimes, except in Cases of Impeachment, shall be by Jury; and such Trial shall be held in the State where the said Crimes shall have been committed; but when not committed within any State, the Trial shall be at such Place or Places as the Congress may by Law have directed.

Section 3. Treason against the United States, shall consist only in levying War against them, or in adhering to their Enemies, giving them Aid and Comfort. No Person shall be Convicted of Treason unless on the Testimony of two Witnesses to the same overt Act, or on Confession in open Court.

The Congress shall have Power to declare the Punishment of Treason, but no Attainder of Treason shall work Corruption of Blood, or Forfeiture except during the Life of the Person attainted.

Article IV.

Section 1. Full Faith and Credit shall be given in each State to the public Acts, Records, and judicial Proceedings of every other State. And the Congress may by general Laws prescribe the Manner in which such Acts, Records and Proceedings shall be proved, and the Effect thereof.

Section 2. The Citizens of each State shall be entitled to all Privileges and Immunities of Citizens in the several States.

A Person charged in any State with Treason, Felony, or other Crime, who shall flee from Justice, and be found in another State, shall on Demand of the executive Authority of the State from which he fled, be delivered up, to be removed to the State having Jurisdiction of the Crime.

No Person held to Service or Labour in one State, under the Laws thereof, escaping into another, shall, in Consequence of any Law or Regulation therein, be discharged from such Service or Labour, but shall be delivered up on Claim of the Party to whom such Service or Labour may be due.

Section 3. New States may be admitted by the Congress into this Union; but no new State shall be formed or erected within the Jurisdiction of any other State; nor any State be formed by the Junction of two or more States, or Parts of States, without the Consent of the Legislatures of the States concerned as well as of the Congress.

The Congress shall have power to dispose of and make all needful Rules and Regulations respecting the Territory or other Property belonging to the United States; and nothing in this Constitution shall be so construed as to Prejudice any Claims of the United States, or of any particular State.

Section 4. The United States shall guarantee to every State in this Union a Republican Form of Government, and shall protect each of them against Invasion; and on Application of the Legislature, or of the Executive (When the Legislature cannot be convened) against domestic Violence.

Article V.

The Congress, whenever two thirds of both Houses shall deem it necessary, shall propose Amendments to this Constitution, or, on the Application of the Legislatures of two thirds of the several States, shall call a Convention for proposing Amendments, which, in either Case, shall be valid to all Intents and Purposes, as Part of this Constitution, when ratified by the Legislatures of three fourths of the several States, or by Conventions in three fourths thereof, as the one or the other Mode of Ratification may be proposed by the Congress; Provided that no Amendment which may be made prior to the Year One thousand eight hundred and eight shall in any Manner affect the first and fourth Clauses in the Ninth Section of the first Article; and that no State, without its Consent, shall be deprived of it's equal Suffrage in the Senate.

Article VI.

All Debts contracted and Engagements entered into, before the Adoption of this Constitution, shall be as valid against the United States under this Constitution, as under the Confederation.

This Constitution, and the Laws of the United States which shall be made in Pursuance thereof; and all Treaties made, or which shall be made, under the Authority of the United States, shall be the supreme Law of the Land; and the Judges in every State shall be bound thereby, any Thing in the Constitution or Laws of any State to the Contrary notwithstanding.

The Senators and Representatives before mentioned, and the Members of the several State Legislatures, and all executive and judicial Officers, both of the United States and of the several States, shall be bound by Oath or Affirmation, to support this Constitution; but no religious Test shall ever be required as a Qualification to any Office or public Trust under the United States.

Article VII.

The Ratification of the Conventions of nine States, shall be sufficient for the Establishment of this Constitution between the States so ratifying the Same.

Index

Adair, Douglass, 49
Adams, Henry, 14
Alker, Hayward, 25
Ambassadors: appointment of, 170,
  182–83; Supreme Court jurisdiction
  over cases involving, 80
Amendments, 189; ratification process
  and, 167, 190
American Revolution, 1, 2, 7
Anderson, Lee F., 26
Anderson, Thornton, 115
Anti-Federalists, 4; Paterson as voice of,
  69
Appleby, Joyce, 7–11
Appointment power: ambassadors and
  Supreme Court justices, 170,
  181–183; removed from state
  executives during the Revolution, 37;
  treasurer, 186–187
Aristocracy, 16; Senate as basis for, 170,
  180–181
Articles of Confederation, 24, 58, 78, 162;
  Hamilton's view of, 51; Madison's
  view of, 36–48; New Jersey Plan and,
  80; support for amending, 201;
  traditional republicanism and, 49
Attendance at the Convention, 20, 65

Bailyn, Bernard, 2, 7–9, 22, 59, 106–107
Baldwin, Abraham, 93; slavery and, 145
Bancroft, George, 1–2, 93; coalitions in
  the Convention and, 5, 24
Banning, Lance, 7, 23
Beard, Charles A., 3–5
Bedford, Gunning, 63, 68, 82, 91–93
Bellah, Robert N., 10
Benson, Lee, 7, 9
Bicameralism, 45
Birkby, Robert H., 70
Blount, William, 191

Bonomi, Patricia U., 13
Brearley, David, 69, 168
Brearley committee, 169–170, 175–181,
  185, 205–207. See also the Executive
Breen, Timothy H., 11
British constitution: Hamilton's affection
  for, 82
Broome, Jacob, 116, 155
Brown, Robert E., 4
Buchanan, James M., i, 15
Burnham, Walter Dean, 19–20, 28,
  196–197
Butler, Pierce, 56–57, 89, 94, 106, 133,
  143, 148, 201

Cabal and corruption, 108. See also the
  Executive, legislative selection of
Canals: power to construct, 187
Capitation taxes, 146
Carey, George W., 42
Carroll, Daniel, 160, 162–164, 188, 191
Cash, W.J., 12
Census, 95, 97–99. See also House of
  Representatives; Representation;
  North versus South
Checks and balances, 204; executive as
  check on legislature, 106–107;
  Madison's view of, 60; separation of
  powers and, 127–130
Citizenship: requirements for, 122, 129,
  131
Clymer, George, 144
Commerce: power over, 95, 126–127,
  129, 137, 165; compromise over
  slavery and, 140–150, 157, 188. See
  also Commerce and Slave Trade
  Compromise; North versus South
Commerce and Slave Trade Compromise,
  312, 131, 140–150; effect on
  southern bloc, 155; proposed by

Morris, 146; reported by committee, 147

Committee of Detail, 111, 120, 122, 129–130, 132, 141, 148, 164, 167

Committee of Style, 186

Committee of the Whole House, 50

Compromise: process of, in convention, 21, 24, 31. *See also* Connecticut compromise; Commerce and Slave Trade compromise; the Executive

Congress, Articles of Confederation and, 54; Jay treaty, 183–184; role in ratification, 165, 167

Congress, constitution and, *see* House of Representatives; Legislature; Senate

Connecticut, 115, 145

Connecticut compromise, 31, 131, 133

Council of revision: preconvention proposal to Washington, 44; proposed in convention, 28, 139; suggested for Kentucky constitution, 38

Courts, *see* Judiciary

Crowl, Philip A., 4

Dahl, Robert A., 15

Davie, William R., 93

Davis, Joseph L., 184

Dayton, Jonathan, 90

Delaware, 47

Democracy, 16; constitutional, 4

Democratic decision making: character of, 18–23

Devine, Donald J., 8

Diamond, Martin, 6, 68; compromise in the convention, 21, 24; impact of Scottish enlightenment, 49; large republic versus small republic, 49–50

Dickinson, John: advocates incremental change, 53–54; convinced by extended republic arguments, 63, 67–68; export taxes, 144; freehold suffrage, 130; money bills, 138; role of the states, 59–60, 67; separation of powers, 60; slave trade, 145–146; troops to quell disturbances, 163–164

Diggins, John, 7, 9, 12, 50

Eidelberg, Paul, 6

Elazar, Daniel J., iii, 9–13

Electoral college, 108, 110, 118, 170, 175. *See also* the Executive

Ellsworth, Oliver, 84, 91–92, 116; Committee of Detail and, 130; slavery and, 140, 145; states to pay national legislators, 87, 90

Executive, the, 16, 103–120, 122–123, 140; Brearley committee report, 167–181, 203; electoral selection of, 116, 119; joint ballot and, 147, 152; legislative selection of, 110, 115; Madison's initial view of, 38, 44, 60; New Jersey plan and, 81; two distinct views of, 107, 111; Virginia plan and, 47, 109

Export taxes, 127, 137, 142–143

Extended republic, i, 49–50, 54–55, 200, 203; executive power in, 107; Hamilton's doubts concerning the, 82; Madison's understanding of, 60, 62; role for the states in, 62, 64. *See also* Small republic

Factions, 4, 42

Factor analysis, 25–28, 32

Farrand, Max, 5, 23–24, 32, 69, 93

Federal Convention, 1, 10, 193–196

Federalists, iv, 52, 58

Federalist Papers, 41, 194

Ferguson, E. James, 9

Fiske, John, 24

Franklin, Benjamin, 58, 106, 134, 187; compromise committee on representation and, 93; statement at the signing ceremony, 190–191

Fugitive slaves, 148–149. *See also* Commerce and Slave Trade compromise

Georgia, 155

George III (King of England), 38, 106

Gerry, Elbridge, 63, 94, 128–129, 135, 139, 180, 201; as chair of Connecticut compromise committee, 78, 93; final objections to the Constitution, 166, 189–190; opposes direct popular role, 56, 66

Gilman, Nicholas, 119

Gladstone, William (British Prime Minister), 2

Gorham, Nathaniel, 84, 140, 149, 191;
    named to Committee of Detail, 130;
    prepared to compromise on
    representation, 88
Greenberg, Douglas, 13
Greene, Jack P., 2, 12, 22
Grumm, John R., 25

Hall, David D., 11
Hamilton, Alexander, 53, 86, 88, 136,
    179–180, 194, 201; move to control
    initial statement of alternatives,
    50–52; doubts "extended republic"
    logic, 82; named to Committee on
    Style, 185
Harman, Harry H., 26
Harris, C. W., 25
Hartz, Louis, 7–9
Higher-level issues, iii, 16–17, 32, 49, 62,
    101, 122. See also Levels of
    constitutional choice; Lower-level
    issues
Hofstadter, Richard, 5
House of Representatives, 37, 56, 132,
    181, 191. See also Legislature
Houstoun, William, 119
Human nature, i, 16
Huntington, Samuel P., 10

Impeachment power, 80, 170, 181–182,
    184–185
Individualism, 8
Individualistic political subculture, iii, 10,
    14
Interest-based interpretations of the
    Constitution, i, iii, 1, 3–7, 17, 22,
    193–194. See also Principled
    interpretations of the constitution
Isaac, Rhys, 12

Jay, John, 107, 183
Jefferson, Thomas, 36–37, 193
Jensen, Merrill, 5, 24, 69–70, 107
Jillson, Calvin, 14, 18, 38, 110, 115
Johnson, William Samuel, 86, 185
Judiciary, 44, 80

Kelley, Robert, iii, 9, 11–13
Kentucky, constitution for, 37–39
Kenyon, Cecilia M., 50

Ketcham, Ralph, 9–10, 22
Key, V. O., 19–20, 196
Kincaid, John, 10–11, 13–14
King, Rufus, 183, 187, 191; Committee
    on Style and, 185; presidential
    selection and, 179–180; ratification
    and, 165; representation and, 76, 94,
    96; slavery and, 132, 142, 146;
    support for Virginia plan and, 53, 84
Klein, Milton M., 13
Kramnick, Isaac, 9

Langdon, John, 119, 143, 189
Lansing, John Jr., 81, 85, 90
Large states, i, iv, 35; coalition of, 67, 69,
    74, 90, 92; executive selection and,
    118, 147; representation and, 64–94
Legislature, 37, 44, 80, 138. See also Large
    states; Representation; Small states
Levels of constitutional choice, iii, 14–17,
    32–34, 59, 169, 194–195, 200–207;
    principles and, 49, 62, 101, 122;
    interests and, 63, 117–118, 137, 140,
    154. See also Higher-level issues;
    Lower-level issues
Lippmann, Walter, 6
Lipset, Seymour M., 9
Lockean ideas, effect of in America, 2,
    7–9
Lower-level issues, iv, 16–17, 32, 63,
    117–118, 137, 140, 154. See also
    Higher-level issues; Levels of
    constitutional choice
Lynd, Staughton, 94

McDonald, Forrest, 2, 16, 49, 55, 101;
    Beard's reading and, 4–6; coalitions
    in the convention, 24–26; mix of
    liberal and republican principles,
    9–10
McHenry, James, 53, 165, 188
McLaughlin, Andrew C., 5, 24, 93
Madison, James, 2, 36, 66, 78, 147, 165,
    184, 185, 187, 189, 201; convention
    related correspondence, 22–23, 35,
    39–40, 69, 92, 193; early defense of
    Virginia plan, 46, 53–54, 56, 60–61,
    63, 84; executive independence, 107,
    116, 119, 128–129, 139, 171, 179,
    185; opposes parchment barriers,

134, 136, 138; on protecting the
national government from the states,
86, 88, 90; representation and, 36,
48–49, 89, 91–92, 100; state
constitutions, 37–39; vices, 40–42
Main, Jackson Turner,106
Martin, Luther, 93, 116, 130, 163, 166;
federalism and, 79, 85, 90, 161, 164;
commerce and slave trade
compromise and, 144, 146; small
state caucus and, 153–154
Maryland, 165
Mason, George, 22, 46, 93, 179;
commerce power and, 142, 188–189;
final objections to the Constitution,
166, 189–190; limits on participation
and, 129, 132; small republic views
of, 60, 115–116, 171, 180, 187
Massachusetts, 55
Mercer, John Francis, 132
Middle Atlantic states, i, 10, 12–13;
positions generally favored by
delegates from, 56, 88, 111, 126–127,
131; weakness in coalition of, 114,
117, 122–123, 142, 152. See also New
England states; Southern states
Miller, Perry, 10
Mississippi River, 184
Money bills, 122, 127, 133, 137–140, 171
Montesquieu, Charles Louis de Secondat,
i, 54
Moralistic political subculture, iii, 10–11,
14
Morgan, Edmund S., 10–11
Morris, Gouverneur, 2, 51, 53, 146, 185,
188, 201; admission of new states
and, 160–161; control of the
legislature and, 95–96, 98–99;
independent executive and, 107,
115–116, 128, 155, 179–180;
ratification and, 165–166; restrictions
on government and, 130, 138; the
Senate and, 133, 189
Morris, Robert, 107
Muter, George, 37

National power, 51–52, 59, 101, 126
National troops: entry into states of, 156,
164

Nationalists, i, iv, 58; early agenda
control, 51–53, 65. See also Federalists
Negative on state laws: approved, 58, 63;
Madison's preconvention strategy
and, 39–40, 43–44
New England states, i, iv, 10–11, 45, 201;
impact of Shay's Rebellion on
thinking in, 11, 85; positions
generally favored by delegates from,
77, 88, 106; positions generally
opposed by delegates from, 56, 66.
See also Middle Atlantic states;
Southern states
New Hampshire: delegates arrive, 119
New Jersey plan, 79–81, 84
New states: admission of, 160–163. See
also Western lands
New York, 38
North versus South, 65, 74, 76, 91, 96
North Carolina, 55

Oath: to support the Constitution, 70
Ostrom, Vincent, i, 15

Participation, 66, 122, 133–137
Paterson, William, 82, 93, 96, 201; New
Jersey plan and, 79, 81; opposes early
nationalist thrust, 63, 68–69
Pennsylvania: middle state coalition and,
33, 76, 160
People, the: republican understanding of,
8
Peripheral states, 101, 103, 111–112, 121,
157, 169; adopt traditional separation
of powers view, 127–128; favor local
control, 126; favor positive
constitutional restraints, 129–131,
135; South Carolina shatters southern
wing of, 149–151. See also Middle
Atlantic states
Pierce, William, 36, 60
Pinckney, Charles, 50, 62–63, 66, 115,
133, 201; property qualifications and,
129, 134; ratification and, 165–166;
slavery and, 144, 148; strong Senate
and, 171, 179, 185
Pinckney, Charles Cotesworth, 66, 86–87,
92; slavery and, 144, 148–149;
property qualifications and, 129, 140
Political subcultures, iii, 10, 14

Pomper, Gerald, 19, 21, 24, 70
Pool, William, 4
Principled interpretations of the
     Constitution, i, iii–iv, 5–7, 14, 17, 22,
     126, 193–194. *See also* Interest-based
     interpretations of the Constitution
Property: representation and, 94–95
Property qualifications, 129, 134, 140

Qualifications: officeholders, 131–137,
     204; voters, 131

Rakove, Jack N., 184
Randolph, Edmund, 88, 130, 146; early
     correspondence with Madison, 37,
     39–40; objections, 149, 166, 180,
     189–190; Virginia plan and, 50, 81;
     southern control of the House and,
     95, 98
Ratification, 85, 156; number of states
     needed for, 164; role of Congress in,
     165–167;Virginia plan and, 39, 45,
     65–66
Read, George, 53, 65, 132
Realignment in the convention, ii, 21;
     factor analysis and, 26–29; issue
     change and, 20–21, 23–24, 26;
     representation and, 94–95, 102–103;
     summary description of, 31–34,
     196–200
Rebellion, power to suppress, 163–164
Regionalism, iii; intellectual divisions in
     the convention and, 9–14, 16; strains
     in the large state coalition and, 74
Republicanism, iii, 2, 22; American
     political culture and, 8–14; executive
     power and, 101, 104, 106–108;
     guaranteed to the states, 163,
     Madison's understanding of, 36,
     40–42; new version versus
     traditional, 49–50, 61
Representation, 202; change necessary in,
     35, 39, 43; Connecticut compromise
     and, 92, 99, 101–102; electoral
     college and, 118; initial debates over,
     52–53, 64; large states versus small
     over, 65–94
Rhode Island, 165
Riker, William H., 107
Robinson, Donald L., 141–142

Robinson, John (Speaker, Virginia House
     of Burgesses), 12
Roche, John P., 5, 93
Roll-call voting in the Convention, i, 20,
     30
Rossiter, Clinton, 4, 6, 10, 23
Rummel, Rudolph J., 26, 28
Russett, Bruce, 25
Rutledge, John, 57, 86, 140, 201;
     executive selection and, 106, 117,
     147, 153; representation and, 90, 93,
     96, 130; restrictions on citizenship
     and officeholding, 132, 136; southern
     interests and, 144, 184

Schattschneider, E. E., 18–19, 104,
     197–198
Schubert, Glendon, 25
Scottish enlightenment, 49
Sedgwick, Theodore, 194
Senate, 37; fear of, 171, 179–180;
     qualifications to serve in, 133–134;
     role of the states in, 67, 93–94;
     Virginia plan and, 37, 57. *See also*
     Legislature; Senate
Separation of powers, 44, 157; checks and
     balances or, 127–130, 137–138, 204;
     Dickinson versus Madison over, 60;
     executive/legislative relations and,
     106–107, 170
Shalhope, Robert E., 8, 12, 22
Shay's Rebellion, 11, 56, 66, 85
Sherman, Roger, 82, 136, 145, 187, 201;
     executive selection and, 179, 181;
     opposed to popular influence, 56–57,
     66; representation and, 76, 92–93;
     state focus and, 61, 85, 87
Signing of the Constitution, 190–192
Simpson, Alan, 10
Slavery, 95, 127, 129, 132, 137; slave
     trade compromise, 140–150;
     southern conflicts over slave trade,
     141, 144, 157
Small republic, 50, 54, 61, 68; delegates
     favoring, 62, 106; supporters' lack of
     alternative to Virginia Plan, 55, 200.
     See also Extended republic
Small states, i, iv, 203; executive and, 118,
     147, 153, 171, 179; representation
     issue and large states versus, 35,

65–94, 99; small state caucus,
152–155; western lands and, 161,
163. *See also* Large states
Smith, David G., 23
Smith, J. Allen, 3
Smith, Page, 2
Social choice theory, i
South Carolina, 38, 66, 149, 151
Southern states, i, iv, 10–11, 45, 151, 201;
and the Virginia Plan, 56–57, 77, 88;
population trends and, 70, 76; South
Carolina and cohesion among, 151,
173; treaty power and, 183–184. *See
also* Middle Atlantic states; New
England states
Sovereignty, 39, 42
Spaight, Richard Dobbs, 57, 119
State ratification conventions, 166–167,
190
State governments, 4, 37, 64, 157, 162;
federalists' view of, 49, 59, 80;
nationalists' view of, 40–42, 61, 78,
128; ratification role of, 166
Strong, Caleb, 78, 128
Sundquist, James L., 19, 196, 199
Supreme Court, 80, 170
Sydner, Charles, 12
Szatmary, David P., 11

Thach, Charles C., 104, 107, 109–110,
113–114, 117, 119
Thomas, Robert E., 4
Three-fifths compromise, 77, 96–99. *See
also* House of Representatives;
Representation
Tocqueville, Alexis de, 194
Tolles, Frederick B., 13
Tonnage duties, 189
Traditionalistic political subculture, iii, 10,
14
Treaty-making power, 181–184
Tullock, Gordon, i, 15
Tyranny, 1; checks and separation will
cure, 60, 129; extended sphere will
cure, 62

Ulmer, S. Sidney, 25–26

Vermont, 161
Veto power, 37

Vice-president, 175, 182. *See also* the
Executive
"Vices of the Political System of the
United States," James Madison, April,
1787, 37, 40–42
Virginia, 11, 33, 157
Virginia plan, 77–78, 207; as Convention
agenda, 50–51; Madison's role in, 36,
43, 45; first trip through, 65; second
trip through, 84; third trip through,
120
Virtue, 8
Voting coalitions in the Convention, ii, iii,
17, 121, 126–127, 135; commerce
and slave trade issues and, 140, 142,
149–150; executive issues and,
103–104, 107–108, 111; initial
identification in this study, 28–34,
195–197; northern majority and,
169–170; representation issue and,
73, 92, 94–95, 102; several traditional
views of, 24–25; small state isolation
and, 155, 157

Wallace, Caleb, 37
Warren, Charles, iv, 3–5, 207; executive
issue and, 104, 107; representation
and, 24, 94
Washington, George, 2, 46, 191–192;
correspondence with Madison, 23, 37,
40, 43–44
Western lands, i, 140, 162, 172
Williamson, Hugh, 87, 191; presidential
selection and, 179–181;
representation and, 89, 93, 97;
restrictions and, 138–139, 143, 148;
Senate and, 135–136, 171
Wilson, James, 2, 88, 128, 130, 160, 187,
190, 201; executive selection and,
106–107, 110, 179; proportional
representation and, 63, 76–77, 81,
88, 91–92; ratification and, 164–165;
restrictions, 134–135, 138; role for
the people and, 56–57, 66, 87, 110;
role for the states, 62, 86; Senate
becoming too powerful, 182–183
Wolfe, Christopher, 24
Wood, Gordon, 2, 7, 9, 50, 59, 106–107

Yates, Robert, 89, 93